PRAISE FOR *ENDING THE SEARCH*

"*Ending the Search* is a delight to read. Dorothy Hunt writes beautifully about her own search and discovery, while sharing the wisdom she has found. She points out the traps of seeking and guides us to our inner teacher. Highly recommended book to remind and reassure us that we are already home."

LOCH KELLY
author of *Shift Into Freedom* and *Effortless Mindfulness Now*

"Dorothy Hunt's latest book, *Ending the Search*, is a call to our deepest heart's desire: our longing to be truly awake, alive, and authentic human beings. Her writing is food for our soul, wherein she invites us to turn in and tune in to not just the silence that arrives when we stop identifying with our thoughts, but to the Stillness that is present, whether the thinking mind is quiet or active. Her writings are living prayers, not for some 'thing,' but for awakening beyond the shore of separation to our essential nature, to knowing the underlying Mystery that has given birth to each of us, and the entire universe.

In *Ending the Search*, Dorothy beautifully reveals how enlightenment entails a shift in identity, where we discover how our true identity as essential nature lies in all movements and moments of life. This is a profound guidebook for those sincerely wishing to end their search for enlightenment. It is full of inspirational stories, exquisite signposts, and wisdom born of a life where no leaf remained unturned in coming to realize what enlightenment truly is. And most of all, this is a book of love, for love pours through every page. Love of truth. Love for how all things can be pointers to our essential nature. And most of all, love for no reason at all, because, as Dorothy so beautifully shows us, our essential nature is love incarnate."

RICHARD MILLER, PHD
author of *iRest Meditation: Restorative Practices for Health, Resiliency, and Well-Being*

D1053866

"From the beginning of seeking to the embodiment of awakening to our true nature, this book has something for every person on a journey to freedom from suffering and the delusion of being a separate bounded 'me.' This book is both a guide and an encouragement. Read it slowly and enjoy the clarity of a truly awakened guide."

TEAH STROZER
head teacher, Brooklyn Zen Center, and lineage-holder in
the Soto Zen tradition of Shunryu Suzuki Roshi

"This wise and compassionate book does what all great teachings do: pull the rug out from under your spiritual enterprise and drop you again and again into the groundless ground; the luminous essence; the timeless, ungraspable Now. Yet it does this dismantling with utmost grace and love, with parables, poetry, and the author's personal experiences, so you feel yourself being lovingly accompanied to your own demise. *Ending the Search* strips away everything you thought you were—and leaves you with the indescribable richness of what you actually are."

STEPHAN BODIAN
author of *Wake Up Now* and *Beyond Mindfulness*

"In *Ending the Search*, Dorothy Hunt offers us the profound wisdom of her amazingly broad and life-long engagement with the world's quintessential spiritual wisdom, especially as this culminates in the boundless vista of serene nondual awareness. The nectar of Dorothy's words reveals a living truth that quenches, satiates, and finally dissolves all forms of struggle and entrapment. Dorothy weaves together rich experiences from her own life and exquisite teachings from ancient masters. She opens the loving jewel of timeless awareness in a myriad of ways that dissolve all needs whatsoever. You will be profoundly rewarded by joining Dorothy at the end of the path and basking in the delicate and loving way in which she shares her timeless wisdom."

PETER FENNER, PHD
author of *Radiant Mind: Awakening Unconditioned Awareness* and
Natural Awakening: An Advanced Guide for Sharing Nondual Awareness

"This is a beautiful, gorgeous book, written from the Heart. Dorothy is authentic, genuine, down to earth, wise, and deeply attuned to the subtle nuances of life. Her words invite the listening silence and the spacious openness from which they have emerged. The whole book is an expression of the unconditional love that embraces everything. Dorothy sees and writes with an exquisite tenderness and sensitivity, illuminating with great clarity what is always already fully present—our True Nature, simply waiting to be noticed. She doesn't get stuck on one side of any apparent polarity or in the language of any particular tradition. At once transcendent and most intimate, delighting in the simple wonders of everyday life while also opening to the no-thing-ness of it all, Dorothy's teaching moves freely between relative and absolute. I love the ways she shares her own journey in this book, and it's obvious how her work as a spiritual teacher is informed by the richness of her own life as psychotherapist, poet, nature lover, cancer survivor, wife, mother, grandmother, and much more. This is a book that I very highly recommend, one that can wake you up to the wonder that is right here, right now."

JOAN TOLLIFSON
author of *Bare-Bones Meditation*, *Awake in the Heartland*,
Painting the Sidewalk with Water, and *Nothing to Grasp*

"*Ending the Search* is an eloquent, lucid, and compelling invitation to deeply inquire into who you really are and to fall into the Heart of Awareness. Whether you are a new or seasoned seeker, Dorothy Hunt's wisdom-infused prose, poetry, and teaching stories will invoke your deepest knowing. A beautiful and inspired offering—highly recommended!"

JOHN J. PRENDERGAST, PHD
author of *In Touch: How to Tune In to the Inner Guidance
of Your Body and Trust Yourself* and retired adjunct professor
of psychology, California Institute of Integral Studies

"A very inspiring must-read! When one truly takes Dorothy's book to heart, you'll absolutely die before you die. In one way she describes a step-by-step journey of taking inquiry all the way, and in another way the utmost humanness of her direct experience made me laugh out loud or cry. One will be pierced by the felt sense of her expression— very sweet and unwaveringly clear.

Dorothy is an elder who needs to be listened to, one who brings a much-needed feminine flavor of connectedness down to earth, encompassing Love, realness, and true spirituality. Knowing Love is kissing you from the inside will help you move from a comfortable awakening experience to total surrender to Love, leaving no stone unturned."

MARLIES MYOKU COCHERET DE LA MORINIÈRE
psychologist and spiritual teacher, interviewed in the
book *Ordinary Women, Extraordinary Wisdom*

"Dorothy is our guide on a delightful journey of calling off the search of striving to be anything other than what we already effortlessly are and have always been. She opens us to our true essence as the pure presence of Being. Through heartfelt personal stories, examples, and exquisite wisdom, she helps us open our hearts and rest deeply in the still, silent spaciousness at our core as the Heart of Awareness. This is a must-read and a book that is a treasure to us all!"

DIANE STEINBRECHER, LCSW
nondual psychotherapist, teacher, and coauthor of the forthcoming book
The Treasure Within: An Archetypal Unfolding to Our Greatest Potential

"Reading Dorothy Hunt's book *Ending the Search: From Spiritual Ambition to the Heart of Awareness* is to experience the nondualism she writes about, a difficult task accomplished through images, stories from wisdom traditions, and her own experience. A compassionate, accepting companion who through her palpable presence invited me to enter the deep, silent dimensions of my being, trusting the deep spiritual impulse within."

DIANE DEUTSCH, PHD
Jungian analyst

ENDING THE
SEARCH

ALSO BY DOROTHY HUNT

Only This!

Leaves from Moon Mountain

ENDING THE
SEARCH

*From Spiritual Ambition
to the Heart of Awareness*

DOROTHY HUNT

sounds true
BOULDER, COLORADO

Sounds True
Boulder, CO 80306

Published 2018

Cover design by Jennifer Miles
Book design by Beth Skelley
Photo of Ramana Maharshi © Sri Ramanasramam
Photo of Adyshanti and Dorothy Hunt by John Prendergast

Printed in Canada

Library of Congress Cataloging-in-Publication Data
Names: Hunt, Dorothy, 1943- author.
Title: Ending the search : from spiritual ambition to the heart of awareness /
    Dorothy Hunt ; foreword by Adyashanti.
Description: Boulder, CO : Sounds True, [2018] | Includes bibliographical
    references.
Identifiers: LCCN 2017033569 (print) | LCCN 2017057377 (ebook) |
    ISBN 9781683640646 (ebook) | ISBN 9781683640639 (pbk.)
Subjects: LCSH: Mindfulness (Psychology) | Spirituality. | Love.
Classification: LCC BF637.M56 (ebook) | LCC BF637.M56 H86 2018 (print) |
    DDC 204/.4—dc23
LC record available at https://lccn.loc.gov/2017033569

10 9 8 7 6 5 4 3 2 1

This book is dedicated to
seekers of truth
and to those beacons of light
whose Presence invites us to awaken
to what cannot be spoken
yet shines brightly in the Heart we share.

What is seeking
And the end of seeking?

Who is the seeker?
What has he found?

What need is there
For striving or stillness?

What is freedom or bondage?

. . .

Nothing is,
Nothing is not.
What more is there to say?[1]

THE ASHTAVAKRA GITA

CONTENTS

CONTENTS

Bhagavan Sri Ramana Maharshi
1879–1950

Adyashanti with the author

FOREWORD

For as long as we human beings have been walking on this earth, we have been searching for a state of mind or way of living that will redeem the sorrows of life and give us a deep and meaningful experience of being. In a psychological and spiritual sense, we are forever on the move, searching for something that we intuitively feel but have a hard time articulating. This restless pursuit of lasting satisfaction, God, or happiness has defined the human psyche for as long as we know. It seems to me that at the heart of this search is a desire for a deeply rich, profound, and meaningful experience of being. An experience of being that not only justifies but embraces the tragic sorrows inherent in life by orienting us toward the greatest love and wisdom that we are capable of experiencing and embodying. The question is, do we come upon such an experience of being by forever searching for it? Or might there be some other way of orienting ourselves toward this restless longing that might prove to be more fruitful and satisfying?

This book that you now hold in your hands, *Ending the Search*, is an answer to these two questions. Ending the search does not mean to simply walk away from it. You may change the mode of your seeking, but you will simply pick it back up again in some other more disguised form sooner or later. Neither does ending the search indicate a form of defeatism or failure to engage in something as important as our human aspirations. Truly ending the search is not a denial of the search but rather a wise and loving way of engaging with the desire for a deep and meaningful experience of being. It is a way of engaging with the seeking energy in such a way that you are not looking for satisfaction in what may happen in the future, or in who you may become, but are instead exploring the deeper nature of your immediate experience here and now. As the subtitle to this fine book says, it is about going *From Spiritual Ambition to the Heart of Awareness.*

There is no future or the exercising of spiritual ambition in this book, nor any attempt to aggrandize or justify the spiritual ego. Nor is this book some sort of cheap shortcut, or clichéd promise of freedom with no price to pay. The price will be your spiritual ambition, and the egocentric orientation that goes along with it. Seeking can become a lifestyle with hidden perks for the ego, but to come to the end of the search is to let go of all that is unreal about your current idea of you, and to step into only what is real. In this sense, *Ending the Search* is ruthless kindness and wise compassion. It speaks of ending the ego's search outside of itself and finding in the Heart of Awareness something extraordinary and immediate. Something of great value and meaning beyond mere words. And something immediately available for anyone who is ready to stop right now and see.

This is not a book to simply be read; it is a book to be contemplated, practiced, and lived. Take this book as good medicine, and as a lovingly offered teaching. It is the product of decades of Dorothy's experience. You will find yourself, your true nature, being encouraged and reflected on every page of it. For it is a book about you—not someone you may become, but something that you inherently are.

Adyashanti

INTRODUCTION

I
f you are a seeker of Truth, God, or Self-realization, you no doubt find yourself driven by your spiritual search but unable to end it even by your most sincere efforts. You are caught by the desire for enlightenment or God consciousness, yet time and again you are acutely aware of your sense of separation. You desperately want to end your suffering or your longing, but no matter what you do or where you look, you are frustrated in your search for liberation. You may have tried all manner of spiritual practices, meditation, guru shopping, chanting, prayer, and spiritual reading, and still you have not attained your heart's desire. You imagine you have chosen the path of being a spiritual seeker, but in actuality, the path has chosen you.

If you are such a seeker, you are in a dilemma. You desire spiritual awakening yet may be told by those you imagine are "awake" that either your desire is not great enough or your desire is the obstacle. You earnestly seek Truth but may be told that Truth cannot be "known" by your mind. You long for God yet continually feel separate from who or what you long for. You are encouraged to practice one or many spiritual disciplines, all of which require the efforts of your ego, but you are told the real goal is to rid yourself of your ego. You search for someone or something to tell you how to get where you want to go, but you are told there *is* nowhere to go. You are told to relax your mind but to keep your body perfectly straight. You are told to love your neighbor as yourself but not how to love yourself.

In your search, you are predictably confused and frequently frustrated. Even when you enjoy moments of expanded awareness, peace, and openhearted connectedness, you have no idea how to remain in such a state. However, you feel certain that if you just search long enough, work hard enough, or eventually find the right teacher, the right practice, or the right path, you can achieve your goal of "enlightenment." Your spiritual ambition is to obtain the knowledge, wisdom, or grace to live in a state of perpetual happiness and bliss, free from anxiety, problems, and pain. You are sure all of the rewards you imagine will accompany Self-realization will be for your own personal enjoyment. Your search could end at any moment because the truth of what you are is never absent. And yet the time-bound, conditioned mind imagines you are on a journey from "here" to "there."

Ending the Search is an exploration of the so-called spiritual journey, both pre- and post-awakening, with an emphasis on inquiry as an invaluable tool in determining the true identity of the seeker. Many, if not most, spiritual traditions and practices direct their teachings to a "self" that is seen to be separate from the awakening, enlightenment, or God it seeks without ever questioning who that "self" is. So the seeker approaches awakening with the ambition of "achieving" enlightenment through the efforts of his or her egoic mind. While the initial impulse to awaken comes from a deeper dimension of our Being, identified mind often begins to seek awakening in the same way it might seek to get an A on an exam or to achieve "success" in the world; and failure to achieve one's spiritual goal is viewed as a failure of the "me." This failure of the "me" to either "get it" or "keep it" is an important aspect of awakening—one that may invite a deeper surrender to Truth.

The funny thing about the spiritual search is that there is no one searching! And yet the search continues. No matter how many times you hear the wise ones telling you that there is nowhere to go and no one to arrive, you can't believe that it is true for *you*. For *them*, maybe, because *they* have already arrived! But not for you! You truly imagine there is a *them* and a *you*!

This book is about the ego's spiritual ambition, its search for its idea of "enlightenment," its frustrations, and its eventual fate, as the seeker becomes the sought. The seeker's quest for Truth becomes the Infinite's quest for you. Woven throughout is the story of one woman's search for God—a search that began in childhood, in anger and disillusionment, took many twists and turns, and suddenly ended in a most astonishing and unexpected way. Yet the "end of seeking" was merely a new beginning. You may imagine that this story is "mine," but it is not. Yet it is no one else's either.

Although for decades I considered myself an ardent spiritual seeker, there were certain ways I imagined the search should and should not unfold. For example, I never sought a guru, never wanted a guru, and in fact would have been repulsed to bow, even in thought, to any human being, because I believed no human was God. However, Ramana Maharshi and Ramesh Balsekar, both twentieth-century Indian sages, no longer in form, as well as the American-born spiritual teacher Adyashanti, appeared from the infinite Heart we share, functioning respectively as guru, guide, and buddha. It turns out that God, Guru, and Self are one and the same.

Once I refused to chant in Sanskrit during a yoga retreat because I did not know what god I was singing to and did not want to be praying to the "wrong" one. Now there is a deep honoring of *all* paths to God, *all* paths to Knowing. Once I imagined that only certain people, feelings, thoughts, and actions, and *not* others, could belong to God. Now it is seen that nothing and no one is separate from God or Consciousness. All there is is God. All there is is Consciousness. And yet no concept delivers Truth, and no name defines the ineffable.

While many methods and valuable practices are useful in one's search, this book emphasizes Self-inquiry, a method advocated by Ramana Maharshi for searching, not for enlightenment but for the source of the ego. It is about the understanding that that which is driving the spiritual search is that which will end the search—or not—and that *none* of it is in the ego's control! It is about meeting Adyashanti, a true spiritual friend and living buddha, years after an awakening had ended my search and learning that awakening to our true nature is only step one on the spiritual journey.

The ego mind cannot explain the Mystery that unfolds the spiritual search. It cannot explain the process by which one person searches for God or enlightenment, another searches for a cure for cancer, and yet another searches for ways to develop methods of mass destruction. And it cannot say why a book is written, or why it is read, or what value it may or may not have. It imagines that we speak or write to express something we wish to share. Actually, one writes because writing happens. One reads because reading happens. Because I am writing, you are reading. But in the world of appearances, this book was written for the so-called spiritual seeker, with deep compassion for the struggles and frustrations inherent in following such a path.

This book says nothing new about the spiritual journey, the myths of the so-called spiritual life, or the perspective that appears with the end of seeking. But if you had truly understood the first time you heard words pointing to your inner Truth—if you believed you were not separate, that God or Consciousness is all there is—and if you lived in that continual awareness, then these fingers would not be typing words and you would not be reading them. But because there are seekers, there are teachers and gurus and books written and words spoken trying to point to the Mystery that cannot really be known. Because there are teachers pointing, there are seekers trying to see. Each thing defines the other, as in all of life.

The entire course of life on earth seems to be about seeking. Plants seek light; birds seek insects; bees seek blossoms; water seeks its own level; energies seek balance; a person searches for a partner, power, wealth, health, a new job, the next meal, happiness, or a moment's peace in a difficult life. Spiritual seeking is just another unfolding of that which drives *all* seeking—one that your body-mind organism seems programmed to do. And that is why we have found one another at this moment.

If any part of this book or the flavor of its understanding seems useful or helpful, know that it is given lovingly to you from your own deep Self. If anything seems true, it is your own knowing that remembers its truth. If nothing rings true for you, toss this book aside and follow your own inner guidance, trusting its process completely. About one thing I have no doubt: whomever you imagine yourself to be, however you imagine your life should or should not look, you have never been separate for a single breath, a single blink, a single moment from the unnameable Mystery you seek.

Ramana Maharshi (1879–1950) is considered by many to be one of the greatest Indian spiritual gurus of the twentieth century. Self-realization occurred at the age of seventeen, and from that moment until his death, Ramana Maharshi continually abided in the Self, teaching mainly through silence. His recommended path to realization was Self-inquiry, a continual referral of the ego mind toward its Source through the question "Who am I?"

Ramesh Balsekar (1917–2009), considered to be an awakened Advaita master, was a native of Mumbai (Bombay), India, alumnus of the London School of Economics, retired bank president, golfer, house-holder, and disciple of Nisargadatta Maharaj. His teaching was simple: Consciousness is all there is, so "who" is to know or seek "what"? All there is is the impersonal functioning of Consciousness or God, reflecting within itself the totality of manifestation.

Adyashanti (b. 1962), a native of California, was an ardent student of Zen Buddhism for fourteen years prior to his teacher's request that he begin to share the Dharma. His nondual teachings have been compared to those of the early Zen masters and Advaita Vedanta sages. Eventually awakened out of any tradition, Adyashanti now teaches around the world, inviting students to stop, inquire, and recognize what is true and liberating at the core of all existence.

Part I

BEGINNING THE

SEARCH

*When God comes in your house
it is only by your invitation,
but even your invitation is God's,
for she has always been
landlady and tenant,
windows and walls,
the fire in your hearth
and the cold wind blowing at your door.*[1]

1

WHAT ENDS THE SEARCH
BEGINS THE SEARCH

Seeker, do you remember?
Listen in the silence . . .
Your own heart is calling you back home.

The spiritual search is a call to remember who or what you essentially are. What ends the search is actually present from the very beginning, beckoning you to come home. In truth, you are what you seek, yet you must make that discovery for yourself.

However your spiritual search begins, you undoubtedly imagine you are taking a journey in time—a journey from wherever you find yourself now to where you hope to arrive in the future. You believe time will take you to the timeless. You want your search to lead you from *here* to a desired *there*, but you do not know the way. And even if you are following a path, you may encounter obstacles that seem insurmountable. Though you are being called to remember the essence of what you are, fear arises when you think about stepping out of your time-bound idea of yourself into the freedom of what is timelessly present here and now. You want to remain in the known, even as you are invited into the Unknown. A tale told in the Sufi tradition beautifully illustrates some of your challenges.

THE STORY OF A STREAM

A stream traveled from a distant mountain to find itself at the edge of a desert. He had crossed many other barriers on his journey, but when he arrived at the desert, his water kept disappearing, no matter how fast he rushed into the sand. He was certain that his destiny was to cross the desert to the mountains on the other side, but he did not know how. A voice from the desert whispered softly that the wind crosses and therefore so could the stream. When the stream argued that the wind could fly but he could not, he was told that he would first need to be absorbed by the wind. But the stream did not want to lose his individuality, fearing he would never regain it. The desert voice, attempting to ease the stream's concerns, put it another way, explaining that the wind takes up the water, carries it across, and lets it fall again as rain, the same rain that becomes a river.

The stream wanted reassurance that this was true; he wanted to remain the same stream. But he was told he could not, in any case, remain the same. He either would be carried by the wind or would eventually become a quagmire dashing against the desert for years. Even his name, Stream, was due to the fact that he did not know what part of him was the essential one.

On hearing a reference to essence, the stream seemed to remember—or did he?—that once he had been held in the arms of the wind. And though he was frightened, he eventually raised his vapor into her arms and was gently carried across, where rain fell as it reached the top of the mountain far away. The stream was learning his true identity, and yet the vast desert sands, quiet and still, simply watched life happen this way every single day.[1]

What do you imagine has begun your search, carried you this far, moved you to pick up this book? Life, in its wholeness, shows itself as stream, desert, wind, rain, and river—movement, stillness, spirit, and form. It moves as your longing, your search, your confusions, and your fears. It even manifests as your ideas about a self that seems distant from its source, distant from its desired destination.

The stream is the stream of life, your life, or the mindstream of Consciousness, your consciousness. It is continually flowing, beginning and ending in its source, coming upon moments of joy, moments of ease, moments of challenge, and moments of crisis, when nothing you have used in the past seems to aid you in crossing a seemingly impossible barrier. And yet if you are a spiritual seeker, somewhere you have a sense that your destiny is to cross the desert, that you will find your home ground on the other side. But you are told you must let go of your habitual ways, step out of your definition of yourself, and allow the wind to take you across.

Like the stream, you do not want to lose your individuality. You are afraid of the unknown; you want reassurance. How can I know whether what the wise one says is true? Do I take the risk and allow myself to be carried without knowing what is on the other side? Or do I stay safe in my identity as a particular stream? But you are told you cannot remain the same in any event. Life is continually moving. In the midst of a crisis, when you do not know the way out, something may open enough for you to hear the One who whispers: *You do not yet know what is most essential about you.*

There is a desert in each of us—not the dryness of our intellect, but a desert called Silence. Eventually we come upon this Silence, and perhaps we fear that we will keep getting absorbed, and lose something important. But it is from the Silence we may hear the whispers of our own knowing, even if that knowing appears to come from someone or someplace "else," inviting us to remember and return to what is most essential.

Hearing the whisper, there is a vague memory of your life as Spirit—or was there? Is it all a lie? To take the next step means trusting, surrendering. It is not necessarily the obvious step from the perspective of your rational mind, and yet something moves in you. There is an impulse deep within that draws your attention toward what lies beyond the known. Something in you says, "I have to find out. I have to know for myself what is true." And perhaps, if you are ready, you let the wind take you, not knowing she has always carried you. You will open to the unknown. Will you learn your true identity?

Before we begin to contemplate the story of a journey—whether it is the stream of birth, life, and death, the mindstream that has been moving from beginningless time, or the story of an individual's spiritual journey—notice something important. Where is it taking place? In the words on this page? On a mountain far away? In the birth of an infant, or in a memory of beginning your spiritual search? It is all occurring in awareness, is it not? Something so simple as being aware we take for granted. We are fascinated by stories—the ones we read, the ones we tell ourselves, the ones we believe about who we are. But none of them would be knowable if you were not aware. Yet do you know who it is who is aware? "I am!" you reply. And I would ask, "Who is that?"

WHAT ARE YOU SEARCHING FOR?

If you consider yourself a spiritual seeker, what are you searching for? What is the deepest longing of your heart? You may have many desires, but what is the most profound one, the one your heart knows is true, even if your mind does not?

You may believe that you are seeking awakening, enlightenment, Self-realization, or God realization. Perhaps you are seeking freedom, peace, love, happiness, truth, or an end to suffering. You may imagine that you know who is searching, who will be the "finder," who will achieve the end goal, and who will be the primary beneficiary. But do you *truly* know what you are seeking, what is motivating the search, or who it is who is seeking and wants the search to end? Learning your true identity is what awakening is about. The identity we have with name and form is not our true Self; it is a costume, a mask we are wearing. What is looking out from behind your mask?

We seek for what we believe is not here now. But perhaps we are searching in the wrong place. Perhaps we are searching in our time-bound mind for the timeless. Perhaps we imagine that the "narrator" of our thoughts is who will be able to end the search through its own efforts and ambition. We may have many ideas about what awakening looks like, who awakens and who does not, what the "end" of the search will bring. But can you open to the possibility that what you are seeking is what you truly *are*? It may seem impossible, but only because you are looking for something "out there" to complete you or love you, rather than looking within for your true Self, that which is already whole and loves its own expression as you and this world more deeply than your mind can imagine. It may seem impossible, because you have never questioned your ideas about the "self" whose identity you think you know.

IMPULSE TO BEGIN THE SEARCH

We may appear to become spiritual seekers in different ways, for different reasons, but at some point, something calls us toward something beyond who or what we imagine we are. Something moves to awaken itself from slumber; an impulse arises from beyond the mind to "know" what cannot be known by thought but can be sensed, felt, intuited, revealed, in the Heart of Silence. Something unknown, yet vaguely remembered, seems to beckon us toward its mystery. Like the stream, we imagine we begin a journey that will lead us from "here" to "there." We begin to want to know God, Truth, peace, or this thing called "enlightenment." The desire to "know" can even begin in anger.

When I was twelve, my mother died suddenly on the day after Christmas. I had asked for a robe that Christmas, my first Christmas that I considered myself too old for a doll, but at the last minute, I had changed my mind and decided I wanted a doll. When Christmas morning came, there was a robe and no doll. Little did I know that within a day, my childhood would come to an abrupt halt. The next April, Easter fell on the day that would have been my mother's birthday. I was raised in a Christian family and was told the biblical story that if one had faith the size of a mustard seed, one could move mountains. I was quite certain I had faith bigger than a mustard seed, and I prayed fervently that she would be resurrected on Easter, the same as Jesus. That Easter morning I set a place for her at the breakfast table. I waited all day for her to come back.

I had been told that it was God who gave life and took it away, and so I became very angry with God. This was a God whom I felt had betrayed my faith. I wanted to know who this was who had the power of life and death. In retrospect, this was the moment that began the search—not for myself, not for my true identity, but for God. As time went by, my anger subsided, but my desire to know God grew, as did my desire to know the truth about life and death.

How did your search begin? And isn't it always about being happier, being someplace else besides here and now? It may seem strange, but the very thing we are searching for both begins and ends our search. It is moving to know itself, to love itself, to wake itself up from its false identification with a supposedly separate body-mind. Whether we call spirit Truth, Consciousness, or God, it has always been "landlady and tenant / windows and walls / the fire in your hearth / and the cold wind blowing at your door."

Just as in the moment of birth, death is already present, and in this moment that we call "time," the timeless is present, so it is that what ends the spiritual search is present in its inception. We may have had a vague interest in spirituality, or perhaps experiences in childhood or beyond that have given us intimations of something transcendent or mysterious. However, a true spiritual impulse begins to draw our attention toward it, with varying levels of intensity, anticipation, curiosity, and/or fear.

Throughout history sages have spoken and written eloquently from the deepest understanding about ultimate Truth. While that Truth can neither be known nor understood through words, masters from every spiritual tradition have provided abundant, profound, and beautiful pointers. One has only to taste the words of the ancient Indian *rishis*, the Taoist sage known as Lao-tzu, the Buddha, Jesus, or countless others to begin to resonate somewhere to that unspoken truth that touches the heart and speaks in the silence between words.

MIND WANTS TO UNDERSTAND
WHAT THE HEART INTUITS

The mind, however, wants to *understand* what touches the heart and to achieve a desired goal. It sends us on a journey. The goal may be to "know" what others seem to know or to have a desired experience that matches what others have described. The seeker's mind wants to discover, label, and define the truth to which the sage's words or life actions point. The mind seeks to know with its intellect what the heart intuits. The seeker or the disciple studies, underlines, memorizes words, and sets up practices and prescriptions based on his or her understanding of the sage's life or the description of the sage's experience.

In the search for what will satisfy the heart's longing, the seeker imagines that it will be his or her own efforts—prayers or practices, sacrifices or service, behavior or beliefs, worthiness or faithfulness—that will ultimately bring about the desired goal. Even if the seeker pays lip service to the mystery of grace, he or she will still imagine that those who appear to have received such grace from God, guru, or life must really be more worthy, loving, earnest, disciplined, knowledgeable, or connected than the seeker.

Seekers are totally convinced that those considered "enlightened" beings are beings very unlike themselves. However, no one truly awake will tell you that awakeness is anywhere else than here and now or that it is not available to all. The Truth you may be searching for is present in you now. What we most deeply are is seeking *itself* in the seeker, seeing *itself* in awakening, and being *itself* in all of Being.

WE ONLY LONG FOR SOMETHING
WE HAVE KNOWN

Because we feel the impulse to awaken, we imagine awakeness is not present. Because we feel deep longing in our heart for Truth, love, the Divine, we imagine longing means lack. But we do not long for something we have never known. We might be curious, as for a food we have never tasted, but we only *long* for what we have known. When a deep spiritual longing is present, it is always for what is somewhere known but perhaps forgotten. We long for our home ground, where all is well, even when the surface of our life may not seem to be.

Rather than believing that a longing means a lack, try following your longing back to its source. Our true heart casts out a fishing line from itself in order to catch the elusive ego, darting to and fro in the Ocean of Awareness like a fish looking everywhere for water when all about there is nothing but ocean. When the ego fish takes the bait, the Fisherman of the Heart begins to reel it back in to itself. Longing is a powerful motivator to begin the search. Our longing is what calls us back home through what T. S. Eliot referred to as the "unknown, remembered gate."[2] We begin the search from the end and end the search where it begins.

The irony is that we have always been what we have been searching for. The truth of YOU is ever present. But like the stream in the Sufi story, we believe we began in one place and need to end up in another, and so we miss what is the most essential. It is in discovering the essential that we taste our freedom.

2

SPIRITUAL IMPULSE AND SPIRITUAL AMBITION

There is a jewel hidden in each heart,
shining from emptiness.
Treasure even the smallest glimpse.

THE JEWEL

Whomever you are, you would not be reading a book such as this if you had not had a glimpse of the jewel. Perhaps as a child you sensed a world that touched a deep and mysterious wonder. You may have had an experience you felt certain no one would understand and so you never shared it, but it has stayed in your heart—some kind of knowing that seemed at once completely true and yet confusing to your mind. Perhaps there was a moment in a temple of trees when a shaft of light from the rising or setting sun struck the jewel of your heart. You may have been hiking on a mountain when you suddenly were stopped by joy, wonder, or a sense of awe. It was not just the view, the misty colors of the many ridges you could see in the distance. Your senses touched the Infinite, and you experienced beauty; something vast touched the vastness within you. Its radiance may have come as moonlight playing on the ocean's waves. It may have shone through a piece of art, a poem, or a dream that touched what connects us.

You may have had a glimpse while sitting in a church or a temple, when the silence and reverence of place seemed to invite you to the silence within your Self. Perhaps you felt it when a baby gazed into your eyes from the eyes of such innocence that all of your defenses melted in such sweetness. The jewel may have shone through the stories you have read, heard, or experienced from great spiritual masters in various traditions. What sparkles is not the stories or words; it is something deeper that touches your heart.

The jewel seems to shine most brightly when we experience love—love for a person, a pet, a moment. When my young grandson lovingly traces with his finger the prominent veins that stand out on the back of my aging hands and tells me they remind him of rivers, we both experience the jewel, though we do not call it by any name.

SPIRITUAL IMPULSE

It is the jewel that gives rise to our impulse to know it more deeply and to want it to be revealed more consciously. Bubbling from the hidden depths of our Being arises an impulse to know what seems to lie beyond our limited ideas of who we are. There arises a sense of mystery, an impulse to know God, Truth, Self, enlightenment, love, or peace. This is spiritual impulse. Infinite Truth or Spirit has placed a longing in our heart, in the heart of our awareness, to know itself, to awaken itself beyond egoic consciousness. This impulse transcends both ego and self. We could call this impulse "the seed of enlightenment," a seed that has been planted deep within and perhaps has lain fallow in the rich soil and silent ground of our Being.

However, at some point, it begins to grow itself, a tiny shoot at first, trying to move toward the light. It begins to be nurtured in the experience of the seeker as it moves toward fruition. But its growth and blossoming are not for the benefit of a single individual but for the benefit of the whole. Awakening is not a feather in the cap of the spiritual ego. The desire to claim it for the "me" is the ego's spiritual ambition, and this ambition can actually hinder the growth of the seed and limit the fullness of its blooming. Spiritual impulse is a gift from our infinite ground; spiritual ambition is the desire to *possess* knowledge rather than to receive it.

EGOIC IDENTITY NEVER FEELS COMPLETE

Egoic consciousness is Consciousness identified with a single body-mind and its thoughts, feelings, senses, memories, will, and conditioned ways of viewing itself as a separate entity. Ego consciousness maintains a self-concept separate from the Divine, the natural world, and other beings, and it frequently feels separate even from itself. Everyone knows the many judgments that an "I" can make about a "myself." But who is who? "I love myself." "I hate myself." "I'm disappointed in myself." "I'm proud of myself." Who is the "I"? Who is the "myself"?

Something in our egoic consciousness knows it is not complete. This sense of deficiency stems from the fact that until we know who or what we are beyond our self-image, we will always feel that something is missing, that "there must be more to life than this," that "I am not enough." As we know, self-images are quite changeable. A compliment or a criticism can inflate or deflate a self-image in an instant.

Egoic consciousness is limited to the finite world of time and space, and all of its productions and experiences are impermanent, as is the form of the body it identifies with. This is not to say there is no place or purpose for ego consciousness. It has very many useful functions in maneuvering a body through life. It is not an enemy; it simply has no *independent* existence, although it "thinks" it does. Egoic consciousness seems to have lost the knowledge that its life belongs to Life, that its consciousness belongs to a greater Consciousness, that it derives its being from Being and not from its idea of separation.

SPIRITUAL AMBITION

Spiritual ambition occurs when ego consciousness takes ownership of the impulse to awaken and assumes it will be the agent of deliverance to what then becomes its own personal goal. While what we call "ego" is actually only a movement of thought, we have come to believe it is more, and its spiritual ambition can often appear as a competitive goal with others who are imagined to be further ahead or lagging behind in the race to the top of Enlightenment Mountain.

What was a gift from the Infinite, a moment of grace, a spiritual longing, becomes co-opted by an "I-thought" (Ramana's term for ego) that begins to look everywhere for what will fulfill its desire—everywhere but in that spark of the heart's longing that arose from the Infinite's fire. Our mind cannot help but look for true knowledge the way it has been taught to look for intellectual knowledge, to look "out there," to look to others, to books, to practices, and to blame its frustrations on its own failures and deficiencies. Conversely, when spiritual insight arrives as a gift in moments of openness, spiritual ego takes credit for its arrival.

SPIRITUAL EGO AND SPIRITUAL EFFORT

Initially, the seeker's ego imagines that awakening is the trophy it will receive for its spiritual efforts. *Who* is efforting? You imagine you know who is efforting when you are sitting on your cushion or trying so hard to be kind or compassionate. You may never even *question* who you are except when your behavior does not seem to match your idea of yourself. You have accepted that who you are is a person, a body-mind with certain traits and characteristics that are judged to be positive or negative, born on a particular date, in charge of your life choices, worried about making the right or wrong decisions. You imagine you know who it is who is efforting, whose ambition will achieve the "goal," whose efforts will succeed or fail on the spiritual path. But spiritual egos face frustrations.

> Friend, please tell me what I can do about this world
> I hold to, and keep spinning out!
>
> I gave up sewn clothes, and wore a robe,
> but I noticed one day the cloth was well-woven.
>
> So I bought some burlap, but I still
> throw it elegantly over my left shoulder.

I pulled back my sexual longings
and now I discover that I'm angry a lot.

I gave up rage, and now I notice
that I am greedy all day.

I worked hard at dissolving the greed,
and now I am proud of myself.

When the mind wants to break its link with the world
it still holds on to one thing.

Kabir says, Listen my friend,
there are very few that find the path![1]
KABIR

What may have begun as a deep, authentic, and quiet spiritual impulse of the Heart to awaken, to know one's Self or God, can quickly be co-opted by the egoic mind, which then becomes the agent of spiritual ambition. Some traditions use this ambition to spur students on. "Sit like your hair is on fire!" or "Don't waste your time, day or night!" might be the exhortation of a Zen roshi. Continued failure at koan study can feel deflating to a mind that wants to "get it" intellectually. The promise of heaven or hell can be the enticing carrot or dreaded stick to an ego wanting only endless pleasure and avoidance of pain. Believing only a few find the path can set up a competitive ego that wants to prove he will be one of the few. Or it can lead the mind to a sense of frustration and futility.

In all spiritual traditions, spiritual practices have developed to help the seeker on his journey. Any one or perhaps several of such practices may have appealed to you over your years of seeking. You have tried one and failed or tried another that seemed useful and continued doing it. There is nothing wrong with spiritual effort or practice. The problem occurs when we imagine that the effort belongs to a separate "self" and that it will take us somewhere *else*.

Spiritual *effort* appears when it appears; it is the action of the moment. The spiritual *ego* believes it is the one efforting. The acting or efforting called "spiritual practice" simply appears in a particular body-mind organism that, at least initially, takes himself to be separate from who or what he seeks. However, identified mind imagines that *you* are creating that effort in order to arrive somewhere else.

Because you seek to be someplace else, you want everything you are doing to be a means to that goal. However, when the Buddhist master says, "Sitting *itself* is enlightenment," she does not mean sitting in awareness of a separate "me" being a good boy or girl, a worthy student of Buddhism, hoping for a reward called "enlightenment" if he or she just sits long enough and thinks the right thoughts. Of course, all of you aspiring buddhas know that these are precisely your thoughts—at least for a while! Realize that effort only refers to mind-body interpretations of experience. The Self does not effort. It simply is itself.

If we are trying hard to be "worthy" or "holy" and thus ensure a place in "heaven" or trying to be "good" so that we will not find ourselves punished in "hell," we may remain totally unconscious of the fact that heaven and hell are productions of a dual mind in Consciousness. Many, many realms or dimensions of thought and experience exist in Consciousness; nothing exists outside of Consciousness. The questions are "Whose Consciousness?" and "Are any ideas of the dual mind Truth?"

NIRVANA IS NOT A PLACE EXTENDED IN TIME

We want heaven or nirvana to be a "place" extended in "time," and thus we often fail to touch the timeless dimension of ourselves, where we are never separated from anyone or anything, and where we are never apart from the infinite and unconditioned love that is available now, if our hearts open wide enough. What is timeless and eternal is Now, not something extended in duration. The mind defines eternity as unending *time*, failing to realize that in the timeless there is *no* time. Our mind continually wants to be somewhere else than here and now because if it were to totally stop moving, it would disappear.

If we are not trying to be somewhere else, we are simply living *as* the present moment. Much has been written and spoken about being *in* the present. You imagine that the present moment is a point in time, rather than timeless Awareness, and then you imagine you can practice being *in* time.

The sense of a separate self requires a sense of time and space. Separation requires the sense of someone in form who occupies space and the sense of someone who is "becoming" or "moving" in time. "One day, in the past, I was born; now I am growing older; someday in the future I will die." Without a sense of time or a sense of becoming, there is only timeless Being, and yet eternal Being and apparent *becoming* share a single essence. All of us have experienced timeless moments in which life or action just seemed to flow effortlessly. In these moments we were not feeling separated from our being or from the moment we were living.

WHAT SEPARATES YOU FROM THE MOMENT?

What is the single thing that continually and without fail seems to separate you from the moment of living? It is the thinking mind, is it not? It continually moves about between memories of the past and projections into the future, interpretations of the moment in the context of past conditioning or anxieties about what might come. It carries on a running dialogue about everything. It is your private tour guide or narrator, incessantly commenting on the passing scene. The thinking mind sometimes seems capable of getting into every nook and cranny of your life without exception. And while the thinking mind carries on its continual commentary, it imagines that its thoughts about the moment are the same as experiencing the moment.

Imagine seeing a flower before you had a name for it. Here is a delicate pink, white, and green shape flowing in a graceful pattern, perhaps delivering a sweet fragrance. Initially, there is simply experiencing, no separate subject or object. Then comes naming: "That is a flower." Before naming, there has simply been *seeing*, without a "seer" and a thing "seen." Now there is a "something" that is seen by a "someone." Both have names, names that are part of the mind's conditioning. This fact does not mean language, names, or concepts are wrong. It just means they are not the reality to which they point.

Separation arises along with the naming. The experience becomes "*I* [a separate *someone*] see a flower [a separate *object*]." Along with this arrives an accompanying mental commentary about whether the flower was pretty, whether we liked it, what it reminded us of, when we saw a flower like that before, when we planted flowers in our garden, how quickly they got eaten by snails, what a poor gardener we were, how we should really remember to feed our indoor plants tomorrow or send flowers to our friend for her birthday, and on and on and on.

Actually, in this experience, *seeing* and its object (flower) arose together. But how quickly the experience of seeing becomes a memory, a concept of a "someone" seeing a "something" about which he has various opinions, associations, and reactions. With this automatic reduction of experience to names and labels, we move away from the freshness, wonder, and intimacy of the moment and begin to believe that the virtual reality we assign to our thoughts is Reality. It is not, and yet neither is it separate. What has been *aware* of both the moment of seeing and the mind's movement to describe?

PERCEPTION IS NOT CONCEPTION

The running commentary of the thinking mind is not the same as experiencing the moment, although thinking may be the experience of the moment. Perception is not conception. Neither perception nor conception could occur without Consciousness, but conceptualization is what appears to take us away from the present moment. Thinking becomes our means of separation from simply *being*, yet thoughts are neither good nor bad. They are simply thoughts. What notices them?

What is indivisible and undifferentiated becomes differentiated by conceptualization, by naming. This is not a problem if we experience ourselves as that which is indivisible and has manifested itself in all forms or functions. But the average person takes his or her conceptualization to be the same as the reality to which concepts are merely pointing. In other words, we take our thoughts about a thing or a person, God or "enlightenment," to be the truth; and we take the *concept* of ourselves to be who we are. We imagine our concepts are the same as what we perceive, and thus we stop being open to the moment in its essential nature of Being—a flowing river of Being. We take our *ideas* about who we are to be the same as the reality of who we are and thus lock ourselves tightly in a separate and rigid identity that cannot experience its true nature.

It is the conditioned mind and its continuous monologue about life that gives experience meaning, interpretation, and value—positive or negative. Without such an incessant flow of ideas—that is, when the mind quiets down or ceases to judge—there is experience of life as it is. This does not mean that the conditioning of the body-mind will not appear, or will not sometimes be quite useful, or will not affect the experience of living. Nor does it mean that no preferences will arise or that thoughts are necessarily an obstacle. They are not—*unless* we believe they are Truth. However, it does mean that concepts are not imagined to be truth about anything, and one's happiness does not depend on having one's preferences constantly met. The truth that quenches our spiritual thirst or longing will not be found in our conditioned mind.

NO ONE ELSE CAN DELIVER WHAT YOU ARE

Spiritual egos want to "know" what the awakened ones speak about and imagine Truth can be found in understanding the concepts. Even though some written or spoken words seem to be alive with *presence* and resonate deeply, it is where the words come from and where they are received that makes them shimmer, not the concepts. Words are used to point toward Truth or Reality. Spiritual ambition wants to take someone else's description and try to live *as if* it understood. But as long as you imagine someone else can deliver the taste of your food without your taking a bite, you will never know for yourself. It is only experiential knowing that nurtures and transforms us.

No one else can deliver truth to you. You may imagine that "truth" or "you" have to look a certain way, based on your understanding of someone else's description. This obstacle will never be overcome until there is a sincere desire to find Truth for yourself, regardless of how anyone else may describe it. "Be a lamp unto yourself," advised the Buddha. "Find out who it is who wants to know," says the Advaitin guru. When we begin to truly taste what it is that feels nourishing to the heart, words become less important. A menu does not deliver the taste of food.

Can we begin to see that our longing for awakening, enlightenment, love, or peace is a gift from the Infinite, a precious thread to follow inward, and that our spiritual ambition drives us away from what is here in this moment, keeps us looking elsewhere than in the heart of our own awareness for the jewel? The place to look for Spirit, for Truth, is in the looking, right here and right now.

As the poet Kabir pointed out, "When the mind wants to break its link with the world / it still holds on to one thing." For me, the important point here is "wants to." When the mind wants something, it generally means it is not content to be where it is. Thus, wanting to break one's link is the assertion of separation that is *itself* separation! I do not dismiss the freedom and truth experienced in transcending our ideas of a world or a "self." Waking up out of the relative into the Absolute is an important first step, but ultimately we find that what is transcendent is also immanent in the world and in our very lives.

Whatever appears in a human life is life unfolding itself in its totality. Effort is not "yours," nor is non-effort "yours," yet it is no one else's either. Through all the ideas, all the confusion, all the desiring, and all the attempts to stop desiring, seeking continues, and spiritual ambition continues. The spiritual seeker imagines himself vying for what he thinks is a *personal* "enlightenment," a trophy for the accomplishments or pleasure of the spiritual ego. Spiritual ambition is the ego's desire to awaken to the Undivided, to possess its wisdom and compassion, *yet still remain a separate "me."* The stream does not want to relinquish its conditioned view of what it is.

3

SILENCE AND STILLNESS: THE GREATEST TEACHERS

All that is required to realize the Self is to be still.
What can be easier than that?[1]
RAMANA MAHARSHI

If you are a seeker of the deepest Truth, silence and stillness are your greatest teachers. Empty of concepts, absent of separation, our own deep silence and stillness reveal what words cannot. The silence I am pointing to is not a concept of silence, not a spaced-out, trance-like, dimmed, or static state of consciousness. It is not the absence of sound. Silence leads us beyond the mind. Silence comes before names. Silence comes before heaven and earth. Silence is your deepest knowing. You will know Silence, for the body-mind will begin to feel very still and may at times seem to disappear altogether, leaving only peace and utter stillness.

But do not imagine the body must be on a cushion or your environment free of traffic noise. Silence is present everywhere, at all times. Stillness does not require the absence of movement. Silence and sound arise together. Stillness and movement arise together. Sounds come and go, but silence remains. Life, energy, breath, thoughts, feelings move about continually, but stillness never ceases.

Silence is a living presence—alive and palpable, intimate and unceasing, natural and whole. Its depths lie mostly unknown because we use noise incessantly to distract us from silence—the noise of our inner talking, the stories we tell ourselves to keep emotions churning, the lies we live due to fear, the ways we continually trade the alive silence of our unborn nature for conditioned thoughts and judgments. Stillness does not resist the moment. Thoughts, feelings, sensations may come and go, but *You* are still. To be still is to touch the deep silence of our true nature. Within that stillness of Being all movement can happen.

If you are drawn to interior silence, this is your soul food. If you are drawn to music, this is your soul food. If you are drawn to service, this is your soul food. I am not suggesting everyone needs to be drawn to silence. But if you are, it will take you beyond yourself. For others, the rhythms of music or dance take you beyond yourself. If you are drawn to science, discovery will take you beyond yourself. We are here to be who we are. Because all there is is God or Consciousness, all of life is holy—all manifestations, all functions, all moments.

In order to walk through the doorway that reveals what we truly are, we must leave our concepts at the door—not because the mind is an enemy of truth or because it is not valuable for maneuvering in the world of ideas, but because the thinking mind will never find the deepest truth. Thinking cannot *see*. The mind operates only in the known and is time bound. What is most deeply true is unknown to the mind, though not unknown to itself, and is timeless. In truth, there is no actual door, but we must walk through it nonetheless. No one can give us our essence or take it away. The journey is one we must take ourselves.

NOTICING STILLNESS AND SILENCE

Have you stopped lately to notice the deep stillness all around you, the unfathomable silence within you? Do you ever stop to listen to the silence in nature, the silence that allows you to hear the wind blowing through pine needles, the sound of the crow calling through the stillness, your own breathing? Have you stopped to notice the freedom, peace, and total acceptance you have for yourself when you do not believe thoughts? Have you stopped to notice what is noticing this moment? Do not pass over this last question lightly, and do not hold on to it too tightly.

An Invitation to Stop

In this very moment lies an invitation to the Silence that reveals itself when you simply stop.

Perhaps your mind is asking, "Stop what?"

Just stop! Stop asking.

Stop trying.

Stop pretending.

Stop believing your stories of whom you are or where you have to go.

Stop thinking you know something or don't know something.

How?

There is no "how"; "how" is more mind activity.

Silence needs no "how." It simply IS.

You simply ARE.

If you want to discover what you truly are, just stop—even an instant is long enough.

What is here when you simply stop?

Stopping does not mean life will cease moving. Silence does not need a special time or place to be what it is. A moment of stopping to enjoy a cup of tea, to listen to birdsongs in your own backyard, or to treat yourself to several days of a silent retreat—all offer beautiful opportunities to stop engaging the restless mind and start noticing the only thing that is unceasing.

AS ATTENTION TURNS INWARD, FEAR MAY GUARD THE GATE

Anxiety and fear may seem to guard the gate to Silence, as gargoyles guard the doors to great cathedrals, or dragons guard the jewel, or Tibetan *thangkas* depict aspects of bodhisattvas looking fierce and threatening. But eventually, we are given the courage to press on and to discover the insubstantiality of our fears. It can happen when we become more interested in being than in improving, more interested in truth than in feeling comfortable, when we prefer listening to "knowing," when we are more intrigued by now than by then or when.

This is a journey into the Heart's cave, a cave that holds a mystery, a precious jewel, but can be reached only by exploring the unknown. Instead of looking out, as we might look out at a sunset or at our most beloved friend, we invite attention to turn inward, not simply to our ideas or memories, but more deeply—deeper than these productions of mind, deeper than feelings, deeper than sensations, beyond all words and concepts.

In stillness and silence, we stop looking "out there" and begin looking within for the truth of what we are. We turn our looking around until we come to a profound "I don't know." In such unknowing, the mind may become frightened and want to return to the known in order to feel safe. It may, indeed, reverse our journey many times before we have the courage to keep going. But once we have entered the cave that leads to the deepest discovery of our essence, we must stand firm, neither returning to the known, nor imagining what is unknown. Thinking cannot reveal the unknown. In the intimacy of silence, beyond anything that can be thought, essence reveals itself to itself as the Source of all that is; this can never be described in words. It is sensed, revealed, intuited. Pay attention to the felt sense of silence, how it dissolves barriers, soothes, nurtures, simultaneously relaxes and enlivens the body.

SOAKING IN SILENCE

Soaking in silence is like being bathed from the inside out. Whatever needs attention, warmth, love, purification, or liberation is invited forth from the shadows to be seen, felt, and drawn back into the wholeness that belongs to our Being. As silence drenches us inside and out, we experience its intimacy, freshness, and responsiveness. We can sense the difference between words and actions that come directly from silence and those that feel stale or conditioned. We feel the subtle currents of silence more readily than before; and we begin to feel a tender love for life in all its distinct expressions—not because we should or because we have become saints, but because we have been transformed by Silence.

SILENCE IS ALWAYS IN HARMONY

Have you noticed that silence seems to be in harmony with everything? It neither judges nor agrees with life, neither rejects nor clings to experience, has no "I" to tell it what it should or should not allow, and does not seem to pay much attention to anyone's inner narrative—the virtual reality of thought. It seems to hold no preference for classical music or rap music, for birds singing or jackhammers pounding. It seems to embrace all creatures equally, those having eight legs, four legs, two legs, or no legs. In its inability to separate from any condition, experience, or form, it has no fear.

Silence is in harmony with moments that seem peaceful and moments that appear otherwise to our conditioned mind. Silence is in harmony with all religions, all peoples, all moments, all experiences. It is equally present in experiences of terror and in experiences of bliss, in sorrow as well as in joy. It presides serenely at every birth and every death. The Western mind seems to be conditioned to imagine life should only be one-half of the play of opposites—the good, the beautiful, the true—and does not like its idea of divine Light to be whole, nonjudgmental, and shining equally on the saint and the sinner, on destruction as well as creation. Nature shows us both aspects.

SILENCE PERMEATES NATURE

Notice how silence permeates nature, how everything has its own quality of silence, the way silence connects us to heaven and earth. Mother Nature is a very wise teacher. She teaches us in silence about life and death, impermanence, renewal, and the connectedness of life. She demands nothing of us in exchange for our enjoying her warmth, shade, food, water, trees, flowers; and her silence never demands we be different from how we are. Of course, she also shows us her power when she sweeps through as a storm, a tornado, a drought, or an earthquake, not picking favorites or targeting enemies. Even these moments arise from her vast, silent nature. Her presence is impersonal.

One of my favorite pastimes as a child was sitting in our backyard apple tree. I could sit for hours just watching the world of sky, birds, and insects and never be bored. The changing seasons delighted me. Mother Nature was a wonderful companion and became a very dependable mother to me after my own mother died. In the arms of her apple tree and in the sweet love of my father, I never again felt so alone as I did that one Easter Sunday after my mother's death. In the great silence of nature, perched high in a tree watching the clouds and seasons change, I grew close to the Infinite once again. And while I let God know I thought he had lied to me about the "faith" thing, I began to pray again, to let in God again. Over the next many decades, the Divine seemed to appear as mother, father, friend, lover, teacher, guide—whatever was needed.

GOD, NATURE, AND CONSCIOUSNESS

The Infinite is not separate from nature and not separate from you. The idea of Divinity being separate from our natural life and our natural way of being seems unbelievable to me, and yet God is the Consciousness of those who imagine their separateness is real, also. A precocious child observed in the book *Mister God, This Is Anna* that God has infinite viewing points, whereas we have infinite points of view.[2] The light of Consciousness shines out of the eyes of ants and antelopes, butter-flies and beetles, honeybees and hawks, dogs and donkeys, monkeys and humans.

When we see from Totality, nothing is excluded, and no one stands outside. Nothing is created apart from or outside of the mystery of Being and the Awareness that is the "knowing" of it. No person, feel-ing, thought, moment; no illness or healing; no breath, blink, hair, or atom; no touch, smell, taste, or sight is separate. None of those apparent "things" has an independent, separate existence. Each arises because of interconnected causes and conditions, and yet none of those conditions can be divided from their formless ground. That is the paradox. Duality says life is "either/or." Nonduality says it is "both/ and." Yet nothing can define Absolute Reality. It is not true to call its nature dual or nondual. How can the nameless be named? How can what is everything and nothing be categorized according to qualities?

Those are tasks of the mind, but the great Silence does not even have "silence" as its name. And yet we try to describe the indescribable.

Look at your reflection in a still pool of water. Are you the eyes looking or the Consciousness behind your eyes looking? Are you the body peering into the pool or the seeing that sees the body, the pool, and the sky simultaneously? Are you the body you call a "self" or a reflection of your Self? Are you the object of your seeing or the subject of your seeing? Who imagines he or she can *know*? Who can tell the difference?

IN NATURE, WE ARE FREE TO *BE*

If we observe nature for any period of time, we may become more and more convinced that there is an action of life that simply happens, that it is mysterious, beautiful, and unknown, and that we are as much a part of that action as a little ant scurrying back and forth between the dead earthworm in your garden and its home under your porch. The silence of nature has no anxieties about its *being* or what shows up in its space. Unlike judging minds, nature makes no demands on its creatures, including ourselves, to be different from how they are, which is why we often feel so much more open, free, and intimate with life when we are in nature.

We can temporarily lose our self-obsession while hiking in the mountains or in the woods, walking along the beach or a lake, planting flowers in a little pot on our doorstep; and when we do lose our obsession, we often feel a great relief. If we allow it, we can be free of the "me" and free to be naturally ourselves. Spending time in nature, we can become more comfortable with many things, including the beauty and unfolding of both life and death and the necessity of impermanence for the continuance of life. Forms may transform, but life flows on. And through it all, silence and stillness remain untouched, at peace, yet always touching the moment exactly as it is.

4

PATHS AND PRACTICES IN THE SEARCH FOR TRUTH

Nothing you do can create enlightenment.
Then why are there spiritual practices?
To encourage your mind to be open and
still long enough to receive Truth's gift.

While silence and stillness are actually all that are required, the egoic mind finds it challenging to rest in these dimensions, and so spiritual practices of all kinds have been developed to help quiet the mind and return it to its original nature. Do spiritual practices lead to Truth, or is Truth moving as spiritual practice?

Whatever path or practice you may follow, there are many ideas about what leads to the end of seeking. But I have yet to meet a single person in whom awakening, and hence a shift of identity, has occurred who did not describe its appearance as spontaneous and unexpected. Beforehand, there may have been practices or devastating life crises. Some had been searching for a lifetime; others seemed not to have been searching at all. There may have been apparent purification of the mind, development of single-pointedness, increasing ability to concentrate, practices that aim at opening the heart or various chakras, kundalini energy moving up the spine, or service (*seva*) that brought humility (or pride). Or there may have been such misery that they were tempted to end their life before something intervened to save it. Any of these experiences, or none of them, may have appeared.

The question is: To what or whom have they appeared? To oneself, of course! And who is that self?

SEEKERS OF TRUTH

There are seekers of truth in many fields—physical, biological, and psychological sciences, for example. Whether seeking objective truth about the physical universe or subjective truth about psychological realities, each discipline will build on what is known but must remain open to what is unknown. Practitioners of each must question their assumptions, test hypotheses, and experience success and failure. Many ideas and theories once accepted as "truth" have been proven wrong. Are you open to the possibility that what you have accepted as the "truth" of who you are might be one of them?

If you are a seeker of ultimate Truth, are you willing to question your assumptions, theories, ideas, or opinions and step openly and nakedly into the silence and stillness of the unknown? It is here that Truth may reveal itself as both the *knowing* and the *being* of objective and subjective realities. It is in being humbled by our failures and in surrendering our attempts to "know" intellectually that knowledge may appear, a knowledge that the finite mind cannot possess.

TRUTH IS NOT SOMEWHERE ELSE

Actually, there is no path to Truth. Truth is not somewhere else. It is here now and requires no traversing of time or distance. Most practices, regardless of the tradition, are designed to encourage the seeker to discover that which is transcendently present in the immediacy of Now.

What is present now in your experience? What knows it? What is aware? The Truth of what you are! But conditioned thought holds that that is a body-mind, separate from all others, separate from life, separate from Truth. This is a bit like imagining a thought, an eyelash, or your fingernail is the whole of "you," when all the while what is timelessly awake as *You* is looking out from one Consciousness at its own body of Being spread through billions of universes.

YET PATHS AND PRACTICES DEVELOP

While Truth is nowhere that you are not, the seeker imagines it is, so paths and practices have developed to aid the seeker in discovering, listening to, and entering the deeper, silent dimensions of one's own being.

We may have a preference for the language and flavors of one particular tradition, practice, set of scriptures, or collection of teachings, but at the heart of the matter, there is no language for the deepest experience or revelations. The attempts to describe them are wrapped in languages and cultures that differ from one another. No tradition and no teachings hold exclusive ownership of Truth. Truth is not a belief, although beliefs appear. It is not created by faith or devotion, yet faith and devotion may appear. Allow yourself to move where you feel moved when you sense it is coming from that deep spiritual impulse.

In my experience, I seem to have been drawn to taste deeply of several traditions: Christian, Advaita, and Zen. Each provides beautiful expressions of the Infinite in unique ways, yet all seem to share in their deepest mystical traditions the same mystery that has no beginning and no end but is present here and now.

GRADUAL AND DIRECT PATHS

So-called paths to awakening can be considered gradual or direct, and each has its strengths and weaknesses. Gradual paths can help the seeker mature; become kinder, more open, ethical, or compassionate; able to concentrate attention; and become familiar with silence and presence. Gradual paths can sometimes leave one searching forever, however, trying to perfect a practice, one's person, or one's actions in order to have a better life or a better "next" life. Sometimes awakening is not even considered, as there is so much emphasis on the seeker's practice. And of course, at times, a seeker's attention to his or her breath may lead to the discovery that there is no one breathing; the breath is breathing itself, as is the rest of life.

Direct paths seek to uncover the infinite ground at the very beginning, directing the seeker to what is ever present and aware. Direct

31

paths begin at the apparent end. Yet at times, early insights or glimpses of awakening that may occur on this path can provide a false sense of attainment for a spiritual ego. Even a very authentic awakening to our true nature does not, *in itself,* confer maturity or infallibility in one's relative life.

WHAT PRACTICE IS THE "RIGHT" ONE?

Our so-called path is actually here, wherever we find ourselves walking. Yet minds are often confused about what path or practice is the "right" one and whether effort or no effort is required for realization. Some spiritual teachers demand great effort on the part of the student or disciple; others encourage following the moment. (For example: "You must sit twice a day every day regardless of your mind's desires; disciplining your mind is the most important practice" versus "If you feel like meditating, then by all means meditate; if not, then don't.") What is right for you? The answers will simply appear as Consciousness moves to awaken itself from its own forgetfulness. The spiritual journey for each of us is tailored to our particular unfolding, preferences, temperament, sensibilities, language, culture, and need. I have always resonated with Nisargadatta's observation:

> When effort is needed, effort will appear.
> When effortlessness becomes essential, it will assert itself.
> You need not push life about.
> Just flow with it and give yourself completely
> to the task of the present moment.[1]

The ambitious spiritual ego does not want to give itself completely to the present moment. It believes the reality it is seeking could not possibly include *this* moment of experience. But tell me, what is absent from Totality? What could be separate from the open, ever-present Awareness that has been awake to every experience? The moment may seem beautiful, ugly, tender, harsh, loud, or soft; it includes rainy days and sunny days, the grocer at the corner store, the child at play in the park, our agony, our joy. What has been *here* in the midst of all changing experiences?

THE QUESTION OF PROGRESS

If you believe that you must sit on a cushion one hour a day or you will never "progress" on the spiritual path, you will either sit one hour a day or you will feel guilty that you are not. The idea of "progress" is always a concept of the mind, an idea that can certainly *appear* to be a motivating force. However, whatever action or experiencing you take to be "progress" simply appears when it appears, the action of the moment. "Progress" is based on memory. You imagine that "you" were somewhere in the past and that now you are somewhere else closer to the place you imagine you wish to go in the future. Such is the play of Consciousness, shifting experiences, but haven't *You* simply been "here" for every experience? Who is the You?

IS EGO AN ENEMY?

In the spiritual search, it seems as though it is ego that searches, that follows practices, makes choices, imagines it is either progressing or remaining hopelessly stuck in its ambition to attain "enlightenment." But it is also considered the "bad guy" in spiritual circles and so it imagines it has to somehow destroy itself. The ego that so earnestly searches and is so frequently frustrated is not a monster, not a demon; the ego is nothing you could destroy even if you wanted to, and it will not end its own life by any efforts it can produce.

The ego is not an enemy; it simply does not exist as what you imagine. Thought has constructed a separate "self," which is an illusion. Even the idea of separation—that collection of thoughts and memories you have determined is "you"—is itself a limited reflection of what you seek. So-called ego derives its consciousness from the universal awareness/awakeness you imagine is somewhere else, but is it? The egoic mind of even the most sincere seeker does not know how to surrender, but is *being* surrendered to Truth, to love, to the openness of not knowing.

RIPENING GREEN WOOD

We might say that spiritual practices such as contemplation, meditation, and prayer are all methods used to ripen green wood so that it can be burned in the fire of Truth, the fire of love. The green wood is our habitual way of thinking, acting, and reacting as egos, as consciousness identified with limitation and the assumption of being separate. Spiritual practices are methods that can begin to soften our stance toward our self, toward life in general, and to open us to what transcends the habitual. They are invitations to become intimate with the wisdom of silence and stillness.

CONTEMPLATION

Contemplation is looking deeply into anything from one's inner silence and stillness. In the spiritual seeker's life it could be a teaching story, a poem, a passage of scripture in various traditions, or koan study in Zen. Koan study puts the student in a pressure cooker because the question asked cannot be answered through use of the intellect. One must become the question and demonstrate the answer, not talk about it. Sometimes the great pressure of the roshi refusing one's answers time and time again can lead to a breakthrough. Contemplating scripture is a gentler process and includes not only thinking and feeling into it but also "becoming" the characters in the story or "being" what is described.

For many years, my spiritual life was centered on devotion to God as I understood God. I was not interested in knowing my Self. The Sanskrit words *bhakti* (devotion) and *jnana* (knowledge) were not in my vocabulary. I was no longer the angry child, wanting to know who took my mother away in death; as an adult, I just wanted to know God. I felt naturally inclined to meditate, although the Protestant church I attended said nothing about meditation, much less offered any instruction. So I bought a book about meditation and decided on the basis of what I read that I must practice it. Counting breaths held no appeal for me, so I decided to begin by contemplating a Bible verse.

The verse I chose was Psalm 46:10. Each morning, as I sat contemplating the words "Be still and know that I am God," something inside gradually quieted down. Each word seemed to deliver a message or engage a question.

 ## Invitation to Contemplation: Be Still

I would like to invite you to join me in contemplating these words and the felt sense of their meaning in your own experience. Let there be space and silence as you quietly allow the words and your experience to merge.

> Be.
> Just *be*.
> Be still and *know*.
> Be still and simply know *that*.
> Be still and know that *I*.
> Be still and know that *I am*.
> *Be still and know that I am* God.[2]

As I contemplated these words over and over for many years, I never for a moment imagined their meaning could lead to a human being experiencing his or her "I am" as the Divine. In becoming still, I imagined it might be possible to come closer to God.

When, years later, I read Ramana Maharshi's words that the phrase *Be still and know that I am God* "sums up the whole teaching," I realized that this verse was not one I had just picked at random, as I had supposed. It had been delivered by my Self, the inner guru, and was specific to the path that seemed to be unfolding in the life I imagined then was "mine." Can you trust how your spiritual life wants to unfold as well? Each of us has a unique path to awakening if we are sincerely longing for Truth. There is no single way that the Divine awakens itself in its own experience of being human.

BHAKTI AND JNANA:
DEVOTION AND KNOWLEDGE

> Intense love is like moonlight and intense knowledge
>   like sunlight.
> The light of the moon—so delicate and healing to gaze
>   upon—
> is simply sunlight in another form. In the infinite sky of
> consciousness, you can always clearly observe sun and
>   moon. . . .
> Knowledge is the flower, love its fragrance.[3]
> LEX HIXON

Knowledge is the experiential knowing or sensing of one's true nature as emptiness, pure awareness, spirit, a "no-thingness" that is undivided. *Love* is the intimate response of the heart to the knowledge of one-ness, the oneness of our single essence with every-thing. The Heart of Awareness does not separate the flower from its fragrance.

We cannot actually separate wisdom from its self-less love or love from wisdom, yet certain spiritual paths seem to focus more on one than the other. In the moment when longing for love finds itself to *be* love, or longing for truth discovers that it *is* Truth, both wisdom and love merge as one. Love flows from emptiness, and emptiness knows itself through love. Neither wisdom nor love can be "known" through books, texts, scriptures, or words of any kind, but only in the awake silence that reveals itself beyond words.

If you are drawn to the path of love and devotion (bhakti), then prayer, worship, service, ritual, chanting, mantra, devotional practices, and action will be part of your path. If you are drawn to the path of wisdom (jnana), then meditation, contemplation, self-inquiry may appear. But at some point, both the heart wishing to surrender to God and the mind searching for its Source will be surrendered to Silence.

The path of devotion is more suited to some temperaments and the path of knowledge to others. Or you might find, as happened in this life, that both may appear at different times. The bhakti path seeks to move the seeker out of self-obsession and toward love and union with God, to serve whatever love one has discovered. The jnana path seeks to drive the seeker inward, toward knowledge of Truth or the true Self, by seeking the Source of the seeker. It is known as an intellectual path and involves removing everything that is not Truth in order to discover the deepest essence or clarity.

The seeker who is a devotee and lover of God, who seeks to surrender all actions *to* God, comes to understand that everything *is* God. The intellectual seeker, "subtracting" all she is *not*, reaches the understanding that nothing exists *except* Truth (or God) and, in seeing the Oneness, comes to the love that flows out from such an understanding. Both paths will eventually end up in the same place—surrender to God or surrender to Truth. Both paths serve the Infinite and involve remembering our divine nature and manifesting that nature in our living.

STRUCTURED AND UNSTRUCTURED MEDITATION

There are many types of meditation practices in various traditions and also outside of traditions. They generally fall into one of two categories: structured or unstructured time sitting in silence and being still. Structured practices include concentration practices, such as counting or focusing on the breath, reciting a mantra, or visualizing the guru, and they are used for gathering the scattered mind and developing the ability to focus the mind in one place. They are useful practices in that they initially show the seeker how very active the mind is. They will frustrate the seeker at first; he will be sure he is not doing the practices correctly because his thinking keeps interrupting his focus on the object of concentration.

Over time, concentration practices do quiet the mind, and they have been shown to have benefits in reducing stress, lowering blood pressure, and bringing moments of calm into a troubled life or a restless mind. If these are the goals, they are quite useful. If you are a seeker of the Truth that frees one from one's "self," however, they may or may not lead to liberation, since the "meditator" may continue to feel separate from the meditation.

Unstructured meditation is an invitation to simply sit without attempting to control anything that arises. It is an invitation to *be*—to *be* the silence, not the one who is trying to be silent; to *be* the awareness, not the one who is trying to be aware. It is not about controlling experience or maintaining a certain state of consciousness. True meditation reveals what IS before any "state" of consciousness. There can be moments where there is no thought, no ego, and no time. We are conscious, if even for a moment, of *being* what we ARE.

This type of meditation occurs when consciousness sinks into the unknown, into the depths of silence, where there is no "meditator." It is a deep listening to silence. Whether thoughts appear or do not appear is not a concern. We are not efforting to maintain a "state," but rather coming to rest in our natural state. This form of meditation does not engage the ego, as do many structured meditation techniques. Of course, in the beginning you will encounter the noise of your "narrator," but you are not engaged in battle with your thinking. In fact, as consciousness comes to rest in its home ground, we discover that thought cannot interrupt the awake silence we eventually discover is our true nature. It is just another phenomenon that comes and goes in the Heart of Awareness.

This type of meditation can render the ego more and more transparent, since we are no longer striving to make something happen. It is a beautiful opportunity to unhook from our digital and virtual worlds, from our goal-oriented minds, and simply rest as what we are. We begin to see that when we are not struggling against our thoughts or feelings, something knows how to realign itself with its true nature. In this type of meditation, we also come to connect with the deep well of silence and wisdom into which we can drop our most important existential questions. Into this depth of knowing, we can inquire: *Who or what am I, really?*

MANTRA MEDITATION

Mantra practice is a form of structured meditation, but one that can help connect the seeker with what is deeper than the mind. It gives the mind something to do as the rest of one's being quiets down. If the mantra includes a name of the Divine, perhaps has been used for centuries, and holds the energy of thousands who have gone before, the sounds themselves seem to invite a deepening into a sense of the Divine. In India, mantra practice has been described as being akin to giving an elephant a stick to hold in its trunk while walking through a crowded marketplace. As long as it holds on to the stick, it does not disturb the market with its trunk swinging wildly from side to side.

In the midst of my early years of contemplation of "Be still," a Hebrew mantra appeared from the stillness whose meaning I did not know, but I remembered the words clearly. In consulting a rabbi, I learned it was a common Hebrew blessing. Those words, "*Baruch atah Adonai, Elohenu*," wove themselves into the very fabric of my life for the next ten years—in meditation, while driving to work, when waiting for a dentist appointment, between client hours. Whether I was feeling distressed or at peace, that Hebrew prayer (translated as "Blessed art Thou, Lord of the Universe") spoke itself and sang itself through a strange melody in the depths of my being. It even showed up in my dreams, so embedded was it in my consciousness. Even now I sometimes sing it as a lullaby to my grandsons, and I sang it the night my husband lay dying. Sometimes we may not seek a mantra, yet one seeks us.

VIPASSANA MEDITATION AND MINDFULNESS MEDITATION

Vipassana, which means "to see things as they are," is also called *insight meditation*, a form of structured meditation that comes from the Buddhist tradition. Initially the seeker is invited to notice the breath rising and falling or to notice other sensations, to pay close attention to the objects of awareness, and to note what is arising in consciousness by naming it. Rather than following the content of a thought or feeling, for example, the meditator is instructed to simply name "thinking" or "feeling." So the experience of naming might appear as: "rising," "falling" (when aware of the breath), or "hearing," "thinking," "feeling," and so forth. In this way one comes to experience being a witness to one's mind and body activity rather than being totally identified with or at the mercy of the changing objects of awareness. This can sometimes lead to a breakthrough in realizing that what is present in all experiences is what you are. Often, however, it leads to the seeker becoming identified with one part of the mind watching another while being continually identified as the "doer." The egoic "doer" now becomes the "watcher."

In true witnessing, we know what is happening in the moment that it is happening, but this requires no effort, no thinking about witnessing. When we are sitting, walking, eating, running, speaking, we know we are sitting, walking, eating, running, speaking. This is called *mindfulness*. Our attention is on the moment, and in that intimacy, we can touch the ground of Being itself. True Presence is not a "someone" trying to be present. Mindfulness meditation can be similar to Vipassana, although it is often applied in secular settings rather than as a Buddhist practice. It can also be a method of relating to one's experience in a more accepting, nonjudgmental way that helps to reduce stress.

PRAYER

Prayer is communing with and listening in silence to the inner voice of the Beloved, in whatever name or form it has been given. Prayer opens the heart to something beyond ego. It may begin as a child's prayer to a Santa Claus God in the sky, asking for things for the "me." It may include devotion to a guru or a spiritual master for whom one has developed a great love. Often we do not come to prayer except in crises, when we are being broken open and have nowhere else to turn. Sometimes that is the value of our suffering; we are surrendered to a deeper wisdom that arises from beyond the egoic mind. In the deepest prayer, there are no words or requests, just a sense of communion or oneness with one's sense of the Infinite.

In working with Mother Teresa, who called herself just "a little pencil in the hands of God," I discovered that when there was a "need," the first stop was not thought or the telephone, but the chapel. It was in silence that the inspiration for whom to call or where to go would come. Prayer is listening from the inner silence, love, knowledge, and wisdom of our deepest nature. It is a vehicle of Consciousness relating to itself, although the individual on the path of devotion will not likely call God Consciousness or Being. Rather, God is experienced personally as a deity, a friend, a guide.

Prayer may eventually lead beyond any and all ideas of a god or goddess, as one comes to know the Beloved as one's Self, one's deepest essence. The Christian mystic Meister Eckhart prayed to rid himself of any idea of God.

TO WHOM WOULD I BE PRAYING?

Often people who are somewhat familiar with the path of Advaita or nonduality will feel they should not pray. "To whom would I be praying?" they ask. But this can sometimes be an intellectual attempt to stop what might be a natural way of opening the heart to a greater love or greater humility in favor of the mind holding on to a philosophical stance. Truth holds no philosophical or religious dogma. It is so much simpler. If you are moved to pray, prayer can move you beyond yourself.

The real question is whether we are living our lives as a prayer. Once awakening has occurred, the prayer may simply be "thank you" for whatever moment is encountered—or, as the Advaita Vedanta teacher Jean Klein once put it, "thanking with no one to thank." An attitude of gratitude is itself a prayer that can transform a life.

MYSTIC UNION

Intense devotion can bring about moments of mystic union with the Beloved. In these moments, separation dissolves in bliss. The problem with mystic union, however, is that in order to have the ecstasy of union, you have to separate, again and again. Bliss and ecstasy can be as addictive as wonderful sex, a heart-opening psychotropic drug, or fantastic food. But like all experiences, these come and go. They do not, in themselves, bring liberation. In my experience, moments of union came unexpectedly and were welcomed deeply, but something kept moving beyond them.

5

PEACE, EGO,
AND INQUIRY

There is no such thing as peace of mind.
Mind means disturbance; restlessness itself is mind. . . .
The Self does not need to be put to rest.
It is peace itself, not at peace.
Only the mind is restless.[1]

NISARGADATTA MAHARAJ

INNER PEACE IS FREE OF CONDITIONS

Peace is what we deeply ARE—the peace that can embrace our troubled minds, the peace that is unceasing acceptance of all that is. It is the clarity that holds our confusion, the freedom that allows us to simply *be*, the love that touches all that has been unloved. This peace lies beyond the illusion of separation and is free of conditions. When we begin spiritual practices, we want to make our egoic mind peaceful, clear, accepting, free, and loving. Even with this good intention, we fail to look beyond our limited identification. We do not seek the truth of the seeker. Instead we try to remake the constructed egoic "self" we have innocently and mistakenly concluded we are.

IS PEACE BORING?

Many years ago, I was privileged to attend a retreat for psychotherapists led by Thich Nhat Hanh. This was one of the first things he said:

"Peace is important, but not as important as our capacity to enjoy it. Peace is right here in the present moment, but we find it boring; so we look elsewhere—drugs, alcohol, sex, thinking, worrying."

IS peace boring? Who would you be in the absence of conflict? Do you notice that your mind often prefers to be entertained, or even agitated, rather than to be quiet? That it continually tries to control life rather than to accept it, projecting a fearful future rather than living in the now? Even when we are touched by a deep and profound peace in the present moment, how quickly thinking wants to reassert itself in time and in identity.

We may long for peace, but only if it looks like our conditioned mind imagines it should look. How do you fill in the sentence that begins, "I will be at peace when . . ."? Can we see how the thought of "peace when" never delivers peace now—not because it is not here now, but because we want something else? We can increase our capacity to enjoy peace when we realize that *this* moment is the only one available for us to touch reality. Perhaps life is neither a problem to be solved nor a destination, but a creation that unfolds endlessly from moment to moment. Peace is boring only when we have not drunk deeply enough from its source.

"I CANNOT MAKE MY MIND PEACEFUL"

In facilitating meditation groups for many years, I have noticed that invariably a beginning student of meditation will report, "I must not be doing it right, because I cannot make my mind peaceful." Indeed, as any of you know who have practiced meditation, the first thing you become aware of when you sit quietly is that the thinking mind is restless. It moves continually in all directions. It especially likes to go backward to memory or forward to planning, projecting, or worrying about the future. It likes to make judgments about everything that happens.

It is very seldom able to touch down in the present moment for more than a fraction of a second. Of course, none of us needs to sit quietly on a cushion to be aware of the thinking mind, but *attempting* to quiet the mind will soon reveal your number one addiction: thinking!

It is our *identification* with thinking that creates the *apparent* separation between "you" and experience, "you" and thought, "you" and feeling, "you" and the moment, "you" and your Self, "you" and the Divine. When I say this, you cannot imagine a moment without thinking, can you? You imagine you would be a vegetable. "I think, therefore I am" represents your experience. Actually, Awareness (Self, the true "I") precedes all thought, including the thought that who you are is only your particular body-mind.

The ability to think serves a necessary purpose for the body-mind organism, its development, evolution, and survival. What we call "mind" is an incredible power within the Self, causing thoughts to arise; yet there is a greater power—that which *notices* thought. While it is the nature of the mind's activity to think, it is not the nature of the mind to quiet itself, and yet without a quiet mind, we cannot consciously experience the truth of our Being.

WHAT IS EGO?

Ego is identification with the body and the thinking mind. In actuality, an ego does not exist as some separate entity. It is a movement of thought, including memory, feeling, will, resistance, wanting, grasping, and reflection. Ego is a state of consciousness caught in the trance of separation. Thoughts, feelings, sensations simply arise, but what we call "ego" is the afterthought that claims them as belonging to a separate "me." While our mind is conditioned, operates in time, and can contemplate its own thought creations, nowhere will you find an entity called "ego." It is the movement of thought that constructs a conceptual "self" that then claims to be the "thinker," the "doer," the "meditator," the separate "me."

While there is a functional necessity for a sense of self, distinct from others, what I mean by "ego" is our sense of separateness from What Is, from the Self, from one another, from the rest of the universe. This sense of separateness from our wholeness is experienced as an energetic field of resistance whose inner narrator continually chats to itself and holds itself the arbiter of what should or should not be happening in reality.

When ego is seen as simply a movement of thought, and not as a separate entity, we discover that it is Consciousness that makes our identification with form and ever-changing experience feel so real. We become emotionally attached to our egoic "separate" identity, not realizing that Consciousness itself has identified with its own form. No one is to blame; there is only an invitation to inquire, to see deeply. Who is the one I have taken myself to be?

SEPARATION DOES NOT TAKE US TO WHOLENESS

The seeker thinks a separate "self" will be the agent of awakening and blames or praises itself for its perceived failure or success. The sincere impulse to awaken that arose from deep within becomes co-opted by our mind in the form of spiritual ambition, the desire or demand to "achieve" or to "get" something for the "me." Many seekers simply desire another experience, another hit of bliss, to be used as one might use a drug. Experiences may come, but one will not be liberated by them for long, for *all* experiences come and go, the best ones and the worst ones. Our freedom lies in discovering what is ever present regardless of changing experiences.

No matter how earnest, eager, or desperate your mind may be to awaken, separation does not take us to wholeness. Yet every day in countless ways, the spiritual seeker is convinced his or her ego is the vehicle of choice for the spiritual search. You think you are in charge of the search and that your lack of progress betrays a lack of effort, worth, or grace on your part. You try harder and harder, become more and more frustrated; or perhaps just the opposite, you are sure you see signs of your spiritual progress everywhere. Why, just last week, "you" rested in pure Awareness, in utter peace. If only "you" could find a way to return there and to stay in that awareness!

WAR WITH EGO IS BOUND TO FAIL

Many spiritual writings and practices take aim at the ego and treat it as an enemy rather than seeing it for what it is—a movement of thought, mixed with pure Consciousness, carrying the scent of both Consciousness and identity, creating the idea of a separate someone. Ego is not an entity with an independent existence. It is the Self with limitations, Consciousness imagining itself bound to a body. When we look for an ego, we cannot find one apart from our identification with our *thought* of an "I" limited to a body.

If we do not know our true nature, we may begin a war with our ego, a war that is bound to fail. How can you have a war with an illusion? Simply investigate, see it for what it is, and it becomes more and more transparent. The only thing that wants to kill an ego is ego. From the perspective of Totality, ego does not exist as anything other than a movement of thought connected with the sense of "I."

But we rarely see through our ego, and so we treat it as a separate body-mind, as a personal identity that needs continual protection and continual improvement. If we have decided ego is an enemy to defeat, then we imagine we are taking up arms against it. But who is trying to destroy the ego? Ego! The thief is pretending to be the police officer, attempting to catch the thief. Often the "spiritual" ego is battling the "worldly" ego and violently judging itself.

Ego is like a shadow, a pale reflection, a false and limited version of the true Self, and of itself it has no separate agency. No one wants to imagine that his or her ego could be rather irrelevant in terms of Truth, in terms of how life moves, in terms of who/what seems to be the mover of this being we have taken ourselves to be. So we try to polish our ego, punish it, dress it up in camouflage clothing, pamper it, abuse it, pursue a better version of it. We want it to be a better master when it is actually here as a servant.

SELF-INQUIRY SEARCHES FOR THE EGO'S SOURCE

However, all is not lost in using the so-called ego for the spiritual quest. The method of Self-inquiry, as taught by Ramana Maharshi, is based on the ego's searching, not for enlightenment but for its Source. What is the Source of the bundle of thoughts, memories, stories, and experiences that you imagine is yourself?

47

It is not possible for the I-thought (ego) to take you to "enlighten-ment," yet it is possible to follow the ego toward its Source. At some point, you will reach "I don't know." At this point, rather than imagin-ing you have failed in your endeavor, remain at the gate of the unknown. Effort will take us only to the edge. But when identified mind comes close enough to the Source, the same grace that took you to the edge of the unknown may deliver a deeper gift. You will not find an ego, nor will your mind *find* the Source, but separation may dissolve along the way.

> The very purpose of Self-inquiry is to focus the entire
>   mind at its Source.
> It is not, therefore, the case of one "I" searching for
>   another "I." . . .
> Self-inquiry is the one infallible means, the only direct
>   one, to realize
> the unconditioned, absolute Being that you really are.[2]
> RAMANA MAHARSHI

Ramana Maharshi was not interested in helping seekers develop yogic powers (*siddhis*), powers of mind or of body. His method of Self-inquiry was for those interested in finding out who or what they are beyond their thoughts. You could have many powers but still feel separate. You could sit in *samadhi* (absorption) for long periods of time, but when you come out of such a state you could still return to the mind's separate identity. Self-inquiry is an invitation to focus the mind at its Source, which naturally stills the mind. A still mind is open to receive the truth about its Being. If you are drawn to powers of the mind, feel free to explore them. But if you are interested in the truth of who you are, taste your stillness. Silence is drawing you to itself.

While Self-inquiry is not the only spiritual practice that is used to quiet the mind and deliver it to the unconditioned, it is quite effec-tive in addressing the illusion of a separate self. Many practices can help quiet the mind, but when the seeker gets up from the meditation cushion, he or she resumes the identity of doer, thinker, and identified ego. Self-inquiry seeks to cut that illusion at its source.

In my years of being a spiritual teacher, it has become clear to me that many, many folks have a sense of vastness, silent Presence, or the Divine when sitting quietly in meditation or prayer or even simply STOPPING for a moment, but the one who has stopped continues to retain a separate identity as ego. And this does not bring more than a momentary sense of peace or freedom. So the search continues. Self-inquiry does not deliver blissful experience, but rather results in the disappearance of the separate seeker/experiencer.

NO SEPARATE ONE TO ENLIGHTEN

In the sudden, intuitive moment when what you are seeking appears itself as who/what you *are*, the search is over. There is no more doubt. A knowing arises that you have always been what you have been seeking, that what you truly are was the agent of your seeking, present from the beginning, moving life and moving you as an expression of itself. You will know that there is simply no separate one to enlighten!

Each wave that arises in the limitless Ocean of Awareness is revealed to be none other than the ocean itself. And in its still depths, there is peace regardless of changing conditions or manifestations. We discover in the very heart of the human being the infinite Heart of Awareness.

NETI, NETI

Sometimes the jnana path begins with exploring what I am not (*neti, neti*), in which the seeker is invited to both discover and disidentify with all the things he has previously identified as himself. "I am not my thoughts; I am not my feelings; I am not my body; I am not my perception. All these come and go. What does not?" The task is to remove the veils of illusion. There is an ancient and well-known Advaita saying:

> The world is illusion;
> Brahman alone is Real.
> The world is Brahman.

Now the strict Advaitin (nondualist) often seems focused on the first two lines and misses the important third line, which sees God and world as one. When we take a path whose goal seems to remain *only* in an absolute view, then our bodies, our lives, our world can seem illusory, which in the absolute sense they are; but it can lead to a disengagement and an impersonal, unconnected stance toward one's embodied life. We remain divided from our wholeness, which includes every dimension of experience. We lack heartful and compassionate intimacy with our humanness.

To come into embodied existence, whether as an ordinary being or as a sage, we will inevitably feel the pain and pleasure, joy and sorrow of human life. Are we to believe that the task of the spiritually adept is to divorce her self from the world, from others, from the play of existence? Wisdom without love is incomplete. It is through form that compassion can express itself. Completion does not come in neti, neti, but in realizing that the no-thingness and the everythingness of our Being are not separate.

A SHIFT FROM RELATIVE TO ABSOLUTE IS STILL NOT COMPLETE

To awaken to the absolute is a dramatic, liberating, and incredibly important first step, but we may discover it is possible to become stuck in the other side of duality. It can become a beautiful, free, and safe place for the spiritual ego to hide. Awakening is incomplete.

Can we come to discover that what is awake does not identify with either absolute or relative? It claims no identity at all and yet is present in all voices, all languages, and all moments. It will shed its light on any manifestation, whether that expression appears limited or unlimited. It will illuminate any role, any identity, and any aspect of its own Being. How freely it gives itself to life!

AWAKENING OF HEAD, HEART, AND HARA

Awakening, which might be described as the opening of one's eyes to our inherent nature, is always the same understanding wherever it appears, although different traditions might use different language to attempt to describe the experience. To use the words of the Christian mystic Meister Eckhart: "The eye through which I see God is the same eye through which God sees me; my eye and God's eye are one eye, one seeing, one knowing, one love."[3]

The moment of awakening is a sudden, intuitive understanding—not originating in the intellect—that all there is is Consciousness, or God, and "I am *That*." But this "I" is no separate "I"; it is not a personal pronoun, but an impersonal one. Later, we may come to understand that the "I" that is *That* is the same essence that is *this*—this moment, this experience. However, the clarity of knowing is free from any acquired answers or doctrine. It appears from beyond the finite mind. The moment of awakening can be dramatic or quiet; there may have been many tastes before it occurs; and some beings seem to come into their incarnation consciously "remembering." But an authentic awakening always carries with it a shift in identity.

Awakening occurs in different ways and at different levels of experience. There is an awakening of the head, out of egoic identity into the absolute dimension, into emptiness, awareness, openness. This is a profound awakening, an awakening to the transcendent, but is still only a partial one. There is an awakening of the heart to Oneness, to unity, and the causeless love, intimacy, and compassion that moves from the true Heart of Awareness. There is an awakening of the *hara*, a dissolving of the existential knot of separation in our gut, a knot that generally continues to be present experientially even after authentic awakenings to emptiness and oneness have occurred.

For those unfamiliar with the term *hara*, it is considered the seat of energy and balance in the body-mind, located below the navel in the area of the lower belly. It can be felt as a place of an invisible strength when we put our attention there in meditation or in the practice of martial arts. But in deep spiritual awakening, this area of the gut is where we feel the existential grip of ego's deepest and most primitive

51

instinct to survive. It is a contracted state of consciousness that is at the very root of the ego structure—beyond thoughts or images of a "self" that we carry in our mind and beyond the familiar feeling states identified with a "me." These may have been transcended or made transparent in the awakenings of head and heart, but the gut-level existential knot remains.

To come upon this existential knot of consciousness is to come into the space where ego fears its annihilation, its nonbeing. If we bump up against this prerational dimension of fear holding up our separate identity, it can feel like we are having a nightmare but in our waking hours. Nothing external is fearful, and yet we may experience terror. When we are ready, we face into this fear, but it is only when something deeper than our instinct to survive has revealed itself. When this contraction releases, there is a sense of falling into that which has no name. In Zen, it has been called "going through the gateless gate" or "having the bottom fall out of the bucket." There is no way to force letting go on this level, and it is unwise to try. It may also be the case that life does not move to release in this dimension. Either way, we can trust the wisdom of Spirit's unfolding. In the Heart of Awareness, we are no more and no less what we truly ARE regardless of the depth of our realization or experience.

With awakening to the truth of our transcendent nature comes an end to seeking, an end to the illusion of the ego's separate existence, an end to the illusion of "doership," and, depending on the depth of seeing, an end to fear. The separate "I" or ego disappears in such an understanding (although it often returns as it continues to be melted time and again back into its Source). The life of the individual continues on being whatever it is. The transformation is a shift of perspective, not of personality. Ordinary life continues, yet it is no longer seen as one's own. Something shines right out of our eyes and right out of ordinary moments. There is a new way of seeing the particularity and infinite beauty of each thing, each being.

Life as it is is seen to be sacred and impersonal, yet it is seen with great intimacy and love. Separation ceases, although it often returns grossly or with great subtlety, only to be seen again. While the initial awakening tends to be up and out of identification with form into that which transcends the body, awakening is not an experience that confers specialness, for we see that the infinite ground of Being, the Heart of Awareness, is shared by all. We awaken to our No-thingness and our Everythingness, our emptiness and our oneness. These awakenings can occur simultaneously or at separate times.

INQUIRY CAN BE USED TO
EXPLORE MANY QUESTIONS

Self-inquiry is not the only way inquiry may be used. We can use inquiry to explore other questions that arise. What is Truth? What is death? What is love? What is rest? What is Being? What is peace? What does awakeness or openness feel like in my mind, in my heart, in my body? "What" questions are much more helpful and effective in the spiritual search than "how" or "why" questions. The latter engage the intellect.

In each of us, there is a deep well of inner wisdom, an inner teacher. We can drop a sincere question into this interior silence and stillness, remaining open and receptive. The answer may or may not come immediately and often comes not as something spoken in our mind, but as an experience, an intuitive understanding, a felt sense. For example, in this moment, ask your Self, "What does awakeness feel like in my feet right now?" Almost immediately, you may feel a sense of energy waking up in your feet. When we have a sense of what it is to engage with or sit as silence and stillness, we can inquire about many things.

ENLIGHTENMENT IS A CONCEPT
BORN OF IGNORANCE

The understanding called "enlightenment" is never achieved by an ego, by a mind that takes itself to have a separate identity. Enlightenment, in fact, is only a concept born of ignorance. When the realization dawns that that which one is seeking is that which one *is*, the question of enlightenment for a "me" disappears. There is simply no "one" to become enlightened! All the efforts, hopes, and fantasies one had about the great achievement come to an end when there is no one left to achieve anything, no separate one to enjoy the great dessert of spiritual longing, fasting, or gorging! A spiritual ego may feel disappointed when this realization dawns, but one soon is grateful for the sense of underlying peace that is present and palpable.

True understanding, when it is authentic, is not met with any sense of personal achievement or reward for one's spiritual ambition, but rather with gratitude and a sense of reverence and awe for the Mystery. The revelation is always a moment of grace, but we may not understand that an ocean of grace is always present.

The very awakeness we hope to find is what is looking—looking for itself, as if it were somewhere else! Looking for true nature outside of your own awareness is a bit like looking for your glasses when they are on top of your head. They are nowhere else than where you are, but you are frantically looking through drawers, pockets, and rooms, trying so hard to remember what happened to them.

"I GOT IT; I LOST IT"

A common experience of seekers is to equate a particular experience of openness, peace, joy, clarity, or love with true nature and then, when experience or attention shifts, to imagine that what they seemed to possess at one point they have now lost.

Anything that you can get, you can also lose, but what you most deeply *are* cannot be gained or lost. The spiritual ego imagines it is either *failing* or *progressing* on the path—"I got it; I lost it" or "I saw light, heard bells, had visions, dissolved in awareness; I'm really getting somewhere now!" One of the last vestiges of separateness to go is the sense that a separate "I" had the experience! Experience happens indeed, but what is the knowing of it? What is illuminating experience? What is constant regardless of ever-changing experiences? What are you, what is your sense of "I am" if you do not go to a single thought to answer?

QUESTION THE QUESTIONER; DOUBT THE DOUBTER; LOOK FOR THE SEER

Do not be too hard on yourself. All of your attempts to shame, degrade, renounce, reject, or beat your ego into submission only serve to strengthen your belief in its separate existence, which is actually an illusion. You might as well allow yourself into your heart. Love is the great dissolver of separation. Yet from the Heart that accepts all and sees with both clarity and love, you are invited to question the questioner; doubt the doubter; look for the seer.

Part II

SEEN AND

UNSEEN

*The footprint of the Divine
stands in your own shoes.*

*Wind is invisible,
yet leaves bow before it.*

*Whatever is seen
flows from the Unseen;*

*Light shines forth
from Darkness.*[1]

6

BACKGROUND
AND FOREGROUND

The world is full of waves,
and the sea is invisible.[1]
RUMI

C an you see awareness? Is consciousness visible? Can you catch it in your hand or create it with a thought? There is an invisible sea in which all experience or understanding appears—the simple and unceasing background to all foreground experiences. The unchanging nature of awareness is so simple, so present, and so incapable of being created by our mind that we cannot imagine it holds the key to liberation. Awareness can be aware of anything; its light does not discriminate. Infinite Spirit animates and illumines the very life it creates. Yet life and what is awake to that life flows from an unseen Source.

We are so used to focusing only on the content of our thoughts, feelings, or experiences that we fail to pay any attention at all to the fact that there is a background out of which life as we know it arises. And to the extent we believe we are consciously aware or being mindful of the moment, we believe that there is a separate "I" in awareness. However, there is no "I am aware" in pure Awareness, and yet no reader reading these words could deny the presence of awareness or consciousness in their own experience.

INFINITE BACKGROUND/IMPERMANENT FOREGROUND: A SINGLE REALITY

In truth, the infinite background, or ground of Being, is never absent from the moment as it is; it is just that most of us imagine it is somewhere else. We are convinced that the foreground of our experience must change in order for us to find the background, and thus we are always moving away from ourselves, away from the moment, trying to control the natural unfolding of our lives. We do not realize that the infinite background is unfolding the foreground *out of itself.*

There is an aspect of life's Mystery that is unknowable to the mind of thought, yet it reveals and knows itself. We call it the Absolute, the Unknown, the dark face of the Mystery. Yet out of this darkness the light of awareness shines. Nothing could be seen or known in our relative life apart from the light or Spirit that illuminates our being. In the darkness of the Absolute, there are no distinctions, no divisions, no coming or going. In the light of the Relative, there is everything that we can see, hear, touch, taste, smell, think, feel, or know. Regardless of the words we may use to point to these dark and light aspects, formlessness and form, spirit and matter, reality is not divided; it is One.

WE ARE THE INFINITE OCEAN AND THE CRASHING OF WAVES

As Rumi and many others have described, this one reality is like the ocean and its waves. Whether they are mild or tumultuous, the waves of our daily life are imagined to be separate from the Ocean of Peace we are searching for. We think that we must stop the waves or change their direction in order to experience calm water. The problem is not that we experience changing waves of thought, feeling, or sensation, or even that some waves are called "fear." The problem is that we are identified as a *separate* wave, a separate someone, experiencing only the surface of the sea and not its depth. We imagine life's waves crash into us rather than experiencing ourselves as the infinite sea itself, which is both still and continually flowing in each moment of our life's unfolding.

We do not dive deeply enough into our direct experience of the wave to discover the peaceful, invisible sea that lies beneath each moment as it is. We are continually trying to get away from certain feelings, people, or experiences and hang on to others. We imagine our peace is somewhere else than where we are because we are identified with the foreground that we take to be separate.

3D STEREOGRAMS

Have you ever looked at computer-driven 3D stereograms? In order to see the forms popping out of a background that appears to have no forms, you have to relax your looking and stare vacantly into space, as if seeing *through* the nondescript background. You have to observe the image without looking *at* it. The image has to come to you, and it can come to you only when you relax your looking. Like other experiences that deliver insights, we have to be open to receive them. When something previously unseen jumps out of the picture at you from the background—an image that did not even give a hint of its presence a moment before—there is a sudden "Aha!" Something that was there all along is suddenly seen, and you experience delight and awe at such a phenomenon.

You might even imagine that such a moment is somehow analogous to an enlightenment moment—but in reverse—when we see that the foreground of what we took to be a "me" has never been separate from what we were seeking. Or, to reverse things again, we might say that the "aha" moment is the delight Divine Consciousness has when it sees, through its *own forms*, all the possibilities of what it can become! *Now I am* this *moment; oh, now I have become* this *feeling! Oh, here is a way I can create conflict! Here I am showing up as confusion, as clear-mindedness, as galaxies and ants! Just imagine—this expression calls itself a name and takes itself to be independent of my gifts of air, water, sunshine, and the life spirit! Look at all the costumes I can wear!* Of course, I am anthropomorphizing the Divine here, but I do so to make the point that everything is ultimately arising from the same ground. Infinite potential is no-thing we can define (although I just attempted to do so!). In itself it is empty of form and yet contains all form.

We realize that, as in the 3D stereogram, the form, the image, the picture, indeed our body-mind and its unfolding life—including the illusion of separation—are constantly being created out of the background. The continual background of all phenomena is Consciousness itself—the invisible sea out of which this world of waves is continually being brought in and out of form. And the apparent "two"—background awareness and foreground content, emptiness and form, absolute and relative—cannot truly be separated. They are like two sides of a single coin called Reality. Just as a painting cannot walk away from the canvas on which it is painted, we can never become separated from the background essence.

IDENTIFIED MIND LIVES IN THE SPACE/TIME CONTINUUM

Most minds live continually in the foreground—the space/time continuum—where one is always searching for experience in phenomena. Attached to its own projections, the mind is caught up in what is manifesting in its universe and, most especially, in what it sees to be manifesting in its "own" life. Because experience is so seductive, we fail to see that whatever phenomena may be arising are not separate from the background out of which they appear. Like a field of wildflowers, each with a different color, shape, and fragrance, all arise from the same ground.

"Form is exactly emptiness; emptiness exactly form," says the Heart Sutra. Awake Being itself may be experienced as eternal Presence, divine love, emptiness, peace, bliss, the creative spirit; it may be called the Background, the Ground of Being, God, the Tao, the Absolute, the Heart of Awareness, the unborn Buddha mind, the true Self. The important thing is not naming the Mystery, but experiencing yourself as *being* the unnameable background as well as the foreground. In this way of experiencing life, there is no doubt about the singleness of background and foreground. Right here and now, Being is manifesting as all moments, all forms, including thought and feeling forms. Different forms, all coming from the same infinite background, made of the substance of that background, not separate from that background in any way.

Time and space are constructs that exist for the purpose of experiencing our Self in form, the one Self that is all and nothing at all. Without time, there is no becoming; without space, there is no form. We see this universe as both becoming and having form. What we do not see is that the Consciousness that sees such appearance is Infinite Being, universal Awareness. This is the invisible sea that neither becomes nor does not become, and *that* is what you are. But you are also *this*—the moving appearances.

Many spiritual seekers may have some intellectual understanding or wish to have some understanding of what is being described here conceptually. What seems so difficult is to know such truth in the depths of your being. It is not the ego mind that will ever be able to discover such truth or to sustain this understanding should it appear. In continuing to identify with the ego's separateness, and not its undivided Source, we can never experience the truth of who/what we are. We will continue to see ourselves as foreground separate from background.

The ego cannot see the ground (or background) of its being because *being* the Self, *being* the ground, we cannot make it an object. We can only *be* what we truly are; we cannot "find" who we are. We imagine the ego is the subject of experience when it is simply a movement of thought that is witnessed. Like the web spinning out of the spider, objects keep spinning out of Consciousness, out of the infinite Source, but we imagine the object (our apparent separate self) is the subject. This is our false identification.

In defense of our sense of separateness, your mind may ask, "But what about our differences? Surely you agree that people are different!" Of course, people are different. Of course there are distinct forms, flavors, and personalities. But differences in form do not mean separate entities. Look at a single tree. It has roots, sap, a trunk, branches, leaves, and blossoms, cones, or seedpods. Blossoms appear when they appear. Buds form and unfold into leaves; leaves turn different colors on the same tree and fall at different times. The leaf does not look like the root; the sap does not look like the blossom; but all arise from the same tree. Unique expressions do not mean separation.

THE PRACTICE OF SEPARATING BACKGROUND AND FOREGROUND

Much spiritual practice is geared toward separating foreground and background in order to help the seeker have a taste of the eternal, unchanging background that is beyond the changing foreground. Many meditation practices seek such separation. But to say life is *only* background or *only* foreground is to stay in duality, and life is simply not two.

Many spiritual seekers with some experience beyond the ego mind or with the desire to identify with the infinite background of Being become attached to what they imagine or experience as "witnessing" or "watching" the events, feelings, or actions of life come and go without involvement. While this practice has immediate value in helping one to understand impermanence and the background of awareness, it is seldom the true witnessing, which is global awareness without a location of consciousness.

The sage is *being* the impersonal witness to all that appears; the sage is not the agent of "witnessing." Awareness accepts all because it *is* all. This is the peace of God. Nothing has to change; there is full openness to the moment as it is and total acceptance of all that appears. This acceptance includes whatever action or reaction the body-mind organism may be spontaneously having to the moment at hand.

THE I-THOUGHT IS NOT THE TRUE WITNESS

I come in contact with many people who imagine they are experiencing witnessing but are simply being aware of one part of the separate mind supposedly watching another. It is the I-thought that thinks it is watching the movement of a "myself." Frequently, it is an attempt to separate themselves from the authentic experience of their lives. In other words, seekers often want to practice witnessing when there is something uncomfortable arising as a way of separating from the moment. There is nothing wrong with doing this, and many people find it helpful in dealing with difficult emotions. "I am not this emotion; I am what is aware of this emotion." This is fine, but anything with a goal of separation is not likely to lead us to an experience of nonseparation. Yes, the sky is not threatened by the appearance of clouds, but do we see that clouds and sky are one? Unity is not found in division.

Of course, it is the goal of many practices to separate from the thinking, judging mind, which is the agent of our sense of separation. But even the attempts to "watch without judgment," which are part of the instruction for certain types of meditation, often reinforce the seeker's idea that her separate self is the witness and that her separate ego will eventually be that which will learn to accept herself or life. The ego, however, is neither the witness nor that which accepts all. The very sense of a separate "doer" that is dutifully trying to practice one thing or another, one idea or another, one type of meditation or another, is the idea that stands in the seeker's way of experiencing her infinite Being and oneness with life. Doing happens; we are inquiring into the truth of the "doer."

CONCEPTS CANNOT CONVEY THE TRUTH OF NONSEPARATION

The minute we make concepts of anything, the moment we label anything, the moment we speak or think about any phenomena, background and foreground appear to be separate, and yet they function as one. Awareness and the contents of awareness are talked about and written about as two separate things, and, indeed, we can conceptualize and experience their different properties. But in truth, there is nothing separate from anything. As the old Taoist saying goes, "Pull out a blade of grass, and the whole universe shakes." Life is one, and all apparent opposites exist as aspects of each other. The ego's very idea of union depends on its idea of separation. The ego's very idea of liberation depends on its idea of bondage.

BEING THE MOMENT

The idea of a "spiritual journey" is that a journey is from one place to another. When you think you must travel *away* from where you are, *away* from yourself, you are bound for frustration. All of life is "spiritual" because all of life is the Infinite's reflection. Not just part of life, not just the parts you like, not just the roles you imagine are the "good" ones, not just the feelings that are comfortable, not just the people who are beautiful, not just the moments of peace. Everything is Consciousness, and this infinite light illumines all. When we stop mentally traveling and stand still, in the midst of the moment we are in, without trying to be somewhere else, the background or substratum of peace, emptiness, awake Being is discovered to be close at hand. Anything, *anything*, can bring us to peace, to our simple true nature, because it is never absent. Where could it go?

A feeling may arise spontaneously in your experience, but the only way to maintain it is to keep telling yourself the story about it. The energy of a feeling has a very short shelf life if not reinforced and reengaged by the story. The story includes all of the thoughts, beliefs, associations and projected meanings that have built up around the experience.

While your mind can go back to all of that later if it wants to, for now, I would like to invite you to explore a feeling without being separate from it, which means without attaching to the story behind it. I am not talking about expressing, generating, or judging feelings, or analyzing supposed reasons for those feelings, or pounding pillows in the case of anger, or acting in ways toward others that are against one's moral code. I am not even talking about *being with* the feeling or meeting the moment, for inherent in those invitations is an implied separation from the moment as it appears. See what happens when there is no separation, when the truth of *You* is at one with your experience.

Inviting Awareness "Inside" a Feeling

Let yourself become aware of a feeling you may be having at this moment. Choose a simple one for this exercise, not one fraught with extreme fear, anxiety, or trauma.

Locate the felt sense of the emotion in your body. While feelings often accompany a belief or thought, for now see if you can sense the energetic component of a feeling as sensation in your body without focusing on its story. For example, you might locate the experience of sadness in the heart area; irritation or resistance might appear as a contraction in the gut.

Now simply invite your awareness inside the experience itself.

Since awareness has no boundaries, it can go anywhere. Rather than being aware from "outside" of a feeling, sensation, or contraction, invite your attention and awareness inside the felt sense of your feeling.

You are not trying to get rid of the feeling, change it, judge it, or analyze it. You are just allowing your awareness to be intimate and at one with the feeling sensation.

Notice what happens when awareness is invited to consciously touch a feeling or sensation from the inside.

If the sensation intensifies temporarily, allow that to be your experience.

If a sensation moves, allow that to happen. For example, you might start out feeling anger, but as you explore its energy without the story, you might find there is sadness, grief, or fear underneath the anger. Anger is quite an effective defense against feeling more vulnerable feelings. Allow compassionate awareness to touch the vulnerability.

If the feeling shifts, let your awareness be intimate with the next felt sense.

Become curious about the truth of a feeling rather than trying to manipulate it. Become curious about what it is made of.

You may discover that the feeling transforms rather quickly when you are not in resistance to it but rather inviting your awareness to be intimate with it. Indeed, the direct experiencing of anything can deliver a surprise. And many people whom I have invited to explore a feeling in this manner have discovered a surprising peace.

When there is no separation, we are at one with our experience. There is an experience of openness, undivided from the moment. This openness is our true nature. When we are willing to *be* the experience or energy even of resistance, we are no longer divided, and there is a softening. *Be* the barrier. *Be* the tears. *Be* the happiness. *Be* the confusion. *Be* the fear. This is how we close the gap between the truth of our experience and the truth of what we are.

Thus, by simply *being* whatever is coming up, rather than being a "someone" who is experiencing a "something" that is separate, it is possible to find ourselves experiencing the background present in any foreground. We discover the calm depths of the same Ocean of Awareness that may be moving as choppy waves on the surface. Direct experience, without thoughts about such experience, can lead to surprising peace, the essence of all experience—Consciousness empty of name and form. Now, be forewarned that ego will attempt to use this method to get rid of what is here, but when we are being the openness, that openness is not trying to rid itself of anything, but rather to see clearly what an experience is made of, to understand its true essence, to transform and not simply transcend our experience.

EVERYONE HAS EXPERIENCED MOMENTS OF NO SEPARATION

Each of us has had many experiences of no separation in our lives. When a sudden moment of awe or wonder arises at the beauty of a sunset or a moment of disappearing into a piece of music—not disappearing into a reverie of thoughts while music is playing, but disappearing into the listening itself—there is the experience of no separation. When one is caught up in the creative process and words seem to be just writing themselves, or a painting appears on a canvas in unexpected ways, or the body is dancing effortlessly, there is the experience of not being separate from the moment itself. Athletes experience being in the flow or the zone, where the action of the moment feels seamless and timeless. Spontaneous laughter or spontaneous action reveals a moment without self-consciousness, without separation, without a sense of time.

BACKGROUND AS EMPTINESS

There may be moments in meditation when the foreground of your mind stops moving, and you feel the great silence and stillness of your true nature as emptiness. The first time you encounter this unknown, you may become frightened because "you" seem to have disappeared momentarily; you might feel you are falling into a realm from which you may never return. Your mind starts moving again, wanting to escape. You squirm, you rearrange your clothes, anything to get back to the comfort of the known.

One day, however, you remain still; you do not try to escape the silence. The thought image of your self disappears; the Infinite is now simply revealing itself, empty of definition, empty of image. For a moment, the body and mind have fallen away; there is only the background of Awareness with no one to claim it. And unless fear should immediately pull a familiar identity back into consciousness, you will experience an unbelievable peace that seems undisturbed by whatever images appear in the foreground of experience.

When the ego is drawn close enough to its Source, its separateness is swallowed up. And from the perspective of the whole, which then becomes apparent, it is seen clearly that Totality is simply unfolding itself always and everywhere. There is really no separate background and foreground, only distinct forms, flavors, and expressions of the one eternal what IS unfolding out of itself what is.

THE MOON DOES NOT GET WET

Once I was teaching in Canada and staying in a cabin surrounded by pine trees. It had been raining in the evening, and the tip of each pine needle seemed to hold its own drop of rain suspended in air.

The clouds cleared, and a full moon appeared in the sky. Every single raindrop hanging on every single pine needle held a reflection of the full moon. The whole tree seemed alive with myriad moons lighting every single branch, present in every single raindrop, like a gloriously lit Christmas tree. It reminded me of how Zen master Dogen once described enlightenment as being like the moon reflected on water, in dewdrops on the grass, or even in one drop of water. "The moon does not get wet, nor is the water broken." Every drop is the height of the moon, and each reflection "manifests the limitlessness of the moonlight in the sky."[2]

One nature permeates all of life, reflecting the light of its jewel in each individual expression—yours and mine and even in the tiniest drop of rain on a single pine needle. The mind imagines enlightenment is something we achieve or something we can hinder. Truth sees it has never been absent. Yet we often imagine that awakening to the Absolute—waking up out of identification with form—is enlightenment. It is profound and freeing to encounter the Absolute, which shifts us out of the dream of a separate "me." However, we can get stuck in another identification when the spiritual ego gets stuck in emptiness or in being only the witness. It is calm, peaceful; there is no suffering, no conflict; but it is a state in which we can hide from our human life and the suffering of the world. It is safe but can become a defense, just as being stuck in form identification can be a defense against the realization of our essential formlessness. Yet as we sense into openness, we may discover the infinite Heart of Awareness that neither divides nor defines itself.

7

THE HEART OF AWARENESS

Enter with Love the temple that is your own heart . . .
silently allowing the deep within to flow
on and into the deep beyond.[1]
RAMANA MAHARSHI

When we feel deeply about something, when we experience love, when something touches us in a way that seems profoundly true, we put our hand on our chest, over the heart space. When we speak with passion about our "I," we do not touch our head; we touch our heart. Perhaps the true "I" resides in the "temple that is your own heart," and yet it is the Heart we share rather than a separate heart. If this is so, where can we enter?

Within you at this very moment there is a doorway to the Infinite. It is so available and so simple that we miss its entrance. We are always unknowingly standing at the threshold. We stand at the entrance with every description about our self, but we are looking out *from* the doorway, rather than turning our attention to look back into it.

Notice the continuous thread in each of our self-descriptions: I am happy. I am depressed. I am smart. I am stupid. I am selfish. I am generous. I am anxious. I am calm. I am a mother. I am a son. I am rich. I am poor. I am a student. I am a teacher. I am improving. I am stuck.

We spend an entire lifetime dwelling on the "I," claiming the "I," beginning every moment's experience with a sense of "I." And this "I" or "I AM" is the center of our universe. The experience of anything is run through the "I" and is claimed by the "me" and

"mine": My house, my body, my experience, my knowledge, my ignorance, my thoughts, my agitation, my journey, my life! Can we look
more deeply into what is seen and unseen in who we are, into what
changes and what does not change in our experience?

THE "I" CARRIES OUR SENSE
OF BEING AND BEING AWARE

In any experience we claim as ours, there is the sense of an "I," the
sense of existing. Whatever we may add to the "I," the "I" carries
our sense of being and being aware. How is it that we search for
something called awakening, enlightenment, the Divine and never
contemplate who or what the "I" of the seeker actually is? Whatever
this sense of being conscious is, it witnesses all of our comings and
goings, all of the changing dimensions of our daily life, all of the
objects that appear in our awareness. While it claims no name, it
has been called our true Self, the Heart of Awareness. This Heart of
Awareness illuminates our mind and our experience of the world. It
is not our thoughts that illuminate experience, but awareness that
illuminates both experience and thought.

Have you contemplated this "I AM," felt into it, put attention
there rather than on all of the objects of awareness—including body,
senses, mind, emotions, and experiences? We are so fascinated by the
objects of awareness that we fail to pay attention to the awareness
that is ever present in our waking state, in our dream state, and even
in deep sleep; but in deep, dreamless sleep there are no objects—no
self, no world, no other, no god. The "you" you imagine yourself
to be disappears in deep sleep. And yet we may be awakened out of
deep sleep by a sound or a sensation that obviously has been witnessed by something within that remains open and aware. At times,
we may even experience being consciously awake while the body is in
states of deep sleep, dreaming, or supposed unconsciousness. What
remains awake?

ARE THERE TWO "SELVES"?

We have been perched at the doorway of the Infinite looking out at objects—a birth date, body, gender, race, memories, thoughts, feelings—and imagining that our "I AM" refers to an ego or a body-mind. We imagine there is a small self looking for something distant called our *true* Self, hoping that someday the one will discover the other. Are there really two selves? In the words of Ramana Maharshi:

> The ego is like one's shadow thrown on the ground.
> If one attempts to bury it, it will be foolish.
> The Self is only One. If limited, it is the ego.
> If unlimited, it is Infinite, and is the Reality.[2]

Where we put our attention creates our sense of reality. If we want to discover who or what we are, what is truth, what is awake, we turn to our felt sense of "I AM," of *being*, of *being aware*. There is something deeper than an I-thought that is identified with form, thought, and emotion. What are we paying attention to? What are we giving our time and attention to? What knows when attention moves?

WHAT IS UNSEEN MAKES IT POSSIBLE TO SEE

In itself, awareness is unseen yet makes it possible to see, hear, touch, taste, smell, and experience our Being. This invisible awakeness is what *sees*, what notices whom we take ourselves to be, what knows our experience, perceptions, dreams, beliefs, or philosophical assumptions. It moves as consciousness in the body-mind, identifies with a body and thought, then comes to believe that a single body is our separate self.

Pay attention to the one whose "self" you claim is you. I am not speaking here about adopting a philosophy or belief or denying that there is a body. I am suggesting finding out, in your own very real experience, who or what is this "I" we all claim. Who or what is it that is always searching for control, for security, for greater knowledge, for a better life, for reassurance about the future, for signs of approval or disapproval from others?

Let's face it: by any stretch of the imagination, the egoic consciousness that takes itself to be separate and limited to a body never tires of thinking about, hearing about, talking about, or evaluating this "self." It is like the old joke about the narcissist who goes on and on talking only about himself, but finally stops, saying, "Well, I have talked long enough about myself. Now tell me, what do *you* think of me?" Use this self-interest, self-obsession, self-centeredness in the spiritual search. Find out the true identity of this precious and all-consuming "I."

SOMEPLACE WE LOVE OURSELVES

Although we imagine we know, we are actually ignorant of who or what this "I" is and remain unconscious of the deep and unconditional love that is present within us. Yet we all want to feel happy or content; we want to experience love and peace; we want to feel a sense of worth. Someplace, regardless of our ignorance, we wish ourselves well. Who is this self? What is this "I" that is aware whether we feel terror or great joy, whether we are truthful or deceitful, whether we remember or are forgetful, whether we feel happy or unhappy?

THE DESIRE FOR HAPPINESS

While all beings wish to be happy, for most, happiness is conditional. It is the happiness you imagine will be created by something external to yourself, the happiness you imagine would come "if only"—if only someone, something, or you yourself would change. The ways we imagine happiness will arrive vary; some ways may seem quite perverted to the average way of thinking. We protect ourselves or try to avoid pain because we want to be happy. We eat or shop or drink to keep ourselves from feeling empty because we imagine "empty" means alone, unloved, unworthy. We seek more and more and better and better because we imagine it will make us happy.

When we do experience moments of happiness, when a desire is fulfilled and the mind is content, we imagine these moments were caused by something outside of our self. But the reason we are temporarily happy has nothing to do with what just happened. We are temporarily happy because we temporarily stopped wishing to be someplace else. Our mind rested for one moment, stopped its craving and straining for one moment, and we simply experienced our natural state, the Heart of Awareness.

WIDEN YOUR DESIRES

Some traditions tell us that the real reason we do not experience happiness is because we have desires. If only we could renounce our desires, we would live happily in desirelessness. *Who* imagines he can do away with desires? Freedom from desire, or nonattachment, is not something the ego can attain through practice, although we may have tried to pretend we had no desires or attachments, only to find we had lost joy and spontaneity. Freedom from attachment arises naturally when one knows one's true nature. Realize that all desire is ultimately a desire for a deeper happiness. As Nisargadatta so beautifully expressed:

> Increase and widen your desires till nothing but Reality
>   can fill them.
> It is not desire that is wrong, but its narrowness and
>   smallness.
> Desire is devotion. By all means be devoted to the real,
>   the infinite,
> the eternal heart of Being. Transform desire into love.
> All you want is to be happy. All your desires, whatever
>   they may be,
> are expressions of your longing for happiness.
> Basically, you wish yourself well.[3]

What knows your experience? The intimacy of true knowing is love. Our mind has forgotten the Heart of Awareness, the Heart of Being, the true Heart that is the source of an uncaused happiness. Where do we enter this Heart? "I" or "I AM" is the doorway. Put your attention on this "I AM" in the Heart. The mind is busy telling you stories about who this is; the Heart is the *knowing* itself of your true nature. It is the Heart of Awareness in which we live and move and have our being. It is what continues regardless of the modifiers—the additions from memory, conditioning, and programming—regardless of the thoughts, emotions, moods, or sensations that are in continual flux.

UNDRESS YOUR "SELF" FROM ITS CONCEPT CLOTHES

The Self (Heart of Awareness, limitless Being) is already present. What is required is to undress our "self," to discover what is beneath the concept clothes our so-called ego is wearing. Egoic identity is maintained through habits of mind and unquestioned assumptions that we are only this body-mind and its conditioning. If we turn our attention inward at the doorway of "I," however, we have an opportunity to step into the Infinite and discover for ourselves whether there really are two selves, whether there is an "other," whether there truly is an independent entity called "me," whether what we call "mind" is the same or different from the I-thought.

Even when we discover the divine "I AM THAT I AM" (Exodus 3:14), there is still something deeper than what we call God. Before a name or a description, what is here? The threshold of the "I" is the beginning of the discovery of the true Heart of Awareness. It has been called "nondual awareness"—pristine, pure, space-like, shining, and illuminating whatever is here. Zen master Bankei called it "the Unborn Buddha mind."

AWARENESS MOVES AS LOVE

Awareness is silent and unseen. And yet its luminosity moves as all that is seen, all manifestations of Being. And in the movements that are free of the veils we call "ego," it moves as Love. Love itself cannot be seen, and yet its movements can be seen, felt, delighted in, and they can melt us out of separation into Oneness. It is not a personal love, or a romantic love, or a friendship love, although all of these are its expressions. It is an unconditional love that is beyond anything most of us have ever experienced in our human lives. It is an intimacy that comes from nonseparation. What the deepest Truth is cannot really be named but can be felt, sensed, intuited. The Unseen has no name but contains all names and forms, including our own.

> Call it by any name—God, Self, the Heart, the seat of
>   Consciousness—
> it is all the same. The point to be grasped is this,
> that Heart means the very core of one's being, the center,
> without which there is nothing whatsoever.[4]
> RAMANA MAHARSHI

Our egoic "me" center is not the center Ramana is speaking about. It is that "without which there is nothing whatsoever." If there were no awareness, would you know, perceive, experience anything at all? If we stand at the threshold of the "I" that is aware, without identifying with any content of that awareness—even for a moment—we will notice a profound silence and stillness. That which is silently awake to all sound and movement makes it possible for all sound and movement to be experienced. If we feel into a sense of simply *being*, without being "this" or "that," we notice that something quiets down immediately.

One reason I use the phrase *Heart of Awareness* in attempting to point to what has no name is to include in the discussion the understanding of love (heart) being the authentic movement of the purity and clarity of awareness. In itself, awareness has no qualities apart from its luminosity, that which both sheds light on and is the knowing of experience. But this knowing comes from oneness, from nonseparation, which itself is a movement of love and compassion. Love beyond any concept of love is the expression of nondual awareness in life. Within you there is a loving Presence that allows all things to be exactly as they are in the oneness of Being.

The Heart of Awareness Is Awake within You

For a moment, let yourself be awake and aware in the following invitations.

Breath

I would invite you to awaken to your breath in this moment, letting it be exactly as it is. What is the experience when you simply allow the breath to breathe itself? Can you separate your awareness from your knowing of each breath?

Body

Become aware of your body right now, noticing sensations, tensions, places of contraction or openness. What happens if you make no attempt to fix anything or change anything, but you just allow a compassionate awareness to become intimate with the experience? What does awakeness feel like in your right leg, your left hand, your entire body right now? What notices? What knows?

Sounds

Can you spend a few moments awakening to sounds? Right now there are many sounds in your field of awareness. Without needing to name the sounds, even if your mind does so, go beyond the names and notice what is noticing sound. It is not your conditioned mind, not your ears, but consciousness itself that is listening. It is Awareness moving in the body-mind as your own consciousness.

Awareness Itself

Can you become conscious of your own awareness? Are you aware of your own consciousness? Ultimately they are one, but they function a bit differently. Consciousness is fluid, can seem to expand, contract, focus attention, change perspective, move as we become aware of listening, sensation, feeling, thinking. Consciousness is conscious of objects and can reflect on itself.

Notice what is aware of being conscious. This appears silent, still, nonjudging, unmoving even as it moves as consciousness in the body-mind to intimately meet the moment. Notice what gives consciousness its strength. That source is what I am calling "the Heart of Awareness," but words are meaningless. Sense it.

For just a moment, can you allow what you experience as *your* consciousness to simply flow into its Source or return to its home ground—without naming, without defining, without needing to control anything or change anything? Simply be quiet and allow your consciousness to melt into its Source. The felt sense might be of attention moving down, down, down into the depths. Or it might be a sense of looking backward from the doorway of the "I" into what comes before. Or perhaps there is a sense of flowing into the vastness of the deep beyond. Stay open to however and whatever wants to reveal itself.

LISTENING IS A PORTAL TO THE HEART OF AWARENESS

Legend states that enlightenment was revealed to Quan Yin, the bodhisattva of compassion, simply by her listening deeply to the sounds of the world. Listening to the cries of the world, compassion arose in her open heart and mind. Our listening is always open. Even in sleep, our hearing is open, although it is not as sensitively attuned to our environment as in the waking state. Of course, we all know the difference between hearing and listening. Listening requires more attention than hearing. True listening comes from the Heart of Awareness.

So often our listening is interrupted by our egoic desire to be heard, to argue, to put forth our own viewpoint, to judge. However, the openness of listening is another marvelous portal to our true nature. Can we begin to listen with more than our ears? Can we listen with our heart to the subtleties of our own experience and to that of apparent others? Can we listen with our whole body and allow it to be an "ear" for listening, for sensing into silence and into whatever is arising from that silence? Can we begin to experience that the song of the bird is happening inside our listening, not "out there"? In listening from the Heart of Awareness, we begin to feel the deep intimacy of our true nature that is simply awake and open.

VERTICAL AND HORIZONTAL

What does not change is often viewed as the *vertical* dimension of life, and what continually changes as the *horizontal* dimension. We could say that where they meet, and the *only* place they meet, is in the present moment, yet what "meets"? There is only What Is. The silent, still, infinite What Is and the appearance of things—life, feelings, movement, action—are simply not two. Time and timelessness are not two. Creator and creation are not two. Manifest and unmanifest are not two.

Everything is occurring Now. Now is timeless and not a nanosecond sandwiched between past and future. The Heart of Awareness contains all in its timeless Presence. As Ramana puts it, this Heart that is our true Self is that "without which there is nothing whatsoever." While it cannot be separated from the moment, it is simultaneously touched and untouched by the myriad happenings—untouched as Awareness itself, yet touched by all that moves in its open, undivided Heart.

8

PRESENCE AND
PERSONHOOD

Are you a person with awareness or the
Awareness that perceives a person?

There is a single coin that can show itself as absolute or relative. What notices which side is up in any given moment? That which neither divides nor defines itself as background or foreground is awake to both. What is it? Can you taste it? Can you touch it? Something is simply and deeply present. Whom does this Presence belong to?

Presence is nowhere that you are not, and you are nowhere that Presence is not. What seems to be somewhere else is actually attention that has moved to the thinking mind, but Presence has not disappeared. In sensing what is timelessly awake and aware in the midst of all time-bound experiences, we experience Presence. When we see, hear, touch, or taste anything innocently, as it is, without the conditioned voice-over of our inner narrator, we experience Presence. Yet freedom does not require getting rid of all conditioning—that would be impossible. It lies in discovering what we are beyond our identification with personhood.

PRESENCE IS AWARENESS
UNHOOKED FROM THOUGHT

Presence is awareness of the moment unhooked from our thoughts, judgments, and interpretations based on separation. Experientially it is a moment of oneness. It is not a quality created by a body-mind or owned by a person. In fact, Presence perceives the layers of clothing we appear to wear over our true Self. Presence cannot be seen; it *is* the seeing and the knowing of experience. Presence is the openness that contains no resistance, no efforting to be somewhere else or to hold on to a separate identity. The sense of "I am" appears inside Presence. Since Presence is the knowing of itself as all appearances, this sense of oneness also moves as love—love for its own expression of *being* called "person."

Being is fluid, dynamic, and an expression of the play of Consciousness. We could see our Self in terms of a trinity: There is the absolute, unchanging, formless, timeless dimension that is always at peace. There is the form (a person, thought, or feeling form) that manifests both the timeless dimension of Consciousness and its expression as being and time. And there is the Holy Spirit, breath, or energy that moves life in and out of its infinite forms from moment to moment. However, what appears to be three is not.

Although Presence is what you are, thought tries to *practice* it. Although Being is what you are, ego efforts to *be*. While Presence is clear seeing and intimate experiencing without the veils of conditioned mind, it sees the movements of conditioned mind. Presence is conscious of itself as *Being* and is experienced as nonseparation, a quiet peacefulness, love, and intimacy. Its intimacy comes from the fact that true Presence cannot separate itself from any moment, any experience, action, or manifestation of Totality. Intimacy may seem to imply two, but true intimacy knows no separation.

If the Heart of Awareness, our true Self, is always intimate with the moment, why don't we experience it? Being awake means being present for *this* moment, for *this* experience, for *this* feeling, for *this* interaction, for *this* birdsong, for *this* sip of tea. Enlightenment is here/now, but from the perspective of belief in a separate person, the seeker often seems oblivious to the moment when the mind is wandering off, thinking, judging, or fantasizing, living in a world of concepts, interpretations, ideas, memories, projections. Indeed, that is the experience of the "person" who is identified with his or her mental or emotional activity. We have all had the experience of suddenly waking up from a daydream to realize that our mind has been "somewhere else." But where were *You*?

What *You* are *is* here, but attention moves. And so practices may be engaged in to try to develop mindfulness or presence to the moment we are in. But can we notice that something is already present before we try to *become* present?

From the perspective of consciousness identified with the body-mind as "person," its light so often shines on mental activity (the experience of being somewhere else) because that is where the attention of identified consciousness has been conditioned to find itself. The "person" finds his or her identity in an *idea* of a self—the body-mind's form, thoughts, emotions, sensations, and memories. Yet these continually change. What has been present to all the changing seasons of your life?

From the perspective of our timeless Presence, the Heart of Awareness that does not come and go, it is simply here now, open and present to your inner or outer environment, to your responses as you read. And, while intimate with the moment, what is simply *awake* is not actually affected by any illusions of "who" or "what" may be imagined in the dream of separation. From this perspective, all is simply happening in, and as an expression of, what has no name, claims no identity, and yet is continually awake and simply *being*. Presence is what we are.

WHO PRACTICES PRESENCE?

Many seekers effort to "be present" in the moment, or at least they imagine that they *should* be practicing such a thing. When we talk about being present, we are usually referring to an attitude of attention and openness in the moment, a quality that is natural and inherent in our *aware being*. It is fine to imagine you are practicing being open and awake in the moment or practicing mindfulness of your breath, your actions, your thoughts, your feelings, but who is practicing such a thing? And when you do not feel present, what notices that your mind is engaged in memory, projection, fantasy, or judgment? Presence is the knowing of your experience.

Presence is the awareness that knows you are reading these words, that the body is seated, that your belly is full or empty. Presence refuses nothing and holds on to nothing. That is its freedom. An illusion called the "separate self" cannot create Presence; it is Presence that sees your ideas of personhood. Our human experience is actually a play of Presence and personhood. It is Presence that pulls the seeker toward Presence. It is not your action that invites Spirit or God into your life; Spirit has invited your expression into its life. Spirit is Presence.

The "I" whom you imagine is practicing presence appears to be a body plus a conditioned mind that is efforting to keep attention on the moment or action at hand. When we follow thoughts that appear to stick like Velcro one onto another onto another, we experience thinking and claim a self as the "thinker." Attention moves, and Presence, or awareness, is now illuminating our mind activity. A moment before we may have been experiencing the flow of life, the flower in front of us, a carrot we were chopping, the movement of our breath, or a moment of deep peace in meditation. Then the thinking mind begins to pull consciousness and its attention to itself. Habitual thought becomes a powerful magnet.

ATTENTION MOVES; PRESENCE REMAINS

While Presence has not gone anywhere, we experience attention moving and the fascination and pull of thoughts, especially the ones that relate to the life, travails, and triumphs of a "me." All of these thoughts are seen by that which is present to its own life and expressions. The light of awareness notices the shifts of attention and is now present to our running inner dialogue, our daydreaming, judging, and fascination with our thinking. However, we do not *experience* Presence—the Infinite aware of itself—when we are living in a virtual world of the mind's thoughts identified with personhood.

All of life's movements—from an experience of a peaceful or focused mind, to a carrot or a flower, to traffic noise or an agitated meditator who cannot remain "present"—are objects in awareness, the awake Presence that has never disappeared. But because it is what we are, it cannot itself be made into an object. The I-thought cannot "find" Presence; Presence has shown us the thought and reveals itself to be much deeper than thought.

 ## Turning Attention toward the Source

Come into the sense of Now, quietly present to your innermost Self.

Invite your attention deep inside, beyond the concepts covering your naked, open awareness.

Bypass all remembered definitions of your self, even for a moment, and come inside your Heart.

Come deeper than any ideas or feelings, deeper even than the Silence that appears to be nothing. What perceives this nothing, this emptiness?

Come inside—beyond your body, your mind, your emotions—to what is Unborn. From this Source comes Presence. A person does not "acquire" pure Presence. It is your natural, empty state of *being*. Presence is intimate with the moment.

Sense this Presence as what is free; the person is not free. Our freedom is freedom *from* the person.

We are neither denying nor devaluing the experience of our body-mind. The body holds great wisdom; we can honor its resilience as well as its fragility. But in this moment we are exploring our deepest and truest essence, the truth of the experiencer.

Turn your attention toward your innermost silent Source; feel its Presence. Let yourself return again and again to this felt sense.

You are living as the form and functioning of the Divine—perhaps not consciously yet, but you may discover the vastness when you stop to notice that silence, stillness, and Presence are already here in your own experience. You imagine you must find ways to connect to that which you seek, but you may never have questioned who imagines him- or herself separate. You simply proceed in your efforts to connect with what you imagine is outside of yourself, separate from who you are. This is the action of identified consciousness.

If you were to relax completely, making no effort, not even think-ing—for that, too, requires effort of the mind—all there would be would be Presence. Of course, you do not imagine that you could stop thinking or find Presence without efforting to do so. The first part is correct: "you" cannot stop your thinking. Ego's attempt to end thinking is more ego. The truth about the second is this: nothing that requires efforting can be who you truly are. How can it require effort to simply *be* who/what you are?

EGO DOES NOT WANT TO STOP BEING THE "DOER"

The ego wants to have something to do. Without doing, it fears its life would end. My friend, that is the point. When the ego gives up thinking it is the doer and rests in/as its true nature, there is no longer any perceived separation from that which you have been seeking. If you investigate deeply your desire to do something, you will very likely find that you do not *want* to stop being the doer. The very idea engenders great fear. You imagine your life would fall apart without a separate "you" as doer at the helm. You imagine infinite Being or eternal Presence might be able to take care of the birds, the meadow grasses, and the movement of clouds in the sky, but not your life. You believe *your* life is separate from nature, separate from its Being.

You do not want to stop imagining yourself as the doer because you do not want your illusory self to die. When you have totally identified with a separate consciousness, the idea of losing that sense of separation can be terrifying. You may imagine that your bills won't get paid or the children taken care of if you did not take yourself to be the doer, but really you are afraid of losing your most cherished illusion: that of being a self in control of its destiny. However, when there is awakening from the dream of separation, the understand-ing appears that there has never been a separate doer for a single moment. It was all an illusion. Doing happens. It is not that life does not unfold in all of its richness or complexity. At issue is not doing versus nondoing, an active life versus a passive one. It is the question of who/what is the doer.

WHO WILL WIN THE OSCAR?

The waking state is a film starring the ego,
directed by karma, and produced by Maya.[1]
H. W. L. POONJA

Each year in Hollywood, California, the Academy of Motion Picture Arts and Sciences nominates actors in a vast array of roles for best performances. Movie buffs watch the award ceremonies with various degrees of excitement, anticipation, boredom, and differing opinions of who should win the Oscar. There is great interest in what attendees at the ceremony are wearing, what jewelry adorns the women, what cut of tuxedos the men choose, how much cleavage shows on certain actresses. There are comments about hairdos and escorts, views about the degree of sincerity in any given acceptance speech, and judgments about the quality of acting that did or did not get awarded an Oscar nomination or win. People who watch films have very distinct opinions about which stories, actors, directors have "arrived" and which have not.

The spiritual seeker is actually quite similar. She looks around at the spiritual supermarket, full of teachers, gurus, books, YouTube videos, and tips on how to "achieve" enlightenment, and she makes judgments about which ones are winners and which ones are losers. Of course, a winner to one person may seem a loser to another. Indeed, the seeker looks around at the vast array of actors playing various roles in life and imagines there will be a winner and a loser. Most especially, the seeker makes judgments about what she must do in order to be a winner. She looks at a beggar on the street and sees a "person" who has failed, looks at a sage and sees a "person" who has attained spiritual success. Seekers often fail to notice the roles they themselves are playing in the film of their own life, the scripts they have memorized and repeat over and over about a self and the world and who that self is. The focus of the spiritual ego is on how to win the Oscar called "enlightenment."

Tell me, in the great movie of life, whom do you imagine will win the Oscar? Perhaps you imagine the prize will go to the one playing the role of Enlightened One, Radiating-Truth-to-the-Masses, with an honorable mention for the I've-Been-Meditating-for-Years-When-Will-I-Ever-Wake-Up Spiritual Seeker. Perhaps there are a few votes for Ms. Perfection, Has-It-All-Together, or Mr. Righteous, I-Alone-Know-What-Is-Right-for-the-World. What becomes of those playing the roles of Ms. Sad and Lonely, No-One-Will-Ever-Love-Me, or Mr. Important, Horn-Honking-Angry-Victim-of-Other-People's-Incompetence, or those cast as Fearful-in-a-Dying-Body? Whom do you imagine you are? Whom do you imagine wakes up? What if all the roles are played by the same One?

The spiritual ego is looking for a prize. And the seeker imagines he can tell who has achieved such an honor and who has not. He can tell by whether the person wears robes or beads or has lots of disciples or can perform great siddhis (powers). The seeker imagines she can tell by whether her own mind goes blank in the person's presence or she finds herself in bliss. The seeker-after-enlightenment imagines that anyone who has received the Oscar will be omniscient, or will have powerful *shakti* (energy) or the ability to heal the sick and raise the dead, or will never become ill and never react emotionally to any situation.

There is a way in which sages know one another, but it has nothing to do with any of the outward signs mentioned above that the spiritual seeker imagines are indicators of enlightenment. And many of these sages live very quiet lives, tending to a shop, playing music, working with the dying, or living simply in remote areas. There are also sages who are public figures. But not one of those persons, whether imagined to be enlightened or imagined not to be, is separate from that which is living itself always and everywhere. And that is also living you.

THE DREAM OF THE WAKING STATE

The dream of the waking state is that we are separate persons, separate from what we seek. Yet, *who* is dreaming such a dream? Spiritual ambition says there is someplace to go and someone to arrive there, waiting to win the Oscar of enlightenment. Self-realization says there is no place to get to and no one to arrive.

In the words of Ramana Maharshi:

> The thought, "I have not seen," the expectation to see, and
> the desire of getting something are all the workings of
>   the ego. . . .
> That which IS is always here. Even now you are That.
> You are not apart from it.[2]

Seekers often imagine that if they knew the sage's experience, they could somehow figure out how to manipulate their own thinking or behavior in order to create the same experience. However, it is when you stop trying to match your experience to another's and begin to investigate your own that seeking begins in earnest. No one else can eat your food for you, digest it for you, or use it to maintain your bodily functions. Likewise, no one else can desire truth or taste it or digest it for you. Truth can only be discovered for yourself.

Without the light of Awareness you would not know a single thing, remember a single experience, or even be able to claim yourself as a separate "person." Nor could you contemplate the possibility that your life of separation could be an illusion. Without air, water, soil, sun, food, heart, lungs, brain, blood, you could not sustain your being for a single moment. Wholeness does not divide itself into parts. Only language and thought make it seem so.

THE ONE IN MANY COSTUMES

When there is awakening from the dream of separation, we realize that this entire universe and everything in it are manifestations or "disguises" of the One. Sometimes even we, or someone we know very well, might be unrecognizable, depending on the costume of the moment. My son performed in many plays during his high school and college days. I remember being really concerned during the first act of one of the collegiate Shakespeare productions he was in. He did not appear on stage even though he was supposed to be playing one of the main characters in that act. I worried that he must have become ill at the last moment. I later discovered he had been performing all along. His makeup, gait, and speech were so different from normal that I had not recognized my own son.

Likewise, in the play of Consciousness, we may not recognize our Self in our many costumes, gaits, and varieties of speech. We do not recognize the Self within ourselves, and therefore do not see the Self anywhere else either. However, once the Self drops its disguise as our separate "self," we will see nothing *but* the Self everywhere. Consciousness is playing all the roles, including those of seeker and the sought. Some moments the Divine appears to play hide-and-seek, hiding and then revealing, but always the dreamer and the dreamed arise as a single unfolding.

DREAMING

In dreaming, our bodies for all intents and purposes remain unmoving, and yet years could go by, many actions could take place, and life and death could appear to be "realities"—"realities" that can happen in an instant of dreaming. Sometimes we are relieved to wake up and find out it was "only a dream." Sometimes we want the dream to continue because it seemed so lovely. When you awaken, you realize that the dream was a production of your own consciousness. It was a movie of your own making that took on, for a time, a sense of reality.

The creation of our dreams is similar to how our mind creates its experience of its world. Even in waking life, several people observing the exact same event will have different views of its "reality." In the larger context, we might say the universe is the dream thought of God or Consciousness. Every moment, form, cell of the body, molecule, atom, particle, nonparticle, pattern, or energy that exists could not be known without Presence, which is itself the knowing. There is nothing that *is* that could be separated from its Being.

Our very life is a divine happening, a both gross and subtle vibration of Consciousness that condenses into form and appears within the light of Awareness or Presence. That same Presence illuminates our world through the instruments of perception.

EGO DOES NOT SEE

To awaken from the dream of our so-called waking life is the same as awakening from a night dream, except in this case the "I" who knows its own dream is not a separate consciousness, not a separate "I." It is the only Consciousness there is, knowing itself within itself, and is *not* the ego's idea of its separate "I." Our true Self—that which is awake in us—is actually universal and impersonal, although also intimate with the experience we imagine is personal. The pronoun *I* actually refers to something vaster and more mysterious that is simply looking out from one of its infinite viewing points. Each individual expression is unique, yet we share one essence, one ground. Our ego, the thought called "I," does not see, but YOU do. YOU are not a thought. YOU are the true "I," the one playing all the roles, creating out of itself the moment-to-moment unfolding of the experience you call life.

THE ARCHETYPE OF PERSONHOOD

As human beings, we are deeply conditioned and identified with the archetype of personhood. We believe each individual person is defined by a body and mind that are absolutely separate from the rest of life or nature. The *person* considers himself either the victor or the victim of life rather than its expression. But just as the hand is distinct from the heart or the liver, having different functions in one body, each one of us is an expression of a single body—in this case, the body of Being, of Totality. Being is always "becoming" as person, but Presence is what is timelessly awake.

Within your sense of being a person, look deeply, and you may find a natural sense of Presence. The *person* will say, "In meditation, I was resting in awareness, but now I am not." You are the Self; you are Presence. You are already here. You are already at peace, already at rest. What is popping up and down is a phantom. The illusory self is a thought-based memory that seemingly freezes experiences in time, rather than opening to the flowing current of life happening now in the Presence we truly are.

IF I AM NOT A SEPARATE PERSON, WHO AM I?

When identified consciousness imagines waking up and discovering his life is a dream, the person imagines this would be demeaning or devaluing to life. "If all of life is a dream, why be here? What's the point? If we are just little robots created and moved by Totality or God, why bother?" This is the view of separation. You take yourself to be separate and then imagine "you" are moved about without regard to "your" feelings, desires, thoughts, hopes, or dreams. You want no part of a life you do not imagine "you" can control. But who is the "you"? Sooner or later we discover that the ego is not in control, but our Being is quite powerful. Presence is actually a much greater power than thought.

Presence is all there is. I am this body and all other bodies; yet no body, no moment, no "disaster" binds my Presence. Wake up and know yourself to BE who you ARE! As Presence, we may experience infinite compassion, love, light, awareness, acceptance, wisdom, being, peace. If you were to discover this as your truest Self, do you imagine you would feel demeaned, devalued, or afraid? It is only our ego, our sense of separation, that imagines our worth and safety require separation. If you knew who/what you truly are was never born and can never die except in a dream, would you still have the same fears?

DEATH AND THE INSTINCT TO SURVIVE

Now, the body-mind of a human being has an instinct for survival, as do other forms of life, and this instinct works equally in the body-mind of an individual in whom the understanding of no separation has appeared. But when it is time for the form to die, the sage will accept death as part of the journey of Presence that truly has no end.

The form may die, but what you ARE does not. This is not a belief in "life after death" for an imagined separate "self"; it is a knowing that who/what you are now is what continues with no beginning and no end. In truth, nothing dies; life simply transforms itself.

HAPPINESS ON THE OTHER SIDE OF PERSONHOOD

Just on the other side of personhood is happiness. Yes, happiness, peace, contentment, love. When we are no longer holding tightly to being a separate person, we can flow with how life is moving back and forth, one moment experiencing itself as a person, with all the attributes we know and think of as ourselves, and in another moment experiencing ourselves as a mystery beyond the thinking mind that is simply noticing the show, the play of existence. And whether Consciousness experiences itself as seemingly limited or unlimited, whether the coin is coming up heads or tails, absolute or relative, there is Presence, present to the moment as it is. As Presence, we experience our unconditioned, timeless Being. As "person," we are humbled in such Presence. Yet to experience the freedom and uncaused happiness of our true Self, our psychological identity and fascination with the "person" will eventually be surrendered into the Presence of Being.

Part III

CAUGHT IN THE

JAWS

OF THE TIGER

At first, God's visits seem so welcome.
She brings tea and cookies and loves you
so sweetly inside your own heart.
You keep inviting her back
by your prayers and meditations,
imagining you have found the one you always wanted
who will hold you on her endless lap
and take away your pain forever.

But pretty soon, she starts arriving unexpectedly,
at odd hours of the day and night,
and every time she comes,
she takes something away—
a pretty picture here, a bookcase there,
maybe even some trash

you are happy to be rid of
in your basement.

But at some point, it occurs to you
she intends to move in completely.
And now the mind starts backing up:
"Perhaps you could come back another day,
after I've worked on my house,
after I've bought nicer furniture,
after I've finished my fight with evil,
after I've planted a peace garden."[1]

9

CAUGHT IN THE TIGER'S MOUTH

Just as the prey which has fallen into the
jaws of the tiger has no escape,
so those who have come within the ambit
of the Guru's gracious look
will be saved by the Guru and will not get
lost; yet one should by his own
effort pursue the path shown by God or Guru
and gain release. One can know
oneself only with one's own eye of knowledge,
and not with somebody else's.[1]

RAMANA MAHARSHI

THE DREAM OF RAMANA MAHARSHI

Eventually the spiritual ego's quest for God or Truth "out there" turns inward and seems to become the Infinite's quest for us. As the tables are turned, this often creates discomfort, as we are getting a foretaste that maybe our ego is not actually in charge. I knew I was no longer in charge (not that I ever had been) of my spiritual life, as teachers, teachings, and experiences I was not seeking seemed to come unbidden. One night I dreamed of a man named Ramana Maharshi. I knew nothing about this Indian guru except his name, but there he was in the dream, his eyes seeming to personify a divine radiance. The power of his gaze made me know that I had to find out something about him.

As I mentioned earlier, I never wanted a guru and felt sorry for those who sought one. Yet in beginning to read *The Spiritual Teaching of Ramana Maharshi* and a number of other books about him, I had the sense I was being exposed to the purest truth I had encountered to that point. Others read the same books and do not have the same experience. Some look into the eyes of Ramana's photograph and see radiance, experiencing love and peace in themselves; others see a kindly looking Indian gentleman whose eyes do nothing for them.

THE EXPERIENCE OF SELF-INQUIRY

Ramana repeatedly advised mature seekers that Self-inquiry was the best means and most direct path for ending the search. My mind equated "direct" with "shortcut," and so the idea of a direct path seemed most appealing. The reason for the ego's interest in a shortcut is that any so-called spiritual path seems to be a way out of this moment and into a better one. This is the nature of the thinking mind. But Life is leading us wherever it is both in spite of ourselves and because of our Self.

Ramana Maharshi's method, Self-inquiry, does not require the seeker to adopt a philosophy or to leave home, family, job, or any tradition, spiritual or otherwise. Instead of trying to renounce life, feeling, perception, or desire, you simply inquire *who* is living, *who* is feeling, *who* perceives. Egoic mind is never the agent of its own demise, but this method is a way of turning the mind on itself—searching for the Source of the "I." At first, it seemed an intellectual exercise for me, but the more I did it, the more I felt the mind withdrawing into itself. It seemed that there was some knowledge already present, a knowing that the Source was within, and so every time Self-inquiry was made, there was a remembering of this knowing.

While the inquiry *Who am I?* is not a mantra meditation, in the beginning it seemed to be used in a similar way. It gave the mind something to do with itself instead of continually following its thoughts outward, spinning more and more. But the difference between a mantra meditation and Self-inquiry is that the latter directly refers the mind to its Source, which is a way of the mind moving in rather than going out. While there is no in or out in reality, in a body-mind organism that has taken itself to be the subject of its objective world, the experience is one of withdrawing into the Self, the *actual* subject rather than the imagined one. Instead of exploring only the manifestations of the Self, which include identification with the body-mind, Self-inquiry pulls attention back time and time again into the Heart of Awareness.

Self-inquiry is also a way of stopping thoughts in their tracks. The moment a thought appears, instead of following that thought, you ask the mind to find the Source of the thought. You are asking your mind to come home. In true Self-inquiry, the mind will find only what it is not. Thoughts quiet down, and the Source simply appears as itself. When the Self *is*, no questions remain. The mind is quiet.

In my experience of maintaining Self-inquiry, it was as if everything would become still, even in the midst of living. Often, this stillness seemed to precede energy moving up my spine. Self-inquiry seemed to take on its own life. I did not compulsively "do" it or even set aside any regular times in the day for such practice. It simply appeared from time to time, at any time or no particular time. "Who is sitting here with her client?" "Who is looking at her reflection in the store window?" "Who is feeling anxious?" But each time inquiry was made, something seemed to slide backward into more stillness. What was sliding backward were the bundles of thoughts that I had taken to be myself.

> Self Inquiry begins as a method and ends as a mirror,
> a mirror in which the timeless perceives its formless reflection.[2]
> MOOJI

GLIMPSES OF THE INFINITE

Once during my early days of being exposed to Ramana Maharshi's teachings, I was on a plane trip when we encountered some frightening turbulence. I decided to try to meditate as Ramana had taught. At first it seemed as if awareness and attention expanded to become bigger than my anxiety; then beyond, to encompass the plane; then more vast, to include the clouds, the sky, the entire universe. In that moment, there was a sense that if the plane should go down and we should all die, "I" would be no different than I was in that moment. Then the direction of attention reversed, and "I" became the smallest speck—a mere dust mote—and still "I" was what I was in the expanded state. Of course, at that time, I believed this experience happened because of my great abilities as a "meditator"! Spiritual ego claimed credit.

A year later, a friend showed me a flyer for a two-week meditation and yoga retreat with Jean Klein at Joshua Tree in the California desert. The inner knowing was immediate: *Go.* But my mind argued. I had never heard of Jean Klein, a European Advaita and yoga teacher, never even seen a photograph of him or read any of his books. Couldn't I wait until he was in my area and maybe go for a weekend—not be stuck hundreds of miles from home for two weeks in the desert? Plus I was not a yogi, wasn't sure I could even touch my toes, and could not begin to imagine going on a two-week yoga retreat. But the inner knowing was incredibly strong: *Go.*

When the information arrived about what to bring and it said no books, I was not happy. I believed my spiritual books were a great boon to my "progress," and surely bringing a few books would not distract me from my path. By then, however, I was used to sitting in front of the photograph of Ramana Maharshi, my projection of my inner guru. So I asked the question *What should I bring on the retreat?* I was shocked when an "answer" immediately came from the inner voice that I attributed to Ramana: *Take nothing; own nothing; desire nothing; be nothing!*

I thought I was asking about what clothes to take, whether I should go ahead and bring a few books, and out of the blue these words appeared quite emphatically. Once again the ego mind began arguing, something to the effect of, "Well, that is easy for you to say. You just wore a loincloth; I wear clothes!" I rather brushed off the profound depth of the invitation I had heard and packed my bag, including a few books. However, when I arrived at the airport near the retreat center, the airline had lost my luggage. I literally arrived at the retreat with nothing. What was being revealed was this: the "I" I imagined I was was no longer in control.

"I WILL DISMEMBER YOU AND DROWN YOU IN AN OCEAN OF LOVE"

Jean Klein demonstrated the incredible Presence that arises when the ego's sense of separation is absent. In the Presence I associated with Jean, the expansive sense of peace I had learned was possible on the airplane a year before appeared again. And during one meditation on that retreat, Ramana appeared in my awareness, saying, "I will dismember you and drown you in an Ocean of Love." Now, the Ocean of Love part sounded great, but the dismembering and drowning part created some moments of anxiety.

Ego believes that awakening will add a great boon to its separate life; it does not know that the whole process is one of subtraction, not addition. But we may begin to receive inklings of the depths to which our Self may take us as the Infinite moves in completely. Of course, the Divine is never absent and is not moving in and out as we may imagine, but our mind does not know what lies ahead when it is being carried by the deeper dimension of our Being. We may begin to realize that the seeker has become the sought, that the ego—once the hunter—has become the prey.

RAMESH BALSEKAR: "WHO WANTS TO KNOW?"

I continued to take egoic ownership of experiences that were actually simply happening. When a member of a group I am part of brought in a copy of Ramesh Balsekar's *Consciousness Speaks*, there was an immediate inner knowing that I needed to read that book. Now, many people bring in books, or speak about books, or encourage the rest of us to go hear one teacher or another, but for me, only one directive was obvious at that time, and that was to read *Consciousness Speaks*. It was just the action of the moment.

Ramesh Balsekar's "appearance" via this book helped me to see that I was still expecting something that a separate "me" could enjoy—this thing called "enlightenment" that I had been praying, meditating, chanting, and burning candles for over the course of so many years. I had never before written to an author of any book, but I was compelled to write to Ramesh about my spiritual experiences and my questions. So began a correspondence with a man living in Bombay (Mumbai today), a disciple of Nisargadatta Maharaj. At first I was conflicted about whether my writing to another teacher was somehow being disloyal to my idea of Ramana as guru. In talking with the inner guru about this, what came was: *Who do you think* sent *him?*

In the early days of corresponding with Ramesh, whom I never met face-to-face, there was a desire to tell him every detail of my spiritual longings, questions, and accomplishments. After all, ego does take all the happenings to be about a separate self! I wrote unbelievably long letters to Ramesh; he wrote unbelievably short letters to me, only a few letters a year, a few words each, and yet each one seemed to strike deep in the heart of my knowing. He never gave answers, but he repeatedly asked one question and one question alone: "Who wants to know?" Once, he simply advised, "Forget the questions."

I was writing these letters to my Self, of course, but I needed a projection of that Self, and so one appeared. The mind will never be able to explain the grace that is present in the relationship between teacher and seeker. The reason is that it is, in truth, not a relationship. The apparent relationship appears in order to teach one thing: there is only the Self, only Reality, only God. A teacher and seeker are not two.

In a nutshell, Ramesh's teaching was this: All there is is Consciousness (Divine Mystery, God). Of your own self, you can do nothing. There is not one single thing anyone can do to "achieve" enlightenment. If, in the functioning of Totality, such understanding is to occur, it will occur. However, achieving something is the very idea that stands in the way of our knowing. The seeker is the sought.

Knowing that my idea of myself as some separate "I" could do nothing to make anything happen, I began to let go more and more of whom I thought I was. Over many months, I began to have periods in which life simply happened effortlessly, sometimes without any sense of a separate "me" living it. Life, breath, words, cooking, driving, working were simply happening. But still the ego would sweep in to claim the experience. There would be some kind of excitement that "I am really getting somewhere now!"

I was beginning to intuit that there might be only one Awareness, but billions of beings who were experiencing it as "their" consciousness—a single seeing, but many viewing points. Still some doubt remained. However, the many tastes of a different, deeper, and wider perspective showed me that when the separate "me" was not imagining she was in control, there was just what is, occurring without choice. My prayers seemed intense when directed to the Mystery that seemed outside of me. Self-inquiry was intense when the mind was searching inward for its Source. Self-inquiry and devotion appeared to be merging, as the Infinite seemed to be calling "me" to know my Self. The longing was so intense that I felt I was willing to die to know the Truth.

This was no suicidal ideation. I loved my husband, my children, the life I was blessed to live, and yet the desire for Truth was so deep, so overwhelming at this point, that I felt I was willing to surrender my life in order to know. Where does such a desire come from? What moves us? What moves your own search?

I do not believe the jaws of the tiger necessarily have to be an outer guru. Actually, in reality there is no "outer" separate from "inner." We eventually discover, as Ramana taught, that "God, Guru, and Self are one." Therefore, however Truth is calling you, in whatever ways you are being surrendered to the Divine, the true guru is your Self. The inner teacher calls forth the outer one when one is needed. But at some point, we will no doubt have to face our fears of disappearing. Since the ego cannot know what "die before you die" actually means or how it could be lived, our mind will conjure up whatever fantasy it has and may scare itself with its own imagination.

10

DYING FOR TRUTH, YET AFRAID OF DISAPPEARING

*Mind fears the Emptiness
that is itself our freedom.*

THE EMPTY TRUTH

When our mind is looking for Truth, especially the truth about its Self, it seems to come up empty-handed again and again. We have imagined we will find something our intellect can know and define, something beautiful that will be seen and admired by others. However, we keep bumping up against what cannot be defined with words or known by the mind of thought. When this happens, we believe Self-inquiry has failed, or we substitute an intellectual answer that we have read or heard about—even though it does not deliver liberation. We stand at the edge of the unknown, ashamed to admit we do not know and frightened to look into the empty truth.

A children's book called *The Empty Pot* tells the tale of a Chinese emperor who was getting old and had no successors, so he devised a contest to determine his heir. He loved flowers, and so he gave all of the children in the land special seeds and told them that whoever could show him their best in a year would be chosen. One little boy named Ping also loved flowers and was sure that he could grow a beautiful flower. He planted and tended his seed very carefully, but the seed did not sprout. He watered it, tried a bigger pot, richer soil, but still nothing. When the year had passed and Ping's seed had never even sprouted, he was sad and ashamed of his empty pot. As the other children made fun of him, racing with their big, beautiful flowers to see the emperor, Ping did not want to go with his empty pot. But his father encouraged him, reminding him that he had done his best.

The emperor was frowning as he looked around at the flowers; then he saw Ping's empty pot. Ping began to cry, telling the emperor that, despite how hard he had tried to care for the seed, still it had not sprouted. It was the best he could do. Smiling, the emperor told the crowd that he had found the person worthy of being the next emperor. He said he did not know where the others had gotten their seeds, for all the seeds he had given them the year before had been cooked, and so it was impossible for them to grow. He admired Ping's courage to appear with the empty truth and rewarded him with his entire kingdom.[1]

I love this story for many reasons. When we are looking into what is important in our search for Truth, telling the truth is imperative, especially telling the truth to ourselves. So often the spiritual ego pretends to be somewhere it is not, to "know" something it does not, and so repeatedly misses opportunities to look deeply into the moment or into one's feelings, missing the ways awareness has of liberating difficult emotions or thoughts when we expose them consciously to the light. Ruthless honesty—seeing clearly and without judgment—is required in the spiritual search. Spiritual egos want to be seen in a certain way. Egos want their "truth" to look a certain way, to feel a certain way, to look like a big, beautiful, blooming flower. Egos do not want to admit they do not know, and so intellectual knowledge is substituted for experiential knowing.

When the ego looking for its Source realizes it does not know and comes face-to-face with the unknown, it often makes a hasty retreat. Egoic thought is quite certain that Self-inquiry is not working because it has not delivered an answer to the intellect. It would rather continue its identity as seeker than to disappear into what has no name. What has no name is empty of definition. Who am I if I cannot think myself into existence?

Nowhere does the ambitious ego feel more out of its element than when faced with an unknown emptiness. To the ego, *emptiness* means being alone rather than "all one." It means being unloved rather than being the empty Mystery out of which love flows. In the moments when one's inquiry or one's stillness erases the familiar, revealing as empty the many ways we have held on to definitions of our "self," the ego often becomes quite frightened.

The process of awakening and beginning to embody what may have been realized is a process of emptying our pockets, emptying our minds, emptying ourselves of separation. The truth of what we are cannot be gained or lost; nothing can increase it or decrease it; we are being lived by a Mystery we cannot know as an object, because it is what we are. What, then, is left for the ego?

THE TRUTH THAT SETS US
FREE MAY ENGENDER FEAR

If you are a true spiritual seeker, there is a part of you that is dying to know the Truth. Somehow you intuitively know that "the Truth will set you free." And you want it badly. Now, everyone desires happiness. In this way, all of us are spiritual seekers, regardless of the means we may imagine will bring about the happiness we long for. But the so-called spiritual seeker cannot imagine a *lasting* happiness unless she discovers the Truth about her most important existential questions.

Some people have to paint or make music. Their lives would have no meaning for them if they could not create their art. Happiness, for them, depends on allowing the creative spirit free rein to express itself. However, if you find yourself on the path of knowledge, you are being drawn to eliminating, which means, to the ego, some sense of dying. If you find yourself on the path of devotion, you are being asked to surrender yourself to God (or Guru), which means, to the ego, the same thing. And for most of us, losing any sense of separation, autonomy, or imagined control involves a visit with fear. Fear is a very difficult demon to invite in for tea.

Our experience is usually that fear does not knock gently. And yet fear is always knocking as long as there is a sense of separation. In fact, fear is a powerful *instrument* of separation. You may not know until there is no longer a sense of separation, but then you may realize that fear and separation arise together. I am not implying that there is anything the "me" can do to ensure the end of fear. Fear will come when it comes; it will go when it goes. It is a stern teacher at times, overwhelming at times, barely noticeable at times. But it appears to be part of the action of separation. Of course, I am not speaking about an instinctual fear that arises in the face of bodily harm; I am talking about the psychological fear of losing a sense of being a separate "somebody."

This particular body-mind has not much acquaintance with terror. There have been moments of extreme fear: when an airplane appeared to be going down in the Irish Sea with myself and my family on board; when the automobile in which my husband and I were passengers stopped within inches of spinning off a cliff on a winding, rain-drenched dirt road at Tassajara Zen Mountain Center; when my husband shared that he had just been held up at gunpoint right outside of our house in our supposedly safe neighborhood; when I was a child passenger in a car driven wildly by a drunken uncle. But apart from these incidents, my experience of fear has been milder, sometimes so subtle that I did not even notice it was there until it wasn't anymore—fears about how I was seen, how I was performing, if I was making the "right" decision, whether I could ever "perfect" myself in order to be worthy in my own eyes.

Even though there may be a point in the spiritual journey when you realize it has a life of its own—quite apart from anything you are doing or not doing—fear may still be a steady accompaniment to the times of your "disappearing" out of separateness. Despite my thoughts that I was a willing victim to the spiritual search, fear arose on a regular basis as "I" was being surrendered to the process. By the time your head is in the tiger's mouth, there is no retreat possible, although there may be apparent reversals in what your mind imagines is its progress toward liberation.

During those first times in meditation when I felt the sense of a separate "me" dissolving, the fear was that I was dying. I prayed to every god I knew—God, Jesus, Shiva, the Buddha, my teachers—to save me. I was terrified. But when there was a jumping into the chasm of no-thing, there was exquisite peace. The ego is not in charge of jumping, for in truth nothing jumps; and while "you" have disappeared, there is no fear. But as soon as the sense of separation returns, so does a fear of disappearing.

Sometimes I would talk to Ramana Maharshi about this fear of dying, and he would "tell" me with utter conviction and utter love, "You absolutely *will* die." I knew he was not just speaking about this body. Gradually, as the "disappearing" and "returning" alternated more frequently, there was a lessening of fear that the body would disappear and never return. When there was a sense of life simply happening, there was no effort and no anxiety. Life lived itself and connected to itself in ways too numerous for the mind to even fathom; it just seemed to flow easily from one thing to another, without a sense of separation. But then something would always happen that brought the separate "me" back to life. That something was the fear of disappearing.

DYING FOR TRUTH BUT AFRAID OF DYING

The spiritual seeker is in a quandary. He or she is dying for truth yet afraid of dying, dying for truth but afraid of disappearing. The ways the sense of separation is triggered are endless. Expansive awareness will appear, followed by a thought about what you forgot to do yesterday or what you need to do today. You will be going along feeling open, loving, connected, when suddenly you remember the sister who drives you crazy. You will have a flash of intuition from your deeper knowing about how illusory the panic is you are experiencing over "time," and then you will judge that knowing to be a defense keeping you from getting your taxes done! As Kabir said so well, "When the mind wants to break its link with the world, it still holds on to one thing."[2]

But the funny thing is, it is only when the mind *wants* to break its link with the world of separateness that aspects of human life appear to be problems! None of these thoughts are actually ending expansiveness, or openness, or our knowing. When our perspective changes, there is simply the witnessing of it all without the involvement that takes it to be something about a "me." The ego uses thoughts, feelings, and events to remind itself of its separateness all of the time. But when the sense of separation is gone, those same thoughts, feelings, and events are simply thoughts, feelings, and events. That is what is so crazy making for the thinking mind. It thinks, "Well, I'm supposed to get rid of the ego, right?" But one sage says, "Love the ego; it, too, is God's reflection!" And another says, "Destroy the mind!" And another says, "Nothing is up to you!" What is one to do?

Our thinking mind is very industrious. It may spend hours or days going around in circles of its own making; it keeps moving because if it ever stopped still in its tracks, it would disappear. But the only thing that disappears in stillness or silence is the sense of separation. Personality, functioning, body, mind, life—they all continue, but without identifying with a separate self.

One of the biggest factors we use to maintain the illusion of a separate self is our memory. It retains not only the experiences of our living but the stories we have attached to those experiences as well. We imagine that the life or story we remember is who we are. And living so much in the mind of memory and projection based on memory means we often pay little attention to our present perception, the open awareness that is here now.

Douglas Harding designed a lovely experiment that I have adapted slightly for use with meditation groups and others. I call it "Meditation without Memory."[3] Harding's experiment asks a series of very simple questions that you answer silently to yourself on the basis of your present perception and not on memory. Since it is important to experience these questions with your eyes closed, perhaps you can ask a friend to slowly read this to you, pausing when he or she sees the ellipsis (. . .) at the end of a sentence or paragraph. Here is how the adaptation goes:

Meditation without Memory

I would like to invite you to find a comfortable way to sit, close your eyes, perhaps take a deep breath or two, and come present, deeply present now. . . .

I am going to ask you some questions that I'd invite you to answer to yourselves as we go along. These are all questions based on your present experience, your present perception, without the benefit of memory. Obviously, memory may arise, but I would ask you to investigate these questions on the basis of your present experience without going to memory for answers.

We're going to investigate our experience without benefit of vision—just focusing on what is given now, when we don't import into the situation things we imagine or remember or foresee. Answer the questions on the basis of what you can actually perceive at this time. We're not talking about our feelings or understanding or memory, but what you can actually perceive in this moment. . . .

Without benefit of vision (remember your eyes are closed, dear Reader), and without going to memory, what is given now? What can you actually perceive in this moment? . . .

What shape is given now, if any? Do you have a shape now, if you do not go to memory for an answer? You can imagine, or remember, a human shape here, but is it given *now* based on present evidence? . . .

Of course, using imagination you could be anything here. But is it given now, on the basis of present experience, without benefit of memory or imagination? . . .

Is there an interface now between you and your environment? Based on present experience, without the benefit of memory, where do you stop and the world begins? . . .

On the basis of your present experience, without benefit of memory:

- How old are you? . . .
- How tall are you? . . .
- How many toes do you have at this time? What toes? . . .
- Without memory, what sex are you? . . .

Based on your present experience, without benefit of memory:
- What color are you? . . .
- What is your nationality? . . .
- What is your name? . . .

Without going to memory, what is your address? . . .

What is your marital status, if you do not go to memory for an answer? . . .

What is your job? In this moment, without benefit of memory, do you know? . . .

All these things that we base our identity on—our skills, attainments, possessions, characteristics—can you find them in the present moment if you don't import things from memory? . . .

On the basis of present evidence, without benefit of memory:
- Where were you born? . . .
- *Were* you born? . . .

As you sit, there may be sounds, sensations, thoughts that arise. You sense them arising and dissolving in you, but what ARE you in this present moment? . . .

What are you without a name, an address, a shape, a gender? . . .

You don't imagine that you have died or disappeared, do you? Even though in this moment, without benefit of memory, you may not be able to identify yourself with being this or that. . . .

Feel into what is left when the whole host of ways you have of defining yourself is dropped away, except as memory traces. When, without benefit of memory, you may not have a shape but sense yourself more like this awake space, awake silence for the dance of sounds, sensations, feelings, thoughts, experiences. . . .

Is there a sense of coming home, a sense of I AM, the sense of Being, of existing, of being aware? Let yourself have the felt sense of this I AM. Perhaps in this moment one cannot say "what" I AM, but simply *that* I AM. . . .

Sit as this I AM.

Now drop the "I"! . . .

Drop the "AM"! . . .

What are you now? . . . [*Long pause.*]

And now, I invite you to very slowly open your eyes and begin to take in the sights of the world, but notice that you do not have to leave home ground. We don't have to go to memory to define ourselves, even when memory returns. As you look around the room and begin to see what are apparent objects, notice that these are arising in the same space. We don't have to go back to our heads to begin to see. . . .

Likewise, when we begin to speak, we do not have to leave the space of awareness to speak. We don't have to identify with thoughts in order to use thoughts to communicate.

Now, this exercise is definitely of the deconstructive variety, and often when I offer this to a group, one or two individuals will, at some point, begin to feel dizzy or experience some bodily discomfort, need to leave to use the restroom, or have a coughing fit. They may not call their reactions "fear," but the fear of disappearing is being coped with in these ways, by these reminders that "I am the body." When we begin to feel the sense of separation slipping away, the mind will sometimes react quite strongly to it. We do not have a choice. It happens if and when it happens. But you may be able to watch this phenomenon and become aware of how fearful it feels to think of disappearing into the stillness. At some point, you may experience a point when it seems there is a choice possible to remain present to your experience and its energy, rather than retreating from it, refusing it, or trying to manage it.

FEAR'S RATIONALE FOR MAINTAINING SEPARATION

Identified mind will give you all kinds of reasons why it might be afraid of disappearing. "Nothing will get done." "I won't be available to my job, my wife, my children because I will be loving everyone equally." "It is such an inflation to imagine 'I am God.'" (Indeed it is, from the point of view of the ego!) "I have lots more life to live before I retire to the cave and contemplate my navel!" "I'm afraid to 'wake up.'" But whatever the mind is thinking, *thinking* is the activity of separation. That seems impossible to accept, doesn't it? You imagine life as you know it would stop completely if your mind weren't thinking about everything at every waking moment. The thinking mind is the mind that becomes involved in following thoughts, spinning them out, imagining they are true, riding wave after wave of memory, conditioning, judging, interpreting, liking, disliking, planning, or projecting.

When the mind becomes quiet, thoughts may still occur, but they are observed as thoughts instead of as your life. They appear when they are needed, guiding, directing, planning ahead when that is useful, and so on. But continual thinking is what keeps us imagining we are the stories that spin about our life instead of the life that is living it or the Consciousness that is aware of it. We have a deep emotional attachment to our conditioned body and mind, and it seems terrifying that this identification might disappear.

Somehow, without ego's constant direction, we imagine life would stop unfolding. Probably most of us have also had the experience in which life, art, sports, writing, music—whatever—just flowed without efforting and yet, incredibly, the results were wonderful. The problem with those moments is our interpretation that "we" had something to do with our being in the flow. Life is *always* in the flow. It is the thinking mind that imagines otherwise.

I had periods of sadness as interludes of recognition occurred that the one I had always identified with was not who I was. It seemed like I was losing an old friend—myself. I thought I would be elated, but instead I was beginning a grieving process in anticipation of a kind of death.

A WILLINGNESS TO "DIE" FOR TRUTH

Who can explain the intensity some souls have to know Truth? It is a mystery, like the rest of life, but there came a point when I felt willing to surrender my life for Truth. It sounds melodramatic to speak of it at this point, and even at the time it was full of drama, but nonetheless, the whole process of committing to knowing Truth became so intense that I felt willing to let go of everything for this experience of Truth I had tasted only for moments. Do you think for a second such surrender is a surrender of the ego? When commitment comes like this, there is no question that it is not your own. A force much greater than the ego propels such a quest.

For much of my life, I had wanted to be seen to be a certain way—kind, loving, spiritual, giving—and tried to act accordingly. I wanted to become what I imagined I was not already. But now all I wanted was Truth, no matter what it looked like or what "I" looked like. I knew that I could never open to Truth as long as I thought it had to look a certain way or fit into someone's vision of what it was—no matter if that vision was that of the Buddha or of Jesus or of any of the Indian teachers I had been drawn to.

Ramesh Balsekar's writings appeared in my life at this juncture, and they seemed to be what was needed for my intense efforting to calm down. The peak of intensity in the seeking were days I was preparing to offer my "self" for some kind of realization of Truth. There would be wave after wave of grief as I remembered my life, the love of my family and friends, the world I imagined I would be giving up to know God. There was no desire to die—I loved my life—but something seemed willing to let go of everything. Was it a last-ditch effort, a bargaining in desperation, a sacrifice, a drama created by ego, true surrender, a grace? I do not know. The feeling was that I was offering the most I had to offer—*my very life*—for God. What more could I do? In retrospect, I can see that my life was never "mine" to offer, but that was not my understanding in those days.

NOTHING MORE EGO COULD DO

I remember distinctly the moment, in the midst of reading *Consciousness Speaks*, when I saw Ramesh's words saying there was absolutely nothing the ego could do to attain enlightenment. I felt something soften and relax; it was really an enormous relief, a great unburdening. It felt like a healing balm to my soul. Right then and there, I began to accept that the understanding I longed for might never happen in this lifetime.

I accepted, more than I ever had before, that there was nothing this little ego could do on its own power to take me to enlightenment. If awakening never came, I had glimpsed it, and that was blessing enough. Some people go through life without even a taste. I began to feel contented and truly grateful for the blessings of my life as it was, and I saw how my intense wanting to be somewhere else had kept me from the feelings I was now experiencing. I began to accept that my life and the elusive thing I imagined was enlightenment was up to a Divine Mystery I could not create, manipulate, or control with my thoughts. My mind was beginning to realize its limitations, to relax its demands to "know." It was beginning to accept, like the little chickpea in Rumi's lovely poem, that "I can't do this by myself."

CHICKPEA TO COOK

A chickpea leaps almost over the rim of the pot
where it is being boiled.
"Why are you doing this to me!"

The cook knocks him down with the ladle.

"Don't you try to jump out.
You think I'm torturing you.
I'm giving you flavor,
so you can mix with spices and rice
and be the lovely vitality of a human being.

"Remember when you drank rain in the garden.
That was for this."

Grace first. Sexual pleasure,
then a boiling new life begins,
and the Friend has something good to eat.

Eventually the chickpea
will say to the cook,
    "Boil me some more.
Hit me with the skimming spoon.
I can't do this by myself.

"I'm like an elephant that dreams of gardens
back in Hindustan and doesn't pay attention
to his driver. You're my cook, my driver,
my way into existence. I love your cooking."

The cook says,
    "I was once like you,
fresh from the ground. Then I boiled in time,
and boiled in the body, two fierce boilings.

"My animal soul grew powerful.
I controlled it with practices,
and boiled some more, and boiled
once beyond that,
    and became your teacher."[4]

There comes a time when our egoic mind realizes it is not the cook. As the chickpea, we are not asking to be "hit . . . with the skimming spoon" as some form of masochism; rather, we begin to see that whatever way life is "cooking" us, it is for a greater realization, ultimately for a greater service to the whole. We become willing to be "cooked" in the service of a love that leads to openness and compassion. We realize that our time in the soup pot is cooking the seed of separation that leads to the empty Truth.

11

ENLIGHTENMENT CANNOT BE BOUGHT OR SOLD

Blessed are the poor in spirit,
for theirs is the kingdom of heaven.[1]
MATTHEW 5:3

He is a poor man who wants nothing,
knows nothing, and has nothing.[2]
MEISTER ECKHART

If you wish to see the truth, then hold no
opinions for or against anything.[3]
SENG-TS'AN, THIRD PATRIARCH OF ZEN

ENLIGHTENMENT AS SPIRITUAL POVERTY

Enlightenment might actually be described as spiritual poverty. By "poverty" I do not mean selling all one's belongings and living in a cave. Spiritual poverty has nothing to do with having or not having material possessions. The poverty I am speaking of is the emptiness that does not separate itself in any way from life. It is the poverty of our true nature that is free precisely because it contains everything yet in itself is nothing. It is the poverty of a mind emptied of its beliefs in its own identity. It is the poverty of a soul that has no idea where it stands on the so-called spiritual path.

There is a Mystery so unknowable that it stops the thinking mind, and thus it is the poverty of a mind that is surrendered in the face of its limitation. It is the poverty of doing what needs to be done without thinking about the cost. It is the poverty of a freedom so immense that self-image does not even register in its movement. It is a poverty that can be compassionate simply because it does not consider being compassionate, but rather it *is* compassion. It is a poverty that does not think about how the awakened life "looks" because it is *being* the awakened life.

Enlightenment is sought and sold as many things in today's spiritual supermarket. But for many seekers, no matter how often thoughts might insist otherwise, what is really desired, at least in the beginning, is an escape from oneself or from life as it is into a new, improved, transcendent life for the "me." In time, of course, we discover that what is transcendent reveals itself in direct proportion to the *absence* of the thought called "me." If egos truly believed there was nowhere to go and nothing to be gained or attained for a "me," I dare say the multi-million-dollar industry involved in selling spirituality or enlightenment would face a hard hit. And, ironically, you might not have purchased this book.

The mind of thought is engaged in the known. The Mystery the mind is seeking is unknown. Yet the mind keeps looking to itself to discover, understand, and unravel the Truth that is unknown. Whatever we imagine we are seeking when we begin to seek enlightenment, we are never prepared for what we actually find—or, more accurately, what we don't find. True poverty of spirit occurs when one is not separating oneself from Source, not even to be a "vehicle" of the Divine, but one is free of knowledge, will, or agency—emptied of ideas of God, Self, or Truth. Enlightenment, in its deepest expression, erases separation, holds on to nothing, and moves from unknowing as far as the mind is concerned. An enlightened moment is a moment when concepts have ceased. Yet wisdom and love flow from such poverty. Someone once asked me, "What did Adyashanti give you?" I answered, "Nothing. He gave me nothing, and that was his greatest gift."

A JOURNEY OF SUBTRACTION

As I mentioned earlier, the journey that we imagine will bring us the ultimate gain, the ultimate knowledge, bliss, and peace of mind is really a journey of subtraction, not addition. Rather than adding something to our self-image, it takes away our self-image. Rather than delivering greatness, it lets us discover the freedom of our own nothingness. Rather than bringing the ultimate point of view, it allows an awakening that renders points of view irrelevant. Rather than feeding the spiritual ego with more and more, it takes away the ego's food, the beliefs that fueled its identity and sense of a separate "enlightened me." Rather than becoming more, we become less. Rather than the mind knowing more, it knows less. Rather than answering all of our questions, the questions dissolve, along with the questioner.

If the spiritual seeker actually knew in advance what would be demanded in this so-called journey, he or she might never begin, for what is demanded is nothing short of our attachment to everything we ever thought, learned, believed, imagined, or identified with as a "self." For many, the cost of surrendering these beliefs feels far greater than the money spent on spiritual paraphernalia, weekend workshops, or retreats, and most are not willing to pay the price that true freedom demands. Such freedom unhooks us from attachment to the illusion of what we are not and at the same time deepens our joy of loving, learning, observing, engaging, and being one with the life we are.

THE COST OF REALIZATION

Most spiritual teachers emphasize the beneficial aspects of awakening: peace, joy, love, clarity, contentment, freedom, wisdom, compassion. And these are not false. But few teachers emphasize the cost: everything we ever thought we were or would become. It is rather common for the seeker to have a taste of paradise and imagine that he has "arrived" in the promised land. But the sincere seeker of truth will soon discover he has arrived nowhere and all that the inflated spiritual ego imagined it has gained will, in one way or another, be taken away or rendered transparent, including realization itself.

If we are to embody what we truly are, we must be emptied of all that we are not. We will be stripped bare, invited out of our "self" possession, our "self" cherishing, and emptied of our most sacred and holy beliefs. The "good guys" and the "bad guys" will be seen to be the same essence; the whole universe will be our body; the suffering of the world will be felt more deeply, as will the compassion it arouses in the heart we share.

However we begin the so-called spiritual journey, we feel motivated by longing, by a deep desire for Truth, love, God, Self, Buddha nature, freedom. If we followed our longing back to its Source, we might discover that what we long for is the Truth of what we are. But most minds begin to look outside to books, religions, philosophies, therapies, practices, and teachers.

A TRUE TEACHER INVITES US INWARD

Happening upon a teacher who embodies awakening, within or outside of a spiritual tradition, can be a very lucky thing, a very great thing, as the true teacher will invite us to look within, to take, as they say in Zen, the backward step. Often, however, our minds are hoping to have enlightenment given to us by a teacher or a practice, and we become frustrated when this does not seem to happen. The truth is that no one can give you what you are. Our Buddha nature, what is awake, can neither be lost nor gained, neither given nor taken away. But it does no good to know this intellectually. Each of us must make our own discovery. No one else can do it for us. And it is here that we begin our journey to poverty.

ARE YOU WILLING TO BE A BEGINNER?

What is unknown is what is inviting the seeker out of the known. Are we willing to not know? It is amazing how many people have had deep and authentic awakenings to their true nature, only then to limit themselves by all the ideas their minds carry about how they are supposed to look, feel, think, or not think "if . . ." What is free and awake expresses itself as life, life as it is. The very acts of sitting, walking, eating, speaking *are* the action of enlightenment. As the Buddhist Heart Sutra says so succinctly, "Formlessness is exactly form; form is exactly formlessness." Most minds, based in self-image, imagine that formlessness (Spirit) is exactly form except when it comes to "me," my life, my personality, my feelings, et cetera. But our true nature does not have a separate "me" or "my." It is whole. As long as we cling to a "me," we will not be free. We will continue to see through the prism of an illusory separation.

ARE YOU WILLING TO LOSE YOUR "SELF"?

Are you willing to pay the price even if it means losing your "self"? If you are, it will eventually feel like exchanging a penny to gain the whole universe. But no matter what one hears of the Buddha's discovery of "no self," or Jesus's realization that "I and my Father are one," or Ramana Maharshi's "only the Self," most seekers believe that there is a separate self (a "me") who will become enlightened and live in eternal bliss and freedom. Why else are so many seekers willing to pay so much for the promise of enlightenment? For how-to books, DVDs, teachers, weekend workshops, retreats, trips to India, zafus, the correct meditation clothing, shawls, jewelry, oils, crystals, statues, candles, home altars?

Now, there is nothing wrong with your attraction to any of the above, but beware when what is being sold is eternal bliss, freedom, an end to life's suffering, the solution to all problems, security for the mind, vast knowledge, powerful shakti, special powers available for one's own use (for worthy causes, of course), finding your true soul mate, and whatever else minds imagine awakening will bring. Whatever a mind imagines enlightenment is, it usually includes such ideas as these: it will create an unending experience of bliss; solve all relationship dilemmas; ensure that you will forever be happy and loved and never feel alone again; create a body or a life empty of illness, pain, or a single moment's tension; and, if one is very honest, *that it will allow you to escape from life as it is to a new, improved life for the "me."* But identifying with the thought called "me" is our separation.

WHAT IS NEEDED WILL APPEAR

For the sincere spiritual seeker, whatever is needed will appear. This includes desire, longing, books, teachers, teachings, gurus, practices, glimpses, openings, closings, frustrations, failures, and more. When the true teacher appears, there is an inner knowing that also simply appears. You do not need to worry about whom "you" choose, since it is not your choice. "You" (as ego) are not the one who creates the meeting. There is an inner knowing that the mind does not control. Life moves us. Something is known in the heart even when the mind is unclear or resists. I am not talking about heart in the sense of simply our feeling state. I am pointing to the true Self that is actually driving the bus.

The seeker who longs for Truth or who longs for God will not be left bereft of what is needed, but it takes an open mind and an open heart to follow your deep inner guidance or to imagine that Silence will guide you. Many of us have grown up imagining we cannot trust ourselves to know what is right for ourselves, and we certainly cannot trust life to take care of things. The ego does not like to leave anything up to chance, fate, God, life, or anyone or anything else, believing, as it does, that its safety and security lie in its (illusory) control.

If the Mystery moves for something to happen, it happens, no matter how hard we resist; and if it does not happen, well, that is just what happens. We may not be ready or receptive because of fear or immaturity, or the voice may be the voice of ego and not our deepest knowing.

TRUSTING OUR INNER KNOWING

There are many things in life that we accept just happen without mental turmoil: having a drink of water when we are thirsty, for instance, or leaving our lungs alone to breathe themselves. I am suggesting that everything else just happens as well, including your actions, reactions, decisions, resistance, the course of your life. This does not mean we have no perception of choice. Of course we do. We can live more and more aligned with our inner wisdom, or we can resist it, doubt it, devalue it. The things that appear in our inner knowing simply appear; and it is only by trusting that we discover the felt sense of inner wisdom that can be trusted. Many thoughts appear in the mind, but it is the heart that holds one and not another. If you have developed a relationship of trust of your deep Self, you realize that when the inner push or pull is strong, you cannot *not* follow it. The action simply occurs.

Now, perhaps you have made tremendous progress controlling a certain destructive behavior—addiction, for example. You have had the experience of working very hard on yourself or on a problem and finally getting on top of it. This, you imagine, proves there is a separate "self," because before you had no control over your addiction and now you no longer drink or do drugs. Or perhaps you have had clear intuitions that did not work at all, and therefore the mind imagines it cannot trust the inner knowing. "I thought my last boyfriend was the right one; I thought I knew deep in my heart. Look how wrong I was!"

YOU WILL LAUGH AT THE RATIONALE OF THE THINKING MIND

The thinking mind will come up with all kinds of rationales for believing in its separate life and separate power, and that just happens, also. When you see that nothing is separate, you will laugh at all the ways you imagined decisions were "yours" to make. If you are drawn to theological terms, we could say: Nothing happens outside of God's will, because nothing happens outside of God, because nothing exists that is not a reflection of God. God is synonymous with Totality/Mystery/Awareness. To awaken deeply is to understand that there has never been a separate person doing one single thing separate from the action of the whole unfolding itself, and that all of the happenings are simply appearances in what/who you are. Everything is unfolding from the true Heart of Awareness that we share.

Perhaps you'd like to get back to the important business of "your" enlightenment and how the right teacher or guru appears. There is no separate "you" to enlighten. The understanding and the shift of identity that occur with awakening simply appear, like everything else. And they appear only because of the misunderstanding we live with that we are separate.

Here in this core misunderstanding is where a guru comes in. In Sanskrit, *gu* means "darkness," and *ru* means "to destroy." The concept of guru has not been part of our Western tradition, nor does it need to be. Most Westerners prefer to use the term *teacher*. A true guru does not care what anyone calls him or her. In fact, the guru is not personally engaged with anyone, yet personal relationships appear to exist in powerful, meaningful, and loving ways from the point of view of the disciple.

GURUS, SPIRITUAL TEACHERS, AND CHARLATANS

From the point of view of Totality, gurus, spiritual teachers, and charlatans all exist as manifestations of one Consciousness. From the point of view of the phenomenal world, there are differences in function.

Gurus

The guru is the power of the Self within, an ever-present support shining in the heart of the devotee. The guru is the expression of grace, inviting the seeker into the true Heart of Awareness. As the Self that is the inner guru pulls the seeker within, the apparent outer guru pushes the seeker over the edge of her limited identity with the nonexistent ego. The guru is not a separate person. The guru is the appearance of the Self both within the seeker and in the seeker's world. Like the rest of life, he simply comes as an appearance, and yet the disciple imagines the guru is separate from herself and is in this world to teach her something about the spiritual path or how to transcend separateness. Yet it is the inner guru who has called forth the outer guru.

Even though as I meditated in front of Ramana's photograph, I would feel a deep peace and sense of simply Being, I did not want to imagine he was my guru. I did not want one, and I felt you were really going down a dangerous slope to treat a man as if he were a god. So one day I asked the photograph, "Are you my guru?" The answer immediately came back, "The Self is your guru." If the answer had come back yes, I would not have believed it and would have gone in the other direction. Of course, these were all thoughts of the "one" who took herself to be separate from the action of the moment, from the guru who had appeared, from the unfolding of life as it was. Yet, to me, this is true: the Self *is* your guru. If a guru or teacher is needed, one will appear.

When we have a deep relationship with our inner life, we can ask questions and receive answers from that place of silence, stillness, and wisdom within. You may think that it is just yourself answering yourself, and of course you would be correct. Everything *is* our Self relating to itself, but until we really know who we are, the Self projects itself as God, Goddess, Divine Mother, lover, friend, guru, teacher, et cetera, and the "answers," coming from our deeper knowing, appear as the answers of God or guru. We have not yet fully understood that Self, God, and Guru are one. We are living in the dual world of God or Guru as "other."

Not everyone who is teaching or who seems to have students is a guru. The guru draws seekers by simply Being. This Being is not about having siddhis, being able to manipulate emotions or minds, or demanding money. The guru is not a person with special powers. The guru is one who knows, in fact, that he or she is not a person and that whatever appears or does not appear is only appearance, not reality. The guru does not identify with personhood *or* powers, yet disciples may imagine both. The guru is not concerned with the number of disciples, though disciples may come, nor is the guru concerned with making money, although money may come. The guru is not trying to do anything. He (sadly, most gurus are men) is merely being the Self, knowing that it is the Self that arranges everything, speaks through human lips, brings seekers or sends them away, brings money or takes it away. None of it is the guru's concern.

Spiritual Teachers

Among spiritual teachers, inside or outside of a spiritual tradition, there are masters and there are messengers. A spiritual teacher might be either, but the one Consciousness is guiding truly awakened spiritual teachers to speak from the deep silence of Truth. There are other teachers who may have had glimpses or partial awakenings, including some who seem interested in commercializing their teachings and may be quite concerned with name, fame, money, or numbers. A true teacher, however, is not arrogant, does not claim powers that only he has access to, is not telling folks that he alone is awake while everyone else is not. When oneness has awakened, there will be an openness that does not claim division from others or an arrogant conviction that one tradition alone is the only way to God or Truth. Spiritual teachers may speak to multitudes or have only a very few students. Some masters may transmit their teachings only to one or two deeply engaged students.

Like gurus, spiritual teachers are also manifestations of the one Self; so are their students. But they may serve a slightly different function than the so-called guru. They may be actively trying to teach something. They may believe they *have* something to teach. They may be very skilled at what they do and be very inspiring and helpful to many people.

Truth Cannot Be Taught

However, the wisdom of the guru or wise spiritual teacher knows that *she* teaches nothing, does nothing, is nothing. Everything is an appearance, just as a dream is an appearance in Consciousness during sleep. What appears just appears, and then it vanishes; none of it is the deepest reality. Truth cannot be taught. Take away everything you can take away until nothing is left, and what is left is what the guru is. It is also what the seeker is, but the seeker believes otherwise.

Now, you undoubtedly have your own ideas about what a guru or spiritual teacher should look like, and here I am writing down my ideas about such things as well. But I am not really speaking here about what someone looks like. There is an inner knowing, an inner communication that is communicating with itself all of the time in all of our apparent meetings and partings with various teachers, gurus, or others. What we experience or receive as "transmission" is simply the spontaneous transmitting of where we are in any given moment.

Transmission

We are always transmitting where we are, whether we imagine that is the case or not. The teacher in whom awakeness is deeply embodied transmits the truth of that awakeness without trying to do so. It is received (or not) by the resonance a seeker might have with that energy of Truth in the moment. Truth transmits itself beyond words. Self sees the Self, Love sees love wherever it looks. Even in the realm of authentic spiritual teachers, there may be a resonance with some and dissonance with others. The fact that you have a resonance and someone else appears to have a dissonance says nothing about where you belong or where the other person belongs. Consciousness is *always* relating to itself in the phenomenal world, seeing itself, communicating with itself, and this is true for the teachers we might see as charlatans as well as for revered gurus and marvelous spiritual teachers.

Charlatans

A charlatan is an imposter, one who claims to possess knowledge or skill that he does not have or one whose ego is claiming to be enlightened. An imposter will promise enlightenment, then tell you that you just need to sign up for the advanced course for X more dollars or give all of your savings or your sexuality or your self-respect as part of the bargain. *Enlightenment cannot be bought or sold.* Saying this does not mean that those who function as gurus or spiritual teachers do not need to pay rent or buy food or support families. Some gurus ask for money; some spiritual teachers charge for their time or their teachings; but no one can give you the understanding that will set you free. No one can give you what you already are. It cannot be purchased or delivered like a sack of groceries, no matter how many "advanced" courses you take.

The guru does not believe she "does" anything. The spiritual teacher may imagine she has something valuable to offer, but she is motivated by a sincere desire to be of service. The charlatan wants fame, fortune, or a quick ride to humility. That which inflates also deflates. How can the seeker tell the difference? His egoic mind may not be able to discern, but his heart will know. The fact is, some seekers are looking for the same thing the imposter is looking for—a way to appear as if they know what they do not know in order to try to impress themselves or others or to give themselves a sense of worth they do not otherwise imagine they have. Such seekers will find false sages, and both seeker and "sages" of this variety will be finding the mirrors in life to reflect back what they imagine life is all about.

If we think life is about rejection and abandonment, we will be sure to find people who will oblige our expectation. If all we truly seek is Truth or God, eventually all that we find will be seen to be that. If what you seek is something else, that is what is appearing, also. Everything is an appearance in the Awareness that we truly are.

WE FIND TEACHERS AT THE LEVEL
OF OUR INTEREST OR READINESS

So how can the seeker be protected from false teachers? In a sense there is no false teacher. At whatever level a teacher is teaching, he or she will often attract students looking for that level. Then there are those who imagine they are looking for one thing and end up finding something surprising. I imagined I was searching for God and did not want a guru because no human was God. I ended up finding every man and woman is, in essence, Divine Consciousness, the Self. There is an old saying that when the student is ready, the teacher appears. Egos often spend much more time looking for a teacher than strengthening their devotion to Truth.

NOTHING BETRAYS YOU EXCEPT EGO

Nothing ever betrays you except belief in the ego—the spiritual ego of a false and self-important teacher or the insecure ego of a seeker who wants to depend on something outside to give what can neither be given nor taken away. In functioning as both a psychotherapist and a spiritual teacher, I have seen deep wounding when people who felt they were giving themselves to a "true" teacher ended up being defrauded, sexually abused, or in some other way betrayed in the trust and love they felt for the teacher.

We may not know the causes and conditions or the karmic connections that have led to a certain outcome. But in protecting ourselves from a false teacher, it is our sincerity, honesty with ourself, and common sense that offer the best guarantee for a safe, though not necessarily easy, passage. Many people have abandoned what their inner wisdom knew to be true in order to belong to a group, to a cult, to a charismatic charlatan. The Buddha's admonishment to "be a lamp unto yourself" seems as true today as it was thousands of years ago. Neither your ego nor a teacher's ego can take you to realization. Pay attention to the silence, to a teacher's *presence* (not necessarily powers), to where the teacher's words are coming from, where they point, and what they seem to evoke in you.

AWAKENING DOES NOT GUARANTEE MATURITY

Having even a very authentic awakening does not necessarily guarantee maturity on the level of mind, heart, or body. We have all seen or heard stories of teachers who were incredibly skilled at spiritual teaching, at pointing to Truth in ways that facilitated students experiencing it for themselves, and yet seemed to exhibit immature or even destructive needs, relationships, demands, or behaviors. In time, however, inflation will always be followed by deflation. Inflation happens often to those on the spiritual path—to both students and teachers.

We have all had the experience of being seduced by Truth and then betrayed by ego(s). We are always drawn to moments of Truth, peace, love. We are seduced because these moments are a taste of home trying to bring us home. What gets in the way of realizing the Truth behind these moments are egoic ambition, expectation, and attachments to images. Seduced by Truth and betrayed by ego describes the experience with false teachers and with our false self. Until we realize how much the ego betrays us when it grasps on to the idea that the body, mind, and thoughts are our correct identity, we will not realize Truth as seamless.

You are not the doer. Ego consciousness thinks it is. Thoughts arise; ego believes it is the thinker of the thoughts. Surrender all to know all and to *be* all. And yet your mind does not know how to surrender. The seeker is *being* surrendered—back to the poverty of not knowing. The means of being surrendered may differ, but we may find ourselves in the phase of the awakening process I call "burning in love's fire."

BURNING IN LOVE'S FIRE

Sometimes [God] cleans your house gently,
dismantling it room by room.
But often, she just comes in with a torch,
and you feel in your gut the fire burn
in the center of your separate comfort,
and you watch the contents of your house
melt and turn to ash,
and the roof blow off.

And just when you think
there is nothing more that she could take,
she opens the ground beneath
the barely intact shell of your house,
and all the levels of your being
fall into the space that has no name,
and you are left alone in all the world,
without a map, without a path, without a point of view.[1]

This description of part of the awakening and embodying process does not sound appealing, does it? For some there may be very little resistance and hence a smoother ride, of course; but for strong egos with a great attachment to the "I can do it myself" mentality, there may be many things that need to be dismantled—arrogance, resistance, self-centeredness, separation, and the intellectualization of spirituality, to name a few. Divine Truth has many ways of subtracting what is not essential, of wearing away our attachment to a false self.

LOVE'S FIRE

The love-intoxicated Sufi poet Jalaluddin Rumi frequently spoke of love as a fire, an invitation to be "cooked by God." Thinking Truth only looks like pleasure often misleads us, and so we avoid the fire that is the agent of our transformation. We are the fire and simultaneously the wood that is burning. We are the flame and simultaneously the moth flying into it, scorching its wings, giving itself to light.

It may feel like the opposite to our mind, yet it is love itself that consumes our illusions, burns away our sense of separation, and melts egoic identification in the radiant light of the Divine. The action of love is the action of Truth. Initially, what begins to melt our habitual resistances to life and attachment to separation may seem to manifest as suffering. Desire, longing, betrayal, grief, pain, illness, woundedness—all can lead us inside ourselves and open the heart to its inward journey. Of course, an experience of love in human form or our spiritual practices can do the same. Whatever breaks open our heart, mind, or body can be the very invitation we need in order to look more deeply and be surrendered more thoroughly to the process that transforms our illusions. Love can use anything, including suffering, in the service of awakening. Whatever begins to melt our identification with what we are not could be called "Love's fire."

This is sometimes experienced as a very thorough housecleaning, and the places of our separation—whether they are experienced as ideas, images, stories, memories, feelings, or body sensations—become the fuel for the fire. When these places of resistance are pulled into the action of Love's fire, it causes friction. We feel the heat. And yet the more we resist, the more intense the blaze.

BECOME THE BURNING

The best advice is to become the burning. Welcome resistance as fuel for the fire that purifies, refines, transforms, and ultimately surrenders us to Love itself. Yet, like any fire, at the beginning there is smoke, crackling, heat—experience that is not always comfortable to the parts of ourselves we have determined are separate from Truth. Whatever we have rejected or defended against, held apart from Love, or tried to hide from our own clarity is invited into the fire. But make no mistake, this is not the action of an ego; it is the action of the fire of Truth. Eventually, nothing can remain outside the heart; nothing is separate; nothing is unwelcome. To live in Love's fire is to be open to the moment as it is, to surrender to the greater knowing present inside our heart, to become a lover of reality.

Love's fire can ignite both before and after an initial awakening, once the green wood of our egoic ambition has been dried out and readied to be the tinder for Love's flame. Sometimes our wood burns very slowly; sometimes something is seen clearly and burns up in a flash. Some of us have much more to see through than others; this is just the way it is, and there is no use complaining. We have been given what we have been given. We accept our starting place, which is always the reality and truth of this moment.

Concepts, points of view, anger, blaming, shaming, hatred, grief, prejudice, fear of death—whatever creates the pain of separation—is invited into the fire. But it is not invited into the fire to be "rid" of it, but rather to transform it, to allow it to be seen clearly and melted into Oneness, becoming one with the fire, one with the Truth. This is Love's way. It totally accepts whatever is arising and invites it to return to its true home.

The peaceful waters of Truth can sometimes become a raging fire that consumes our identities, sacred images, and every single idea we've held about how Truth should move. It challenges our long-held positions and flushes untruth from all its hiding places within us and within our relationships. It can crack open our hearts and unwind our bodies. Love returns for the whole of itself—including our suffering, illusions, and unloved places. For some minds, this process can feel blessed; for some, it can feel very messy. Sometimes it can feel like a blessed mess. Often our pain in the process seems to be in direct proportion to our refusal of it.

EGO DOES NOT LET GO WILLINGLY

Identified mind does not react kindly to this heat. But that is the point of the fire of Truth; it dismantles our identification with what we are not—the stories, the separation, the false self. As most of you know, the ego does not let go willingly. It holds on for dear life, because it imagines its separate life is what is most dear rather than the glorious wholeness of one's being.

If, in an attempt to rid ourselves of something unwanted, we are trying to let all things pass like clouds in the sky or trying hard to hold on to an identity we have made of a concept called "awareness," we may not yet know that the clouds and the sky are of the same essence; illusions and Buddha nature share the same ground; heaven and hell arise as concepts that are seen by a single light.

Sometimes Love's fire feels like a wildfire raging through our being. Sometimes it just gently melts something back into its Source with the utmost tenderness. Masculine and feminine, Shiva and Shakti, form and formlessness, light and dark, strength and vulnerability, teacher and student, ignorance and enlightenment—all are being returned to the nameless ground where, as Meister Eckhart noted, "distinction never gazed." Life, or our teachers, will provide medicine for our illusions, for our attachment to a separate self. But this medicine differs depending on where and in what ways we are holding on to our egocentric views, our center as a supposedly separate self, our selfish actions, and our fear of Love. The medicine of the Divine appears to deliver exactly what is needed into our lives, but this cannot generally be seen except in retrospect.

EVEN "REALIZATION" IS BURNED IN THE FIRE

If ever there is a time you may feel you have been delivered into the jaws of the tiger, this time of burning is it. There is fire inside the tiger's mouth. And eventually, the fire will take away even "realization." It is the action of Love and yet can sometimes feel like an act of destruction. The only things that are being destroyed, however, are our illusions.

I once described this process of being surrendered as akin to giving up after fighting a very long illness. There was the feeling that the mind was totally spent, the body exhausted, as both were finally surrendered to fate. There were so many tears, so many years of trying to "get it," so much resisting, so much emptying, so much seeing again and again how separation keeps finding more and more subtle ways to maintain itself. While there is an end to seeking, there is no end to love's fire of Truth or its action within us. There is no end to the ways the Infinite might show itself as life.

The mind is like a spark that keeps jumping out of the flame until it finally knows that its peace lies in remaining at home, home in the darkness of not knowing the next moment, not knowing the next response, not knowing what words or no words will pour forth from our home ground. In the deepest burning, there is no trace left of wood, not even ash. Yet here we are, here is the "I am" once again. Here is an ordinary being living an ordinary life, content in knowing that the wind of grace and the flame of Truth are moving from the Heart of Awareness as its own expression as this moment, this question, this dissolving of the question.

There is no claim to perfection. The process of being surrendered in Love's flame is, in fact, very humbling. That is the point: to empty us of all that stands in the way of being a true and authentic person, not a perfect person. Perfection lies in the wholeness of Being, yet that Being is you, is me, is this very life with all of its apparent imperfections.

THE BEAUTY OF IMPERFECTION

The description of being burned in Love's fire sounds very poetic, but you may wonder: What about my imperfect life? What about my faults, my flaws, my weaknesses, my unskillful moments, my doing and feeling things that I know are not aligned with Truth? What am I to do with all that? There is a form here, a body here, a life here as a person in the world. And what about this very imperfect world of ours—filled with wars, greed, poverty, hunger, slavery, racism, global warming, inequality, broken political systems? What about this

HUMAN thing? Aren't these concerns real and important? Will my passions for justice, peace, and equality be burned in the fire?

We don't know, do we? We do not know how life will express itself in us once the Infinite has awakened within. We *do* know how it is moving in this moment—the only one where we are truly living and the only one where we can be awake. What are you moved to do? What does your heart open to? What is it afraid to open to? What do you love? What is your deepest desire? How might you live if Love instead of fear were living your life? These are questions that may help us open to the Truth within and how it wants to move in our lives. When we want Truth more than fleeting forms of happiness, Truth will show us the way to a deeper dimension.

We may imagine that we cannot awaken to Truth until we have perfected a "self," until every conditioned illusion is burned in the fire. In our desire to try to be a better, more peaceful, loving, or wise person, we often find ourselves locked in an ongoing inner battle, feeling anxious about our own and the world's imperfections. In taking ourselves to be a separate entity, we do not see our wholeness.

In my first private meeting with Adyashanti, I asked to hold his *mala*. As I did so, he told me that in Buddhism the 108 beads of a mala can stand for the 108 illusions, but that those beads were the same as the Buddha bead (the so-called guru bead that begins and ends one's counting of breaths or mantras with a mala). He spoke of a passage from Seng-Ts'an's *Verses on the Faith-Mind* that describes how the one and the many "intermingle without distinction," and that to live realizing this is to be without anxiety in the face of imperfection.

Our resistance is melted in many ways; this continuously delivers us to an acceptance of the moment as it is. To be without anxiety in the face of imperfection is to know that there are myriad interconnected causes and conditions for life moving as it does, but that ultimately life moves as *itself*, as a single unfolding in a timeless reality. To accept life or ourselves in the impermanence of any given moment says nothing about what will occur in the next moment. Openness gives us the ability to remain open, not simply to the suffering and insanity of our world or the seeming imperfections of our reactions to it, but to how our deepest nature might want to move in response.

We begin to see the beauty of imperfection—like the chipped cup that we love in our cupboard or the misshapen bowl that seems somehow soulful and beautiful. There is an entire Japanese aesthetic, known as *wabi-sabi*, that celebrates imperfection, incompleteness, and impermanence. Perhaps it is our imperfections that make each of us unique and deeply loved *exactly as we are* by our true Self. What is perfectly whole is simply seeing its own expressions, its own reflections mirrored in the Heart of Awareness.

Part IV

THE SEARCH
ENDS
IN WHAT NEVER ENDS

At this point,
what you are inside your house
is simply What is looking out.
Nothing's left but what is looking,
yet everything you see is you.
Now your life turns inside out.
Your body is the world of being
looking out of just What Is.

And strange as it seems
to the mind of your memory,
you enjoy each dance of yourself,
even the pains you hoped to be rid of,
you experience fully without regret,
for everywhere your eye may look,
all it sees is infinite love
displaying itself in creation.

But just to be completely honest,
there are times you might be tempted
to rebuild your house of concepts,
for the mind just loves to think;
but the fire of Truth resides within you,
where it always lived before you knew,
and it keeps revealing moment to moment
what is false and what is true.[1]

13

THE END OF SEEKING

The one who awakens is not the "me."

What ends the search is realizing who/what we truly are, and yet the end of seeking simply begins the continued embodiment of what we have always been. When the moment comes that convinces us there simply is no separate "one" to enlighten, it is a profound realization to the seeking mind, but to the Heart that was never separate, nothing actually happened! Life has always been unfolding life, but now you know you ARE that life in its totality.

There is a danger in sharing an awakening story. Seekers may imagine this is how it will (or should) look for everyone. This is not true. The Infinite has many different ways to wake itself up within the experience of its human beingness. Remember, we are talking about the infinite potential of the *Infinite*. So, while I will share one story here, do not hold it as a template or prototype of what awakening will always look like. There is one constant, however, in an authentic awakening, and that is a shift in identity. Sometimes the shift is very quiet and does not come with any bells or whistles; sometimes it seems dramatic.

Prior to what I would call "the first awakening," life had seemed to relax. I was no longer expecting that my efforts could bring about awakening. I had accepted I might live my entire life without ever knowing what it was like to live in awareness of God or Self continually. I accepted that there was nothing more I could do. This did not mean that there was no more desire, but somehow, it all just seemed less important as I felt more and more open to the moment I was living. I seemed to accept or to begin to see that all of us—the people I had judged as obnoxious, the ones I felt were beloved, the animals and birds in nature—were sharing the same sentience. God, Mystery, Consciousness was in them, too.

In the spring of 1997, years before I met Adyashanti, I went on a private retreat to the Vedanta Society Retreat Center, near the town of Olema on the Northern California coast. There, in the open fields, walking with the deer on the property and hiking up in the hills, I began to experience the life around me as my life. "I" seemed to be one with the butterflies, bees, trees, flowers, the other people. The only moment that existed seemed to be the one I was in; thoughts seemed to diminish, and there was simply *being* in the present, *being* silent in nature.

Still, when thoughts appeared to move attention out of the direct experience of the moment, I seemed to be waiting for something, imagining there was something to get or be given. One night, as I was meditating in the meditation room before the photographs of Ramakrishna, his wife, Sarada Devi, and his disciple, Vivekananda, the energy I had been experiencing rushing up my spine became quite intense. I felt I was plugged into an electrical socket, exploding and releasing energy in my head, throat, and heart.

SOMETHING IMPORTANT WAS GOING TO HAPPEN

Then a directive seemingly came from Ramakrishna that if I were to stay awake and meditate until 10 p.m., something important would happen. Well, of course, I was excited and curious and had no doubt that I could stay awake until 10. I was not a disciple of Ramakrishna and knew very little about his life, but, before my eyes, Ramakrishna appeared to come out of his photograph and began to transform into the Divine Mother Kali. The cloth thrown over his shoulder seemed to move to cover his head, and in this moment, he appeared as the Divine Mother, then alternately as himself.

Now, I had never particularly liked Kali, the destroyer goddess; those traditional fierce images of her were rather off-putting to my sensibilities. I wanted my mother sweet and innocent and loving me, not destroying anything. But the image of Ramakrishna told me in no uncertain terms to "surrender to the Mother." Soon I was chanting to the Divine Mother despite myself, and the energy was intense. So here I was, swept up with all this energy, chanting to the Divine Mother, feeling my heart wide open, and certain something big would happen at 10 o'clock, maybe what I had been waiting for all these years. Of course I would stay awake!

But Ramakrishna, who seemed to manifest in form in my consciousness, came over to me and tapped me between the eyes, and I went unconscious. I do not know to this day what happened, whether I simply fell asleep and dreamed or was knocked unconscious, but the long and the short of it is, of course, that I was NOT awake at 10. When I did come back to consciousness, it was 10:15 or even later—I don't remember. At first I felt angry at being set up that way, but then I began to laugh and laugh because I saw what had been in the way all along!

The ego, wanting something to happen in some moment other than now, was the problem. That ambitious one was not in charge of anything, never had been, never would be. I went to bed that night with a smile on my face, grateful for the gift of the evening's meditation and humbly recognizing that "Dorothy" was not the one doing anything, that no matter what "I" intended, there was a greater power that was really in control of all my action or inaction. "I" could do nothing apart from that Divine will—not even keep myself awake.

AT THE TEMPLE SITE

The next morning I hiked up to a place called the temple site, a beautiful open circle of sweet grass in the midst of a grove of cedar and redwood trees. There I sat on a stump and gazed at the sky through the tops of the trees. On this occasion, I sensed God as an inner feminine teacher, and asked, "What is my lesson for the day?" The answer was, "Time and space."

By a force over which I had no control, I sat motionless looking at the tops of these magnificent trees for some period of time. I have no idea how long I sat there, but my neck got sore, and still I could not stop gazing. I sat lost in timelessness, really. And in one sudden, unexpected flash of knowing, a veil seemed lifted between what I was looking upon—these trees—and who I was. I knew at once that now is the only time that exists and that the illusion of time and space had been created so that "I" could see my Self. This was no intellectual insight, and this "I" was no separate "I." This "I" was the only thing there was or ever had been, manifesting as myself and every other self that ever lived, as these trees, this sky, this sun, this warm earth. There was a sense of waking up, of being born again into a world that was simultaneously totally the same and totally different from the one I had always known.

SHOCK AND JOY

There was a sudden shock at knowing the truth of *being* what I had been seeking for all these years. The power of this truth was so great, my body seemed knocked over by it, and I lay on the ground breathing my Self, seeing my Self, knowing my Self, and this Self had no separate existence whatsoever. I knew without a single doubt that there was no "one" to enlighten and never had been. What I had taken to be a separate "me" was in no way separate from its Source. The Source of all was separate from nothing. It was even the Source of the Consciousness that could think it was separate from itself, except now it could no longer think or experience itself (myself) as separate. There seemed to be only this moment and only what is unfolding as a seamless whole, and there simply was no separate "me" observing it.

The sheer happiness experienced in this moment of recognition was beyond description. Never had there been a taste of such profound joy and humility. There was joy in knowing I was what I had been seeking all along. There was humility in knowing the "one" I had taken to be the seeker—in charge of her life, responsible for her "spiritual" choices, serving, praying, meditating, willing to die for Truth—was not for a single moment whom she imagined herself to be, separate from what she had been seeking, serving, praying to, meditating on to experience, and willing to die for. It is the ego—the illusory part of ourselves so conditioned by our upbringing, our culture, and our fear—that imagines itself separate from God, yet this, too, is God's manifestation. It is only in the absence of that sense of separation that Truth can be experienced.

There was such love and connectedness, love for the one who imagined herself separate all these years, love for the recognition of the Truth she had longed for, yet the clear and unequivocal knowing that there simply is not, nor has there ever been, any "one" to be enlightened. The concept had no meaning whatsoever for me. We are *all* awake Consciousness. A profound shift in perspective occurred, but the perspective was not "Dorothy" seeing her Divine Self; it was the Divine Self seeing itself, being itself always and everywhere. This Consciousness has no location and yet sees out of my eyes and the bee's eyes—Consciousness alone IS. This world is reflected in who you are.

THERE IS ONLY THE INFINITE

In the Totality of functioning, some are led to seek a cure for cancer, some to milk cows, some to compose music, some to be warriors, some to struggle to improve themselves, some to seek spiritual understanding. Prayer, wherever it is found and whatever it is seeking, is a turning to the Infinite. But when the discovery is made that there is *only* the Infinite, life itself becomes a prayer. All seeing is a seeing of the Infinite. All tasting is a tasting of the Infinite. All listening is the listening of the Infinite. All forms are forms of the Infinite. And all lives are lives of the Infinite.

The day I was to leave the retreat, I was walking in a wooded area and suddenly was surrounded by a dozen or more enormous vultures, flapping all around my head. I was startled by the suddenness of their appearance, but I was not in the least frightened. My movements had apparently interrupted their dining on a dead deer lying at the foot of a tree. The eyes of the deer had already been eaten, and there was blood oozing from its partially consumed body. I gazed at the sight for quite awhile, a sight that earlier in my life would surely have repulsed me. Now, there was a deep knowing and a simple accepting that God was eating God.

On this last morning I visited a meadow alive with life itself—buzzing, humming, blowing, warming, chirping, hopping, dancing. I wept in gratitude for the ability to experience my Self in all things: the new growth of the pine trees, a slender blade of grass, the rainbow light around the sun, a deer grazing in the meadow, the song of a redwing blackbird. There was no questioning my experience. Doubt had vanished. Who can say how or why? "Shoulds" and "should nots" vanished along with doubt. There was no more wondering what or if or how. There was just the simple fact of life unfolding itself each moment. "Should I do such and such?" no longer appeared in consciousness. If I did, I did, and if I did not, I did not, and there was no separate "me" choosing.

PERFECTION IS NOT REQUIRED

Recognizing true nature did not require perfection of body or mind. It just required being quiet, being still, being open, being here. What I *am* is free to be myself as Dorothy and every other object in awareness. Awareness/Presence is one. These body-minds are objects in that awareness and are loved and accepted exactly as they are by what we truly are. To know this is to be free of your "self" and thus to be free to be your Self.

Feelings come and go, preferences exist, but the peace and happiness of the moment do not depend on preferences being fulfilled or certain feelings being present and not others. The conditioning of the body-mind is seen more and more clearly to be what it is. Biological fear (the organism's instinct for physical survival in the face of physical danger) is present, but it no longer is felt to be identical to the fears we feel when our psychological "self," or ego (self-image), is threatened.

We do not lose our values as human beings; indeed, they deepen in the face of our shared essence. But they no longer need to be upheld by "shoulds" or "should nots." Rather, in knowing that the world and those in it are your very Self, we are not moved to harm, divide, or separate. And to the extent we allow ourselves to simply *be* and to be authentic, we give that freedom to others as well. Discrimination about wise action comes from a deeper dimension of Being. Life does not need to be different, and yet when we take a seat in our true Self, when we are moving more and more from our home ground, we do not become passive—rather, we become more clearly responsive. Freedom comes, not in life or a body-mind looking a certain way, but in not needing the moment or the body-mind to look or be different than it is.

I am the pattern of light on the wall right now; I am also the writing of these descriptions of the life that Consciousness has created and identified with, temporarily, as Dorothy Hunt. If I am sad when a friend is in pain, I am sad; I do not take it to mean I haven't "arrived," because there is no place to arrive. Whatever appears, including the conditioning of the body-mind based on its experience of living, means nothing about who I am essentially and truly. It is simply an occurrence.

·

FREEDOM FROM THE "ME"

Freedom is not found in renouncing desire; desire leads us to the next moment's unfolding. When the body needs water, thirst appears; when the body needs to move, it exercises itself. When the mind wants stimulation, it reads a book. When the heart is full of love, it may want to hug a friend. Freedom is in realizing that your happiness has nothing to do with desires being fulfilled.

Likewise, freedom is not the end of feeling. We are *Being* being human. What a gift to experience the full range of human emotions. We do not have to rid ourselves of anything, even if we could. What seems to bind us are not feelings or desires but our idea that we are separate selves. Self-inquiry seeks to cut the root of difficulties, the idea of a separate self. It is not interested in developing yogic powers, or seeing past lives, or awakening kundalini, or balancing chakras, or becoming omniscient, or learning how to create states of consciousness, though these things may appear. It looks beyond all that to the understanding that truly ends suffering. And this understanding/realization is not of the mind. It bypasses the mind, though the mind is involved in attempting to describe it.

THE ABSENCE OF AMBITION

After the understanding appeared that seemed to end my seeking, the loss of drive and ambition was very surprising. For so long, my passion had been the so-called spiritual journey—the yearning, praying, meditating, spiritual reading, the intense desire to "get it." There were moments of missing the passion of that search, and yet no "one" was missing it. There was incredible peace in everything that happened; drama, passion, intensity, longing were no longer present. There was no sense of depression about it, no sense of wanting or needing things or myself to be different.

I actually played solitaire quite frequently in the beginning, having so much more time now available without the efforting of the spiritual search; and in playing, a certain knowing appeared having to do with life itself being a game of solitaire. Possibilities unfold. Winning or losing is merely a production of mind that imagines a beginning and an end to the game. But in this divine *lila*, this game of infinite solitaire, beginnings and endings, winners and losers, births and deaths are simply illusions. In the manifestations of the Self, anything may appear that appears, and anything may disappear that disappears, but the real does not change. Life is a single unfolding. God/Consciousness/Mystery is playing all the parts. Life's moments appear because of causes and conditions that go back to beginningless time. Life is a giant game of solitaire being played in the limitless Heart of Awareness.

PERSONALITY DOES NOT MEAN IDENTIFICATION

There are those who say or imply that awakening looks a certain way, and by that they mean an "awakened person" looks a certain way. It is not a "person" who "wakes up." The understanding that I wish I could describe changes perspective; it does not necessarily change personality. Seekers are often confused because a spiritual teacher or guru may display moments of cultural conditioning or distinct personality traits. The body-mind carries conditioning, and its personality could be seen to be a unique flavor or perfume of one of life's human expressions. Personality is not identical with egoic identification, though of course the two can intertwine. There is a commonly held belief that if identification with ego were gone, the personality would be gone. And certainly around some people there seems to be such an absence of "self" that the seeker can scarcely imagine this guru or that teacher needing to eat or go to the bathroom, or ever becoming tired.

The freedom you seek is not dependent upon becoming someone else. It is knowing that the essence of what you are is the Mystery you seek, without any need for you or the world to be different. Such acceptance is the starting place for the much more challenging aspect of awakening—embodying the Truth that has been realized. Embodiment, which we will explore in a later chapter, refers to how and to what extent we are actually living consciously from our true nature, the Heart of Awareness. This aspect of the spiritual journey requires continued devotion to Truth, ruthless honesty, and clear seeing. It is an invitation from our Self to see and experience life from our inherent wholeness and compassion rather than through the veils of the judging mind.

LIFE IS NOT AN IDEA

In some respects, life seems too simple to talk about. Things are just what they are. Everything else is an idea. When you see ideas clearly as what they are rather than as the truth about anything, you can discuss them or not, but the power of life is no longer imagined to reside in any idea, no matter how lofty. Everything I have written is an idea. I cannot communicate my direct experience of living, and neither can you. The minute words, thoughts, or ideas appear, direct experience ends and there is an attempt to communicate *about* it to yourself or to someone "else." Yet all relating is to our Self; all speaking is to our Self. And in not imagining separation, there is simply *being* your Self.

AN AWAKENING EXPERIENCE IS NOT THE SAME AS LIVING AWAKE

Liang-shan, who would become the Forty-Second Patriarch of Zen, was once asked by his teacher, T'ung-an, "What is the business beneath the patch robe?" (Meaning: What is here beneath our clothing, our skin?) The priest had no answer.

His teacher said, "Studying the Way and still not reaching this realm is the most painful thing. [Now], you ask me." So the priest asked, "What is the business beneath the patch robe?" His teacher replied, *"Intimacy."* At this the priest was greatly awakened.[1]

Don't you love these Zen stories? It is always a moment, isn't it? A pebble hitting, seeing a peach blossom, hearing a turn of phrase. Initial awakening *is* only a moment, a moment in which there is such a revelation, such a remembrance, such a deep understanding that one's whole identity shifts. But often the intimacy of such a moment can become merely a memory if we lose the freshness, spontaneity, and deep presence of Now. Regardless of any past experiences of awakening, are we awake in *this* moment? Are we intimate with *this* moment, *this* experience, *this* sensation? Or have we returned to our stories, our memories, and our habitual conditioning of mind, which separate subject and object, "self" and "other"?

With the end of seeking comes the much bigger challenge of expressing what we are in our human lives. This is where devotion to Truth continues to be strongly needed. But in the initial awakening, we may be so enamored with our realization that we think nothing more will ever be needed! Life will eventually show us otherwise, but at each stage, enjoy the moment that is here. There is great freedom when spiritual ambition comes to an end, even though truly nothing has ended.

What has become of the one who
searched and chanted, read and prayed,
and hoped for enlightenment?
She still laughs with her family,
sips champagne with friends,
and sings in the shower.

What is life when seeking ends?
Just what is, nothing more or less—
an ordinary person doing ordinary things,
not wishing to be more or less,
content to simply be herSelf.[2]

14

AWAKENING IS ONLY
THE FIRST STEP

To be attached to things is illusion;
To encounter the absolute is not yet enlightenment.[1]

THE SANDOKAI

hree years after an initial awakening had ended all seeking, I met my teacher Adyashanti when we both were speakers at the same conference. As soon as he spoke, a transmission began that I knew I needed. Because my spiritual search had ended, I rather naïvely thought I was "done." Life seemed simple and satisfying. Just as I had not been looking for a guru when Ramana Maharshi showed up, I was certainly not looking for another teacher at this point. And yet, shortly after this conference, life moved for me to attend a retreat with him in the high Sierras. During that retreat I began to feel a deep and mysterious remembrance of, and pull toward, the Zen Buddhist lineage that seemed to flow through Adya's words and being. I felt that grace had delivered a living Buddha into my life.

I had no thought that I would actually be able to meet with him one-on-one after the retreat, but I summoned up courage to write and ask, and in a happy surprise I was able to do so. When we met, I told him I had a fantasy that one day he would give me a mala and a name. He said he had the mala but not a name, and he gave me a wrist mala made of seeds. He also gave me an article on the ten Zen Ox-herding pictures, which are descriptions of the stages of enlightenment, including the letters of a young woman to her Zen teacher. She was ill and traversed many stages of the post-awakening process very quickly before her early death. This article made me a bit uneasy, as I had just been diagnosed with breast cancer, and I wondered if he knew something I did not about my life expectancy.

AWAKENING TO THE INFINITE IS ONLY HALFWAY AROUND THE CIRCLE

In spending time with Adyashanti, I soon learned that awakening to the Infinite—beautiful and profound as that is—is only coming halfway around the circle of awakening. How does the Mystery that awakens itself within us want to function within the body-mind? How does it want to be embodied in daily life? I saw I had been stuck in emptiness, caught in identification with the Absolute, seeing everything from that perspective, and not paying much attention to the relative world.

Adyashanti seemed to light a fire to the dry grass I did not know needed to be burned within me. It was a time of seeing the many places in myself that were continuing to hold on to a separate identity, even in the face of realization that all was One. It was a time of great humbling and of increasing acceptance of and tenderness for our humanness.

CORE BELIEF

During one retreat, I came face-to-face with a core belief around separation—so many losses over lifetimes and in this life as well. Grief spilled out and out until at one point, the Truth in me asked, "Is this grief, now, authentic, or am I wallowing?" At the time the question arose, I knew it was the latter. Truth seemed to force me to look into each one of my "separation" stories and ask, "Is it true?" Then, when I had been through them all and had seen through the illusion of each one, Truth held my beliefs to the fire and made me go through the old stories all over again to confirm the understanding.

Here the inquiry was: Is it true? Can you *absolutely* know your beliefs about separation are true? What is the truth about this belief, this feeling? Dropping the questions into the silence of true nature led to the realization that in the Truth of what we are, we have never been separate or separated. To maintain the *story* of separation, we must identify ourselves as separate.

Core stories or beliefs may be encountered before or after an awakening. They are the conditioned ways ego essentially sees itself and the world. We maintain them by rigidly holding them as true while ignoring evidence that might contradict them. Core stories often include such beliefs as: I am flawed. I am deficient. I am unlovable, stupid, weak, a failure, invisible, a mistake, and so on. They can exist consciously or unconsciously, but as the Truth that has awakened within begins to move more and more consciously in our system, we will see these stories when they appear and will be invited to inquire into the truth of the beliefs and feelings that maintain them.

The willingness to see the stories that maintain suffering and to allow them to be dismantled is actually a movement of love. The love that moves from the Heart of Awareness sees clearly, without judgment, our places of contraction, identification, or holding. It moves us to see what holds the stories in place, what they are made of, and whether they are actually true. As awakening unfolds to live itself more fully in its human expression, it is not enough to simply know that deep truth and love exist as our essence; we are invited to BE that truth and love more and more consciously in ourselves and in the world. The end of the search means only that we are invited to BE the truth, love, peace, understanding, compassion, and clarity of our Buddha nature in our daily lives.

HOW DO TRUTH AND LOVE WANT TO MOVE WITHIN YOU?

Are you moved to tend your vegetable garden, smile at a stranger, spend quality time with your friends, children, or grandchildren, or simply to be deeply present to the moment? Do you feel moved to feed the hungry, work for peace, help refugees who come from countries ravaged by war? All of these are actions that may appear spontaneously from the love you are. There is no "should," but there may be a movement that compels you to address issues or give attention to causes or people you feel passionate about. What might it be to address them from a place of peace and love within yourself? Some people march for peace with no peace in their hearts. Begin to sense in yourself where an action is coming from. Are we serving Truth or ego? Ego will not be able to know. That is why we spend time in silence, becoming familiar with the felt sense of this Heart of Awareness. It illuminates egoic thought but is not caught by it. It seems to love even what our mind may have imagined was unlovable.

NO STRATEGIES

It would be foolish to imagine that there is a prescription or strategy one could use for living awake. What is awake is that which sees its own infinite potential unfolding in infinite ways, moment to moment. It is not the egoic mind that figures out "how to" live awake. Egoic thought is what is always trying to control both inner and outer life, trying to improve a "self," trying to "become," trying to be the agent of "awakened" living.

Of course, from an egoic perspective, it is preferable to live among egos that want to be present, kind, compassionate, and loving, but these qualities are actually inherent in our true Heart. The "how to" playbooks—while they might be helpful or inspiring—often arouse our judging mind, which then compares our actual experience with the "high" or "holy" guidelines we might read about. It is more helpful to keep returning again and again to the Heart of Awareness for guidance. Life has moved itself up to this point; does our mind imagine it will stop doing so because we now know we are more (and less) than we originally were conditioned to believe?

After an initial awakening, many return to ego—now spiritual in flavor—to try to figure out *how*. It seems innocent enough in its inception, but over time this reifies a separate self that will once again try to assert its importance as a major player. This is a bit ironic, since the discovery may very well have been that there IS no separate entity, only a movement of conditioned thought, feeling, and so forth.

This is not to say that after an awakening there is an automatic knowing of what it feels like to live awake in any given moment. In fact, the ambition for a self to be consciously aware of awareness in every moment is more ego. What is awake has no ambition to become itself. It cannot be anything else! Yet, as my teacher's teacher used to say, we start out like baby Buddhas, not yet knowing how to walk in our newfound freedom. Here is where one's integrity, deep and authentic intentions, and devotion to Truth come in.

AWAKENING REVEALS WHAT HAS BEEN HIDDEN

Whether before or after an awakening, most of our challenges deal with what is born and dies, suffers, is changeable, and often is confounded by its human incarnation. Truth seeks to bring into the light the dark, repressed aspects of the human psyche to heal us of our divisions. This can often feel confusing to the seeker who imagined awakening would only bring bliss, peace, or joy. Yet it is frequently the case that after an authentic awakening, many things we thought we had dealt with or we did not know even existed will come forth to be seen and transformed. Such transformation is not about improving a "self" but, rather, is the outcome of our sincere desire to see the places and the moments where we may not be aligned with the Truth we have realized. Seeing these moments does not mean we could not be awake. This post-awakening investigation is not to rid us of what arises but to enable us to see with clarity, love, and compassion our innocent misunderstandings. It is deep seeing and experiencing from the openness of Presence that transforms us.

DIRECT EXPERIENCE

Awareness moves as consciousness in the body-mind, but in itself it has no boundaries whatsoever. Thus, when we invite our own awareness into a difficult or painful felt sensation in the body or into our emotions, there is direct experience of what is awake, as well as of the moment itself. Right away, there is a softening, a lessening of judgment, an openness to feel whatever is here. Transformation begins immediately—not because we are trying to rid ourselves of anything, but because we are no longer separate from the moment, separate from our Being. Even if what we experience in the moment is a feeling of resistance, we are able to feel the energy of this resistance as simply what it is. We have allowed ourselves to have a moment unburdened from "shoulds" around our feeling state.

The fact that awareness has no boundaries does not mean that in our human interactions we do not sometimes need boundaries. Our inner knowing will sense when the well-being of the body-mind requires our moving away from toxic environments, whether physical or psychological.

HARMONIZING OF BODY AND MIND

Part of the post-awakening experience is bringing our body and mind more and more into alignment with the truth of no separation—from ourselves, from one another, from the Divine, from the moment as it appears. Healing of separation concerns itself with melting frozen concepts or frozen experience back into direct experiencing. When there is no resistance to the natural movement of life, we experience the flowing freedom of Being itself. Harmonization begins to happen on the level of mind, heart, and body. Life moves spontaneously, directing itself and continually harmonizing itself.

15

RESTING THE MIND IN THE HEART OF AWARENESS

When the mind is not needed for functioning,
it rests in the Heart.
When thoughts emerge, we do not need to leave home.

When I speak of "resting the mind in the Heart of Awareness," I am simply inviting *You*, Consciousness, to become aware of the felt sense of living from your home ground rather than being identified with the thinking mind. No one can tell you where to find your home ground, since it is not a place in time, but there is a felt sense in the body. For many, there will often be some sense of attention dropping down from the head to the heart or the gut, of the body relaxing, of the mind quieting, of the heart opening, of being more sensitive to energies moving in the body or to sounds in the environment. But do not try to feel these things. Just allow yourself to have your own experience of your home ground. This is not an attempt to control the mind, tether it to a place, or try to maintain a state. No efforts by an illusory "self" can produce our natural state of awake being, nor can they "make" the mind "stay" in the Self.

Even after profound openings, many people remain at war with their mind, or at least with certain conditioned productions of the mind. They imagine that living from the Heart of Awareness, from one's true nature, must be separate from the changing faces and functioning of the mind of thought. Let's experiment a bit to see if this is true.

Remaining at Home Even as the Mind Moves

Let yourself experience thinking consciously. Any thoughts will do. Notice what the energy is in your body, your mind, or your emotions when attention is focused on thinking. You may notice the energy of your entire body seems to rise to the region of your brain. Your shoulders may move up; your jaw or your forehead may become more tense. Let yourself really get a sense, a feel, for the *energy* of thinking as it shows itself in your body.

Now let yourself come home, however your home ground appears in your experience. I cannot tell you how to come home, but *You* know. Familiarize yourself with this felt sense of home. Even if your home ground does not have a location, you will feel yourself experiencing this dimension of your Being through your awareness. Rest your attention in the experience of your true home. Allow your attention to remain for a while on the *felt sense* of this home ground.

Now, let yourself have a thought while remaining in/as this home ground. Thoughts do not require a separate "thinker." They arise from emptiness and actually need not interfere with the unfolding of life or the movement of your body-mind in it. Keep playing with your experience for a few minutes, moving from thinking to your home ground, then remaining at home even while thoughts are appearing. The latter could be called "resting the mind in the Heart of Awareness." Thoughts do not have to disappear for *You* to remain at home. Who or what is thinking your thoughts, knowing your sense of home, witnessing attention moving, being aware of the whole show?

Thoughts arise from the Self. The thought "I" arises in the mind of a human body; this, too, arises from the Self. However, this I-thought is then taken to be our whole identity and embellished with all kinds of descriptions. It is recreated from memory each morning when we wake up. Some of you may have had the experience of being very open when you first awaken, before thoughts appear to tell you who you are and what you have to do that day. This is a lovely time of day to investigate your experience of the moment before the I-thought so boldly returns. You may still have sensations, feelings, thoughts, the urge to stretch, but all of these simply arise in your awareness and are known by it.

Even when we have had many glimpses of our true nature or even one or more authentic awakenings, egoic consciousness may very well continue. Usually, even if our ambitious spiritual ego has not claimed the whole of the awakening process, it will reappear to rebuild a structure around the emptiness that was revealed. We can have many experiences of being awake, and yet the mind retains its separation from Totality; it holds on to its core identity of "self." The Buddha referred to that which holds up our separarte identity as the "ridgepole."

THE RIDGEPOLE

During the Buddha's search for an end to suffering, he tried many different methods of reaching his heart's longing. He studied with the most revered meditation teachers of the day and mastered each level of meditation being taught. Still he did not reach an end to his search. He tried becoming a total renunciate, an ascetic, eating only one grain of rice a day, according to legend. His body became emaciated; he was near starvation. Still the search did not end. Finally he sat down under the bodhi tree and vowed not to get up until he attained full enlightenment.

Mara and his forces, ego's inner voices of limitation, delusion, and fear, came to visit, appearing as angry demons, tempting him with dancing girls, appealing to lust; still he was not moved. The awake silence that was/is the Buddha's true nature saw through every guise, every identification. It delivered knowledge of the Buddha's countless lives, the understanding of karma and the cycle of causality. The Buddha saw that there was no independent "self" in anything, but rather that everything was dependent on every other thing. Shortly after enlightenment revealed itself, the Buddha uttered these words:

House-builder, you have now been seen.
You shall not build the house again.
Your rafters have been broken down;
your ridgepole is demolished too.
My mind has now attained the unformed nibbana
and reached the end of every kind of craving.[1]

Investigating Your Ridgepole

I want to draw your attention to the image of the ridgepole. The ridgepole is what holds up our illusion of a separate self. For a moment, consider the ridgepole of a tent or a house. Imagine the structure is yourself, your own mind, and there, in the center of your idea of yourself, is a ridgepole, holding it all up. What is your ridgepole made of? What keeps your idea of a separate "me" standing? What do you experience on a daily basis that holds up your identity?

Stop for a moment, inquire, stay open, and see what wants to be revealed as you contemplate your own ridgepole. . . .

When you have seen a bit of the truth of your ridgepole, imagine that it comes down. You are the tent or the structure of your own mind, and the ridgepole of what has been holding up your idea of a separate self is taken down, demolished. What is your experience? What remains without the ridgepole?

What is still here when everything you have thought or felt about your "self" is (at least temporarily) removed?

One man told me that he saw his ridgepole covered with sticky notes about all the ways he had been told he was "supposed" to be by parents, grandparents, teachers, and others; and when it was taken down, there was a sense of tremendous freedom.

SEEING INTO THE STRUCTURE
OF YOUR OWN MIND

Until we see into the structure of our own mind, we will likely not be free, even if we have had authentic awakenings to the *absolute* nature of mind, Being, life, God. We cannot see what we are, because that is what is seeing; but we can begin to see more clearly how and in what ways we continue to "unenlighten" ourselves through our attachments to certain beliefs, ideas, feelings, and the like. Truth will continue its thorough housecleaning if we remain open. Such thoroughness comes from clear seeing and carries not one speck of judgment from our true nature, but we will bump up against many things that our thinking mind will want to judge. As soon as this happens, we are thrown off the scent of liberation, because now our attention has moved to the judging mind and not to what holds up our separate identity. Begin to see in what ways and for what purpose your mind keeps putting the ridgepole back up.

Part of the embodiment process includes getting to know the nature of our own mind, its habit patterns, its preferences, its places of holding or of separation. Anthony de Mello once advised that when you are looking into your own mind, be like a bird watcher rather than a dog trainer. Can we *see* how often and by what means our mind pulls attention to itself, away from the deeper truths of our being? Can we become familiar with the things that fascinate our mind without judging that we should not be fascinated? The more deeply we simply *see*, the more things become transparent.

Seekers often imagine that when thought appears it means they have "lost" the Presence that they felt at some other point. Attention has simply moved. Presence has not gone anywhere. Thoughts appear, but what notices them? What notices your feelings, sensations, and interpretations of life? Thinking does not see. Keep noticing that thoughts come and go, but freedom comes in discovering what does not. The Heart of Awareness has nowhere to go, no goal to achieve, no judgment of what should or should not appear. This perspective does not appeal to the identified mind, which has lots of places to go, many goals to achieve, and innumerable judgments daily. But it is possible to begin to have a felt sense of returning the mind and attention again and again to the Heart of Awareness, to the openness of "not knowing" mind, to our home ground.

Resting our attention in the Heart of Awareness begins to bring that awareness forward from the background it always occupies. We feel its presence, sense its vastness, experience its peace. The mind of thought is seen as simply mind and not our true identity. Life becomes an adventure. How will it move here? How will it move in this situation, in the face of this feeling or this challenge? The Heart of Awareness, which is itself awakened heart and awakened mind, will move.

> As mind merges inside the heart, true understanding awakens.
> You are the invisible inside the visible, the unmoving inside all movements.
> Like space moving in space glowing inside a thin skin called human being.[2]
> MOOJI

Part V

UNDIVIDED
LOVE

*Until we have fully embraced
our humanity
without relinquishing
our divinity,
we have not yet come Home.
Love is the invitation
beyond separation.*[1]

16

LOVE FLOWS FROM EMPTINESS

Every moment love is gently knocking
from inside, longing to flow out;
but we are busy looking elsewhere,
searching in the market place of "me's"
to fill the Emptiness that is, itself, vast Love.[1]

The truth that is our essence may be called many names, but it is ultimately nameless. It is empty of definition, empty of separation, and yet this Mystery apparently loves to BE, creating out of its single essence infinite expressions of being, which it loves unconditionally as *itself*. Awakening to the truth of our oneness will invariably lead to love. Love seems to be the first movement of our true nature. Truth moves through mind as wisdom, insight, understanding, and discrimination. Truth moves through the heart as unconditional love, compassion, happiness, joy, and gratitude. The Heart of Awareness is the inseparability of Truth and love.

Isn't the gift of love really the gift of being received fully? The only thing capable of seeing and receiving life in its fullness, loving it for what it is rather than for what it can do for us, is the Truth of what we are. The ego wants something to fill itself up, yet Truth's indefinable emptiness is what moves as wisdom and love. Are we willing to be emptied so that Truth can shine through us and move in us? Can we receive the love that is trying to empty us of untruth? It has sometimes been said that love is blind, but actually love sees clearly; it simply has no attachments.

Love has many faces, but the deepest and most powerful love is beyond any feeling state. It is an unconditional love that does not discriminate, judge, grasp, or reject. Of course, our love of friends, partners, children, pets, art, mountains, or trees are all expressions of a kind of love, but I am pointing to a deeper love. It is a love that is not exclusive, a love that flows from Oneness. It is a love that flows right out of emptiness, a love that touches both our joys and our sufferings. Emptiness is the Heart of Awareness, the limitless and undivided heart that sees clearly and loves without exception all that it appears to create in its own dream.

WHAT IS EMPTINESS EMPTY OF?

In itself, Emptiness is infinite potential, or Source. Yet Emptiness cannot be separated from the fullness or forms of life itself, so what is Emptiness empty of? The Emptiness that becomes love is empty of concepts, empty of self, empty of distinction, empty of resistance. It is a seeing of the moment and an intimate sensitivity to it that is empty of "me." To be empty means we are open, available for whatever or whoever is in front of us. To be empty means we are not stuck anywhere but can experience the flow of life. Awareness in itself is empty, is it not, until it lands on an object? Emptiness allows the world to appear and separation to disappear. Our freedom, inherent wisdom, and selfless love arise right out of Emptiness. Another word for Emptiness is *Openness.*

Minds fear emptiness, imagining it means loneliness, detachment, absence of love, unconnectedness, lack. The psychological experience of emptiness is based on a sense of deficiency—being devoid of nourishment, connection, or loving warmth on the level of heart or feeling a lack of purpose or meaning on the level of mind. To the conditioned mind, emptiness is regarded as a failure of love, worthiness, or purpose; egos want to avoid such feeling. We fill our lives, homes, bellies, minds, and free time with "stuff" to keep from feeling empty, or we may succumb to feelings of despair.

But have you ever allowed yourself to truly experience emptiness without a story line, to be undivided from emptiness, to *be* emptiness? Emptiness is nothing like our mind's ideas or fears. There is a vast difference between the mind's peering into its *idea* of emptiness and actually *being* empty of self, empty of definition, empty of concepts.

LOVE REFUSES TO SEPARATE

In those moments when we are free of identification with ego, oneness reveals itself and, from that sense of unity and connection, love and gratitude move naturally. Strange as this seems to our conditioned mind, this is a love that has no conditions. It does not demand that we agree with or even like the person or thing we find ourself loving. As Nisargadatta put it, "Love is the refusal to separate."

LOVE IS KISSING YOU FROM THE INSIDE

This love can be discovered in your true heart, and when it is, you cannot believe how deeply loved every speck of you actually is. Every part of you and the world is seen clearly as what it is, but nothing is judged unworthy of being loved. There are no conditions for this love, and its felt sense has nothing to do with approval—an addiction that begins in childhood for many as a poor substitute for love. This unconditional love, a divine love, *agape*, comes from your own true nature. It is the love you have been longing for outside, but here it is kissing you on the inside with a tenderness and warmth that melt separation.

We may have awakened to Spirit or to empty awareness, but realization is incomplete if it lacks love and compassion. Buddhists use the term *prajna* to point to the true heart wisdom that does not divide emptiness from love.

WHAT DOES AWAKENESS
FEEL LIKE IN MY HEART?

Just as we can inquire deeply, "Who or what am I?" we can also inquire, "What is love?" or "What does awakeness feel like in my heart?" or "How does love want to move in this situation or with this person?" Awakening to the heart's deepest love delivers an experience of oneness, but with or without an awakening, anyone can begin to have a felt sense of his or her own warm and compassionate heart. What we give our attention to, we give reality to. Put your attention on your heart space and stay open to what is revealed. We may see the ways we are defending our heart, trying to protect a "self" from being hurt, but we can inquire whether love actually needs protection. Can love itself be harmed or threatened?

A QUIET "I LOVE YOU"

We may find there is tremendous fear around love or loving—fear of being rejected, fear of feeling vulnerable. Adyashanti once observed that there is something people seem to fear more than death, and that is love. We can stay "separate" until our last breath, but in the deepest, truest love, it is impossible to maintain separation. It is often in relationships that we find the most challenge to *living* from our home ground, the emptiness from which love and Truth flow so naturally.

Adyashanti once gave a very simple practice for connecting with our heart and connecting with one another through love rather than fear. The practice was one of saying "I love you" quietly inside before having a conversation. Before engaging or even just encountering someone or something, we pay attention to the field of our shared essence and connection. Saying "I love you" can open our experience of the true heart. While this exercise was initially given as a way of connecting in conversation, I found myself engaging in this practice with every single aspect of life. Just saying a quiet "I love you" to everything, in random moments, began to happen spontaneously, and it pulsated through my whole being. It kept opening the felt sense of the heart beyond my wildest imaginings, and with each pulsing of love, there was a moment of deep joy.

Here are some examples. A stranger walking down the street: "I love you." The person I am sitting with in my office: "I love you." The waitstaff and cooks in the restaurant: "I love you." The driver of a taxi-cab: "I love you." The belly I am washing in the shower: "I love you." The knee that has a twinge of pain: "I love you." The empty bottle tossed on the street: "I love you." The grass growing in the sidewalk crack: "I love you." A moment of worry about the future: "I love you, little thinking mind." Sitting with other women waiting for results of a mammogram: "I love you." Reading a news story about a victim and perpetrator: "I love you both." The sound of rain on the roof: "I love you." Ramana Maharshi: "I love you." Adyashanti: "I love you." Before going to sleep at night: "I love you to all who come to mind."

MIND IS NOT THE AGENT OF LOVE

Now in this exercise, the quiet words "I love you" are simply evoking a remembrance, a felt sense of the love we are. The words are inviting Consciousness out of its identification with thought and judgment and into its deeper expression of love. It is not that a separate "I" is trying to love a separate "you." The one you may imagine is supposed to be trying to love everything is not able to do so. This is not an affirmation for egos. The truth in *You* sees through the eyes of love. Our mind is not the agent of love, but our unique expression of Being can become a clearer and clearer reflection of the emptiness and love that are synonymous with the Heart, the Self. We cannot really "love our neighbor as ourself" until we know the truth about our Self.

After inviting a meditation along the lines of saying "I love you" quietly inside toward anyone or anything that comes into view, one man told me, "I used to think that I had to feel love first *before* I could say 'I love you,' but saying it first, inside, seemed to evoke love and expand my heart." A woman who had been using this simple practice for a while exclaimed: "It's so efficient! For years, I tried using affirmations, therapy, all manner of things to try to become more loving, but this opens the heart immediately. And I find that now, even my mind seems to be getting on board. And you don't have to even like or agree with the person you are loving!" You may prefer just using the word and felt sense of love, dropping the "I" and the "you." This may be a more accurate reminder of the love that flows from oneness.

.For those who think this is a "fake it till you make it" practice, I see it differently. The one who feels he or she would be "faking it" will never be the source of love; we are simply directing our attention and our consciousness to the Heart that is already love and loving. The reason the mind may eventually "get on board" is that it feels so much better to love than to judge.

EYE GAZING

Another useful practice, for those open to doing it, is an eye-gazing exercise that is actually a form of meditation with a partner. Quite simply, we quietly and innocently begin to look in the eyes of a partner, a friend, or our beloved as that person gazes back into our eyes. This is not a staring exercise, and we are not trying to fall in love with anyone; we are simply looking into the looking. We may find ourselves feeling vulnerable, afraid our partner may see something we don't want seen. Or we may find our mind getting caught up in trying to figure out what is going on in our partner. We can close our eyes for a bit and notice what is happening inside, perhaps inviting ourselves to pay attention to our heart, but then perhaps open the eyes again and simply look. Notice, when you pay attention to simply the looking itself, whether there is any place "your" looking or your partner's looking stops or starts, any place it divides itself.

Regardless of our mind's thoughts, is there any separation in the looking itself? We may discover, as Saint Francis of Assisi did, "What you are looking for is what is looking." In using this form of meditation for many years myself and inviting it in groups, I have found it a powerful way to wordlessly touch and open the heart—even if what we may initially discover are fears or defenses against loving. In doing this practice, the emptiness that is simply aware of whatever arises will begin to become conscious of itself in the looking and becomes love just gazing at love.

BEING LOVE RATHER THAN SEARCHING FOR IT

We may be longing for love but afraid of love, afraid of being seen to be flawed, unworthy, unlovable; we may fiercely guard our separation. What is frightened is a false self. We fear being seen as we see ourselves: limited, unworthy, imperfect. But true seeing is identical with loving. The love you *are* sees its own radiance in you and in the apparent other. To truly *see* is to love. When we open our heart to anything—a flower, a person, the sky, grief—we feel alive, touched, tender, and often vulnerable. We may feel we have been hurt in love, but love itself is eternal; it cannot be harmed; it cannot be destroyed. In love, there is no "other," only the appearance of another. Understand that longing for love is a divine longing. We are searching for our deepest Self without knowing it.

Contrary to the lyrics of many love songs or the lyrics of our life story, real love has no beginning and no end. It arises spontaneously in freedom. It is indiscriminate and, like the sun, "shines on the just and the unjust." It gives itself to the moment without asking for anything in return. It is unselfconscious. Love's sensitivity to life excludes nothing and no one. It has no opposite called "hate." This is a love that knows no division. It touches life as it is. It is undivided.

Consider what it is to *be* love rather than to seek it. Consider doing the small things in your daily life lovingly instead of grudgingly. Love's gifts are endless; your life is one of those gifts. Love's greatest gift is itself. It has a wisdom that moves with no one to figure it out. It does not see an "other." In the deepest love, there simply are not "two." And yet love pretends to be two in order to dance. The dance includes both joy and suffering.

17

LOVE CONTAINS BOTH
JOY AND SUFFERING

What is suffering if not that which
draws us to seek what is truly beyond suffering?
What is joy if not a taste of liberation?
What is love if not the container that holds both
and knows that in the sacred dance of life,
either can bring us home?

To be human is to know both joy and suffering. While it is natural to prefer our joys, our sufferings often deepen our insights, increase our compassion, or lead us beyond whom we thought we were. Our difficulties do not necessarily arise from either pain or pleasure but from being stuck in one place or another. We may clutch so tightly to pleasure that, in the fear of losing it, we destroy the joy we might have known. Or we may struggle so fiercely against our pain—armoring ourselves against it, or raging at it, or judging ourselves unworthy because of it—that we increase our suffering. Yet joy and suffering are simply changing faces of a love that calls us to go beyond our limited definitions of who we are, a love that points us toward one seamless reality that embraces both.

One of the thorniest questions in spirituality, religion, or human experience is the question of suffering. We cannot reconcile in thought the question of suffering, although there are many theories, many views of suffering. Here are just a few:

Suffering is inevitable. "The world is full of suffering," observed the Buddha in his first Noble Truth.[1] Birth, old age, sickness, and death are suffering. Suffering is created by attachment and aversion.

Suffering is illusion. The eldest son of the Tibetan teacher Marpa was killed, and Marpa was spotted weeping in grief by one of his students, who then questioned Marpa's teaching that everything is illusion. "Yes," Marpa replied, "everything here is illusion. And the death of a child is the greatest of these illusions."

Suffering is redemptive. In the Christian view, suffering can be redemptive. Jesus suffered on the cross to redeem the world; and one's own suffering, if joined with his, is sometimes viewed as "coredemptive."

Suffering is punishment for sin. Many believe illness, loss, and poverty to be punishments for sin.

Suffering is karma. This view is similar to the previous one, but with the addition of a belief in past lives that determine the experiences in the current life. Here the view is that suffering is karma, punishment for sins from past lives.

Suffering is transformative. Rumi's poem "Chickpea to Cook" (see chapter 10) is a tale of suffering being the agent of transformation to a new life. Suffering may serve the transformation of our ignorance into true understanding.

Suffering is grace. Martin Buber, the Jewish theologian, said, "All suffering prepares the soul for vision." In this sense, suffering is seen as grace, a gift; and it is the case that many who experience misfortune do not seem to be suffering, but continue praising the Divine for all moments.

The limitless One is suffering. Whoever sees that all is One—by whatever name—holds that it is the limitless One who suffers with us, as us, yet simultaneously is free of suffering. So it is the suffering Buddha or the suffering Christ that is seen.

VIEWPOINTS ARE IDEAS

Suffering has also been imagined to be a choice, an accident, the result of an unjust society or poor parenting. But the one thing all of these viewpoints have in common is this: They are all ideas! You may hold to one or more of them, but understand that each one is an idea. Each believes it points to a truth about suffering. Each view may also have evolved from experience. Yet in holding our viewpoints as "truth," we may miss the deeper truth that each of us is simply a "viewing point" of the Infinite.

SUFFERING COMES WHEN WE PUSH PAIN OUT OF OUR HEART

Pain is inevitable in a human life, but suffering occurs when we push our pain out of our hearts, out of our loving awareness, imagining it speaks about our lack of worthiness. When pain is judged, we increase our pain. The body may be in pain, but it is often our beliefs that add suffering. When pain is touched by the experience of love, however, it is frequently transformed. Someone simply being deeply and compassionately present in the face of your suffering can bring comfort. There is also your own compassionate and warm heart that can pour its love into the places of pain in your body or mind.

Sometimes the reasons for suffering seem apparent, but often suffering is a mystery. So is love. Yet no matter how we view suffering, no matter what spiritual traditions might speak of it or in what ways, most seem to agree that suffering is deeply healed by love.

Suffering and pain are not necessarily the same. And many of us suffer greatly for such things as not getting somewhere fast enough in our automobiles or not liking the weather or having to wait for our child or our spouse to get ready to go somewhere and it is taking "too long." We suffer when we refuse life as it is.

WHEN TRUTH FEELS UNCOMFORTABLE

Most of us are happy to be touched by the truth of joy, goodness, happiness, love, peace—moments when truth feels comfortable. But what happens when we find ourselves face-to-face with the truth of the shadow in ourselves or in our world? Do we stop wanting truth when that truth feels dark, hidden, uncomfortable, confusing, or painful?

When our desire to know truth becomes greater than our desire to appear a certain way to others or ourselves, the Truth within begins to reveal itself. On the way to discovering the Truth about our essence, we begin to see with greater clarity our own places of holding, of suffering, of attachment to ideas about how life should look or how we should look. Sometimes it can be a painful process to see the truth about our defenses, our sense of unworthiness, our hidden motivations, our lies. Yet when Truth is what we want, the light of Truth comes to illumine whatever lies in the shadow.

What has been hiding in the shadows, fearful of being seen? Self-ishness? Anger? Pain? Power? Exuberance? Sexuality? Neediness? Self-abandonment? Love? Vulnerability? What about ourselves has been pushed out of our own heart? What are we judging should not be here even when it is? What happens when we invite *all* of life into the light of Truth? We may discover that the place of our greatest fear or our greatest wounding becomes the place where the greatest light will enter to liberate our experiences back into the wholeness of Being.

HEALING INVOLVES OFFERING
OUR SEPARATION TO LOVE

Separation is our suffering; judgment is our suffering. Fear is our separation; thinking "I am the doer" is our separation. That separation may be from others or from ourselves, from our bodies, emotions, or the truth of our own experience. We may struggle with certain feelings or situations, imagining they should not be present in our lives, but they are. So what do we do in the face of such judgment? We either deny the truth of the moment, the truth of our own or another's experience, or we judge one or the other to be unworthy of love.

When you know your Self as the universe and as every moment that unfolds, you understand that your true heart excludes nothing from its love. The body may still experience physical pain, but you are healed of the pain of separation the moment you give your experience to the love in your own heart. Love separates itself from nothing and does not end when people part, nor does it end in the face of so-called death.

The deepest pain comes when we feel disconnected from our true Self, our divine nature. This separation drives all our longings. We suffer every single time we cast ourselves out of our own heart of love. Every single time our fear keeps us from touching *what is* with compassionate awareness, we are separate. We hunger for love and acceptance but continually stop to dine in the mind of judgment rather than the heart of acceptance.

Nothing is as accepting as our true nature, because our true nature never separates itself from the moment in order to judge it. Only a conditioned mind does that; then thought imagines "it" must learn to accept the moment. Minds "trying" to accept the moment can even believe that this means accepting abuse when everything inside is screaming to get out of a destructive or abusive relationship. We continually look to our conditioned mind to be the agent of acceptance or love. We are looking in the wrong place.

Love dwells in our own heart, and when we begin to discover it there, we begin to see it everywhere. It is what we are when we are not afraid. It is the absence of separation. It is a state that requires no conditions and holds no attachments. Love is our true nature, and our life is its reflection. For our true Self, love is natural, spontaneous, and effortless. What is arduous is seeing clearly the obstacles of conditioning, attachments, beliefs, judgments, and stories that obscure the experience of our Self as love.

Hungry for love, many of us search for crumbs under the table instead of sitting down to the sumptuous feast of life. We grieve for the self we imagine unworthy of love rather than opening to the love we are. We become bitter when the universe (substitute *mother, father, friend, spouse, God*) doesn't give us the love we want because we believe love can only come from the places and in the ways we have imagined it. Often, we fantasize that love is a "special" relationship that will meet all our needs and without which there can be no happiness. But happiness arises when we are *being* love rather than seeking it or demanding it.

LOVE IS KNOCKING ON THE DOOR, WAITING TO BE LET OUT

Even if we feel we are "looking for love in all the wrong places," we may not know where else to look. Look in your own heart. Love has been there all along, knocking on the door from the inside, waiting to be let OUT. We may have defenses, walls built over time that we imagine are protecting our heart, protecting a "self" from being hurt, protecting ourselves from feeling open and vulnerable, but we may never have inquired whether love needs protection. We look in the world of opposites, the world of duality, for the love we are longing to experience without ever following that longing to its Source. We are love, looking for love, trying to be love worthy. We are the ocean looking for water.

SUFFERING CAN BREAK US OPEN TO LOVE

Suffering is often the very thing that breaks us open. When we are suffering, we are seeking a way out of suffering. When our habitual ways of dealing with inner turmoil no longer work, we may find that our suffering has surrendered us into the arms of a bigger truth, a deeper wisdom, a greater love. Our heart may open, not because we even wished for such a thing, but because it may feel broken, shattered, betrayed, raw, and exceedingly vulnerable. Love may be trying to lay claim on us through our broken heart. And perhaps we will one day be wise enough to let the heart remain open rather than defended, angry, or closed.

Every day, sometimes moment by moment, we refuse love—refuse to give it or receive it. When we withhold it from ourselves, failing to let love touch our own pain, our own suffering, we may also refuse to see suffering in another. Ram Dass and Paul Gorman wrote insightfully in *How Can I Help?* about the fear some of us have of the compassion in our own hearts. We are afraid to see suffering in the world because we might be moved by the compassion we would feel, and then what might happen? Would we then have homeless people sleeping in our living room? Love seems difficult to touch in the presence of fear, and yet love accepts all, even our fear. In love itself, there is no fear, for there is no separation, no estrangement from our self, no separation from the moment as it appears.

However we view suffering, we might say that love is the answer or at least the response. But what is loving in any given situation? The ego mind often thinks love would be having exactly what it thinks it wants at any given time. But love is not always about getting what we want, as any mother knows who has yanked back her child from running in the street, only to have to comfort him in the midst of tears and fears. Love is not always about comfort, either. There is a greater love than comfort. Rumi points to the paradox in his poem "The Question": Walking into the "fire" or into the lovely "stream," we do not know who is blessed and who is not. And yet we may, often in retrospect only, realize that what we imagined was one thing—the blessing or the curse—has shown itself to be the reverse.

WHEN THE QUESTION OF SUFFERING DISSOLVES

Ultimately, the question of suffering will never be resolved in the mind. It is only when the mind is still that the question itself dissolves. In the phenomenal world, all opposites appear: suffering/healing; birth/death; failure/success; poverty/wealth; good/evil; joy/sadness; honor/dishonor; satiation/hunger; hard/soft; sometimes joy, sometimes suffering. Each flows into the other, creating, defining, and disappearing into the other.

BOTH JOY AND SUFFERING CAN RETURN US HOME

There is no experience that cannot return us to our home ground. We are generally quite happy to allow moments of joy to simply BE, and we do not feel the need to inquire into their Source. Yet joy itself, when traced backward, will be found to be arising in the same aware-ness that is also open to suffering. We might imagine, for example, that the first bite of a delicious chocolate is what brings pleasure, but "pleasure" does not reside in the chocolate. It resides in us. The source of pleasure is within; the experience of pain is within. In spontaneous joy, there is no refusal of the moment. This nonrefusal is the action of our true nature. We discover there is a causeless joy in the Heart of Awareness. And we discover that suffering appears when we feel sepa-rated from the truth of who/what we are.

Find what does not appear or disappear and rest there. The phe-nomenal world, including the life of the body-mind, will continue to come and go, but *You* will not. You will not abandon yourself in failure or promote yourself in success. You will be content to live your life by "not doing," yet doing will happen. What arises you will accept, what returns you will accept, including your body-mind's feelings, actions, and reactions. You will be like the sage, but you will neither need one nor need to be one.

> The sage calls dying young a blessing and living
>   long a blessing,
> calls beginnings a blessing and endings a blessing.
>   We might
> make such a person our teacher, but there's
>   something the ten
> thousand things belong to, something all change
>   depends upon—
> imagine making that your teacher![2]
> CHUANG TZU

The "ten thousand things" belong to what has no name, but the felt sense is an empty awareness that moves as life and love in its own expressions of Being—the living Truth of who you are. When we make that our teacher, we can open to the possibility of receiving grace in even the most challenging moments of our lives.

FIERCE GRACE

God whispers to us in our pleasure,
speaks to us in our conscience,
but shouts to us in our pain.[1]

C. S. LEWIS

Do you know the story of C. S. Lewis, whose life was portrayed in the play and movie *Shadowlands*? It is the story of the British writer and Christian theologian, a don at Oxford, and his relationship with Joy Gresham, the American poet who would become his wife. About his marriage, C. S. Lewis wrote, "God gave me in my sixties what He denied me in my twenties." Soon after the marriage took place, however, Joy died a painful death by cancer. Lewis said that his whole faith crumbled, like a house of cards. Here he was, a famous Christian apologist, but in the face of personal tragedy, he asked himself, "Is God a loving Father or is God the great Vivisectionist?"[2]

We do not imagine it is the Divine shouting to us in our pain, do we? It is in pain and suffering that love most often seems absent. However, when we are in touch with the deepest dimension of our Being, and not simply an *idea* or a *belief* in a concept of Truth, God, or Being, we may come to discover a fierce grace that can appear in times of suffering.

The path that moves each of us to awakening is unique. There is no one size fits all. I have an incredibly energetic friend who was diagnosed with cancer eighteen years ago. During fifteen years of living with cancer, and in spite of debilitating chemotherapy, which first seemed to work and then seemed not to, the types and locations of cancerous growths increased. Tumors were discovered in her pituitary gland, liver, lungs, brain, and bones. At one point she weighed as little as ninety pounds and was confined to a wheelchair, unable to walk, unable to lie flat in a bed because of pain, dependent on heavy doses of morphine just to survive the agonies of her body. She closed the charter school she founded, gave away her belongings, said good-bye to her friends, and went to her parents' home to die. However, she experienced a deep awakening in which she felt her skin unzipped to discover the radiant truth that lay beneath the costume of her sick body. She told me she felt she would never have been still long enough to recognize her true nature if her illness had not been so debilitating. Today, she is cancer free. The unexpected and often unwelcome life situations that appear in our experience—those that rattle us, make us uncomfortable, put us face-to-face with the mortality of the body, defeat us, and teach us the ego is not in control—these challenging times have the potential to take us more deeply into what lies beyond our attachment to separation.

AWAKENING DOES NOT GUARANTEE A LIFE OF EASE

Many believe awakening means that life is always easy, that the body is always healthy, that living awake means life will always look a particular way. Might I remind you that the Buddha died a painful death from food poisoning, Jesus was crucified, Nisargadatta had throat cancer, and Ramana was wracked with pain and died from a sarcoma that began in his arm. What is "awake" is not a person; it is the Buddha nature or Christ consciousness within that wakes up to itself. Living more and more fully and consciously as *that*, one's response to pain, illness, and other challenges may be deeply altered; however, this does not mean an awake life will never include pain or uncertainty.

Indeed, if we are completely honest, we never know what the next moment holds. This is not a reason to live in fear that projects a future that has not happened, nor does it preclude having human reactions in times of trials. Jesus, in his humanness, prayed, "Please take this cup [of suffering] from me . . . yet not my will but Thine be done." And although what is awake in us is not threatened in the face of any movement of its own life, these human forms feel whatever they feel in the face of loss, perceived danger, or the unknown. And these are opportunities to accept the fierce grace that pushes us beyond our comfort zones.

MEETING UNEXPECTED CHALLENGES

The world remembers 9/11—planes flying into the World Trade Center in New York and the Pentagon in Washington, DC. It was a time of chaos, fear, dread and uncertainty. My son was working in a building very close to the World Trade Center on that day, and he witnessed those horrific moments.

In the aftermath, his way of facing into the fear that swept through his mind and the whole city was to envision his own death in various ways, almost as a daily practice. While this might increase anxiety for many, for him, confronting his own death seemed to open his mind to the point that he felt no more fear of it. He said he began to feel at peace with the idea of his death and indeed felt freer than he had ever felt. What moved his method of dealing with trauma and fear? What moved his mind? What began to lessen and erase any fear of death? We don't really know, do we? But I have repeatedly observed and experienced that it is in trying to escape what is here that we move away from the openness that can deliver compassion, love, wisdom, and unexpected healing. It is in the moments when we open wholeheartedly to our actual experience, rather than trying to deny it, judge it, or reject it, that grace seems most available.

One month after 9/11, I was diagnosed with breast cancer. Now, such a diagnosis is a wake-up call if ever there is one. It offers an opportunity to look at mortality straight in the face, but also a chance to discover what is here that does not die.

During this time I was clear that I did not want to be in the energy field of anyone who was afraid of either cancer or death. This left very few people, actually, but I was very happy to have met Adyashanti before this experience. Here was, indeed, someone not afraid of either cancer or death. In moments of uncertainty or fear, Adya often appeared—not physically, but in the Heart where we have never been separated for a single moment.

One evening shortly before I was to have surgery, I attended one of Adya's *satsangs*, where he told me, "You wouldn't miss this for the world!" Of course, my mind was dubious and might have responded, "Easy for you to say," but in fact he was right. I have perhaps never felt held in such an abundance of love as I did while I was waiting with my husband before being wheeled to the operating room. Then I was left alone in the hallway outside the OR, where I watched surgeons coming and going from their scrub room, some with half sandwiches hanging out of their mouths, or laughing, or pulling on their paper booties. It was a totally fascinating experience during which I was astonished that the degree of sterility, at least outside the operating theater, was not what I had imagined. But what was amazing was that I felt absolutely no fear whatsoever, just a curiosity about the moment.

LOVE CAN BE FIERCE AND ALSO JOYFUL

In the matter of birth, life, and death for my immediate family, we have faced two additional cancer diagnoses in addition to my own: my daughter, when her son was only two, and my husband, at the end of his life. Life touches all of us with both joy and suffering within the wholeness of Being. Love wants to touch itself in every experience.

Sometimes in the darkest and most uncertain times for our family, there were moments of beauty, moments of joy, moments of unexpected insight, and a fierce love that showed up for all of it. I say "fierce" because love sometimes needed to show up as a protector, a cook, a strong advocate in hospital settings, a listening ear, a *no* to well-meaning friends bombarding us with advice, a long and silent hug, overnights with our grandson, the open space for our feelings, fatigue, and fears. Love does not abandon us, and it is our pain that is most in need of compassion.

When it was time for my daughter to have her waist-length shining hair cut off and her head shaved, I expected it to be a sad occasion, but actually it was full of joy. Her husband also shaved his head in solidarity, and their two-year-old wanted to have his head shaved as well. (We all thought better of that idea.) She donated her hair to a place that makes wigs for cancer patients. As layers of my daughter's identity began to temporarily fall away—being an opera singer, a healthy mom, someone with long, silky, beautiful hair—she felt herself grow "lighter and lighter," in her words, and at one point seemed to become radiant, despite the fact that, or perhaps because, she was facing into what was left when so many things seemed to have been taken away.

MY HUSBAND'S DEATH AND THE GRACE OF NO SEPARATION

The last example I will share with you of a fierce grace came through my husband's stage 4 cancer diagnosis, and our family dealing with yet another loved one undergoing chemotherapy and radiation and all that that entails physically, emotionally, and spiritually. After months of aggressive treatments, unbelievable fatigue, and dietary challenges for my husband, his oncologist announced that he actually had a clear scan. We were in disbelief, relief, and joy, imagining we might have at least one more Christmas together. However, two months after the wonderful news, he died of sepsis. Where is the grace here? I will tell you.

My husband and I had been married nearly fifty years at the time of his passing. That itself was a grace for which I am truly grateful. We shared the joys and sorrows of life together—the births of our children, the deaths of our parents, the challenges of my cancer diagnosis, our daughter's, and now his. For many years, we had said to each other that we hoped we had many more years together, but if we did not, ours had been a "wonderful ride." Our love was steadfast and sweet, focused on our family and each other. There was hardly ever a day in our lives that we did not share laughter, good food, and music.

He did not want to pass his days dealing with debilitating cancer treatments, and he wanted no extreme measures taken. But he was in a temporary remission when sepsis occurred. Despite the many ways that the sepsis was treated in the ICU, it actually took his life within a few short days. If it could not be reversed in his case, it also seemed a grace that these intense days were not prolonged. Our children and I were with him in a hospice room as he breathed his last breaths. A great calm arose inside as I invited him to let himself be taken to the other shore and assured him that he did not have to DO anything, just to let go and let himself be taken. It was a very peaceful death, and immediately after that last breath, two hawks circled right outside the window. Freedom seemed to be showing itself in flight.

THE BODHISATTVA WAS A HUMMINGBIRD

The night after his passing, I had fallen asleep in exhaustion when I was awakened by someone squeezing my hand. His presence in the room was palpable, and he reassured me that he was fine. I did not doubt that that was so. A few days later I walked to a park where the two of us used to walk frequently, where we took our grandsons on the days that we cared for them over the years. This day, I sat on the bench where we always used to sit, and I felt his presence on that bench immediately. A hummingbird began to circle near me, and while this may sound strange, it felt as though my husband and I communicated through the medium of that hummingbird. In one profound download of insight, it seemed as though we understood what karma we had played out in our lives together. Through my tears, his presence as THE Presence was incredibly potent.

After a while, I thought it was probably time for me to walk home, and so I asked the universe, "If it's time for me to go, let me see the hummingbird one more time." Sure enough, the bird appeared, but as I began to walk in the direction of home, the hummingbird seemed to be flying nearby and beckoning me in the other direction, so I followed the bird to a lovely fountain. Once again, the humming-bird disappeared, and after a time, I sensed perhaps I should go home. Once again, I asked: "If you are really *here*, let me see the humming-bird again." But the hummingbird did not come at once. Instead, what came so deeply, so very powerfully, so very profoundly, was this: "Now you see me in the olive trees; now you see me in the flowers; now you see me in the clouds; now you see me in the sky." And as my whole being seemed to receive and understand this all the way through, the hummingbird appeared not two feet from my face and took a drink from the fountain.

In the years since, hummingbirds have been very much part of not only my life experience but also our two children's, being present in ways they never were before this incident. The hummingbird is the only bird that can fly backward as well as forward, and perhaps it can teach us to look back without getting stuck in the past—an apt teaching for one who feels a loss. But the greater teaching, through a fierce and painful grace, is that I see my husband as the Spirit that we all are—before, during, and after incarnation.

"I AM HERE"

When Ramana was dying, he told his followers, "They say I am leaving. But where could I go? I am here." I feel deeply that my husband is "here" in that same way. What we all are in our essence has gone nowhere; it is here everywhere I look. Death does not end love, and even in so-called death, there is no separation in the Heart we have always shared. Transformation has happened—similar to water evaporating to become a cloud, like the stream in our first chapter—but all that has happened is a transformation, not an ending. At some point before, or certainly at the moment of death, we will all be transformed as well; we will go beyond form and yet lose nothing of our deepest essence that is Spirit.

Part VI

LIVING
AWAKE,
LIVING NOW

*So what can be said about what happens
when God takes over her house?
She laughs and simply sips her tea,
washes her dishes and sleeps when it's time,
then goes to find another house
where there has been an invitation,
an invitation to come in
from the deep, deep love of Herself.*[1]

EMBODIMENT
UNFOLDS ITSELF

You do not figure out how to embody Truth.
Truth embodies you.
You can never see your own shining.
You can only BE what you are.

When the infinite Mystery moves within a body-mind to wake itself up out of time, out of the known, out of the cherished thought called "me," we call its movement "awakening." When it moves to lovingly embrace the entire world of manifestation as its own body in the lived realization that there is no "other," we call this movement "embodiment." Like life, embodiment unfolds itself.

An initial awakening is energetically "up and out" of identification with form. Embodiment is a "down and in" movement as Reality becomes conscious within you. Rather than longing or searching for itself, the Divine now consciously experiences itself in the world of Being as all that is seen, touched, tasted, felt, heard, or perceived. While awakening can happen in a single moment, embodiment is an ongoing process as Truth moves to share, express, and love itself in life—*your* very life, the life of the world. Living awake beyond an awakening can feel simultaneously freeing and challenging.

The profound freedom one feels in an awakening makes it seem as though "this is it! There is nothing that could ever change this experience or this knowing." But as all know who have trod the path of spiritual awakening, the truly challenging part comes afterward. What does it mean to embody what we have realized? If there really is only One and the whole world is my very Self, how does that affect my living, relating, *being*? If the love we may have initially experienced for the whole returns to being self-centered and limited, how does it become reawakened? What does it feel like to live with an open mind, an open heart, an open body—open to the openness that is our true nature?

KEEPING OUR QUESTIONS ALIVE

Finding out what was most important was an essential question before we began our spiritual journey, and it continues to be important as we learn to navigate our life and experiences from a deeper dimension of our Being. Keep your questions alive about what is most important to you about your life or within a particular moment, situation, conversation, or relationship.

While there is an end to *seeking*, embodying our realization is unending. How could there ever be an end point to discovering and living more consciously from the Infinite? Yet as life continues to unfold itself, we will become aware of where our mind continues to want to hold on to separation to stay in control, what wants to come out of the shadows to be experienced or loved, what walls around our heart may continue to remain in place. This is not about maintaining egoic vigilance, ferreting out every moment we may feel out of alignment with our deepest truth in order to judge it. It is an invitation to see more deeply into the fear we may carry underneath our conditioning and to expose it all to our heart's clarity and compassion. Our conditioning does not mean we are, in fact, separate selves. There is no separate self to judge a "self," and yet Truth will shed light in the darkness out of its unceasing love for its own expressions.

SPIRITUAL EGO IS NOT IN CHARGE

If our mind imagines an awakening is a won-and-done game, believing a "someone" has finally "arrived," then what might have been an authentic opening has become co-opted by spiritual ego. While ego is not an enemy, since we see that it is simply a movement of identified thought mixed with Consciousness, we must realize that its conditioned ways of viewing itself as an entity often find more and more subtle ways to reclaim a separate identity. There is an emotional attachment to this identity, even when it has been seen through time and time again.

After understanding ego has no separate existence, our mind still functions. It may now claim to be "enlightened" and imagine there is nothing more that is needed, nothing more to discover. It can innocently feel that way temporarily because in an authentic awakening, the moment egoic consciousness shifts to the Heart of Awareness, there is a shift in identity that is Self-authenticating and experienced to be profoundly true. However, the experience of an awakening is not the same as living it. If the mind is expecting an unending experience that feels identical to an awakening moment, it may become disappointed and doubt the revelation. Returning to daily life, the mind may become confused about how to "stay" awake, as we experience the ways our thoughts, feelings, or behavior may continue to induce contractions or some degree of suffering.

Living awake as truth and love in the midst of an egoically driven, divided, and conflicted world can be challenging, and especially so to any aspect of our conditioned identities that have not become transparent. We will, in all likelihood, continue to see the ways the ego mind wants to reassert control. Egoic thought may now decide it is the captain of the ship called "embodiment" and continue to try to "figure it all out." But now ego is operating in the realm of living a realization rather than seeking one. Here, again, our invitation is to return over and over to the Heart—not the heart that is simply the feeling organ, but the true Heart that contains wisdom, love, compassion, and discernment.

Awakening was not up to an ego, and neither is embodiment, yet many folks return to their old ways of seeking to "know" with the intellect rather than opening and surrendering to what is unknown. Without a fixed point of view or a set of beliefs that are taken to be "truth," we find ourselves thrust into "not knowing." Not knowing contains our intimacy and also our vulnerability. Freedom lies not in getting rid of anything or fixing a "self," but in clear seeing and experiencing what is here now.

POSTPONING SURRENDER

Part of the embodiment process is seeing the myriad ways egoic thought has of postponing surrender, of "unenlightening" ourselves. We may imagine we can only be awake when we no longer have any "issues," when we have perfected a "self." We may use strategies of self-improvement—working on a "somebody"—in order to postpone facing into the truth of being "nobody." Yet the human part of ourselves is an expression of our Divine Being, and when we see it as such, our judgments and our suffering begin to melt. In no way am I suggesting that if you are suffering from depression, anxiety, addiction, or trauma you should sit idly by if and when it is obvious you need to ask for help. But realize that trying to remove conditioning piece by piece can be an endless process. The real task is letting go of the illusion of a separate self *defined* by that conditioning.

YOU WILL FIND WAYS OF RETURNING TO TRUTH

With the end of seeking, there are no guaranteed prescriptions or strategies for living awake. While you may imagine that the clear and instantaneous moment of awakening will bring immediate knowledge of how to live from the realization of who/what you truly are, it is rarely the case. However, when someone wants to "stay" awake, there is a return to the wanting mind of separation. The Heart of Awareness cannot be gained or lost. We have only to notice what is ever present regardless of the forms of expression that continually change.

And yet all of us will face conditioned thoughts, emotions, and reactions arising. Likewise, each of us will discover our own ways to return again and again to the Truth of what we are and to see what we are not. For example, the spiritual teacher Byron Katie developed the questions that make up the method she calls "The Work" as a way to continue to see what is not true while dwelling in/as the truth of what IS. While I am not moved to develop a school or deliver techniques for staying awake, what I can do is share with you a few ways that I have found helpful. If any resonate, use them. If none seem applicable, know that you will find your way.

THE ONE WHO WANTS TO "STAY" AWAKE IS NOT WHAT IS AWAKE

First of all, the one who wants to "stay" awake is not who/what is awake. Stop frequently to notice that what is awake is already present. Silence, stillness, and peace are already present. Presence is already present; it is the *knowing* of your experience. There is no one who creates this. What we are talking about here are ways of seeing and inquiring with great love and understanding into the beliefs (or emotions upholding those beliefs) that *appear* to obscure experiencing or living more consciously from what is already our alive, awake Being.

Remember that any seeming obstacle is simply an appearance that our conditioned mind has given power to. The "power source" is always our consciousness and habitual ways of drawing consciousness toward perceived problems, negativity, attachments, and fears. Awareness is untouched by the body-mind's beliefs, feelings, judgments, or innocent misunderstandings. Yet at the same time it is intimate with them and can begin to liberate these movements by clear seeing.

Seeing, being, and loving are more important than doing in unwinding the conditioning that leads to a change in attitudes and behavior. We may begin to notice the essential qualities of various emotions when their energy is seen with precision in the field of silence and stillness. We might find that anger shows up as aggression when it moves through ego, but its essential quality is actually clarity, giving us strength to remain steadfast in confronting the causes of suffering within ourselves or injustice in the world. We might discover that the essential quality of fatigue is actually relaxation.

SHIFTING ATTENTION FROM PERSONHOOD TO PRESENCE

Like jumping a fence, our attention can shift from one perspective to another in an instant. Both the perspectives of personhood (the thought of being separate) and the perspective of Presence (unidentified, undivided Consciousness aware of itself as Being) are available. While ultimately nothing is separate, we can be identified with the "person" or we can see and experience the person/moment/experience through our Presence, which is not identified with thought. Many, after an awakening, find themselves sitting on the fence—no longer completely identified as "person" only and yet not able to leave that identified perspective in order to embody Presence.

We are not talking about denying we have a body, thoughts, feelings, or experiences in the realm of human beingness. And we are not talking about a spiritual ego adopting an Absolute "stance." ("I am nothing and nobody, and so nothing matters.") We are talking about where our Consciousness is learning to hang out. It has been so used to living in the story of a "me," in the ego mind, that it takes a while for that mind to merge with the heart mind. It is a bit like living in a different atmosphere for a while. There is a natural adjusting to the altitude, a natural way that the Heart of Awareness begins to move in the body-mind. It moves to harmonize itself in our body and mind when there is less judging and worrying and more trust in what we are.

What I experienced is that the moment attention jumped the fence from personhood to Presence, there would be an immediate sense of peace, stillness, clear vision, love, and even happiness. This was different from shifting to the dark (unknowable) face of the Absolute (a nonview). The same Source is the essence of the Absolute, of Presence, and of its movement as ego. What is awake is aware of every dimension and of the shifting perspectives. Yet when we become more and more familiar with our inner territory and its many dimensions, there can be a natural shift to Presence—or a seemingly more deliberate choice point—when we find our consciousness returning to a limited, false home in ego land.

THE QUESTION OF SPIRITUAL BYPASS

Spiritual bypass is a term that describes using spiritual concepts, practices, or transcendence techniques to avoid facing difficult emotions, serious psychological issues, or actions that are based on separation, repression, and unconscious beliefs. Spiritual *concepts* and Spirit are not the same thing. I would like to make clear that *Spirit bypasses nothing*, since it is the essence of all. In fact, it is Presence alone, being intimate with what is arising, that has the power to bring understanding and liberation to the experience at hand.

It is the ego that wants to bypass what it is uncomfortable seeing or feeling. While this may seem necessary at certain points, our true Spirit clearly and unflinchingly sees what is before us or within us, but in the context of great compassion, acceptance, understanding, and love. It is the use of an *idea* of spirituality as a defense that supports our continuing unconsciousness. The compassionate Heart of Awareness is what makes it possible to bring those unclaimed, painful, angry, sexual, fearful, or even exuberant and joyful parts of ourselves back into a state of harmony and wholeness.

Pain of any kind is a call for attention. It is not, however, a call for identification with delusion, division, or victimhood. Presence or Spirit is what both tenderly holds and fearlessly sees our conditioning and can begin to unwind it. Often, it is love that we have bypassed, fearing, as we do, being hurt, being abandoned, or not having our love returned. Yet the greater abandonment—and the greater cause of suffering—is abandoning what we truly are and denying what is authentically *here*.

Many people use the truism that "stories are not truth" to intellectually dismiss or judge some pain in themselves that is wanting loving attention in order to be liberated back into wholeness. "Since there is no 'me,' I don't have to care for this rage/fear/suffering inside." Yet it is the "me" idea that is holding onto rage, fear, suffering, and judgment.

Another example would be using a belief in a concept of nonduality to serve ego. In working with couples, I once encountered a man who was trying to manipulate his partner into having sex with multiple partners, since "there is nobody here, no right or wrong, everything is love, so why would you object?" His partner was confused; she was a spiritual seeker and considered him to be "more advanced," but this arrangement was not aligned with her inner truth. While he might have been undivided about such behavior, she was not, and his use of spiritual concepts to pressure her did not honor how relative truth was moving in her. We have also seen this attempt to twist truth in order to serve ego used in cults by charlatans.

KNOWING OUR EDGE

Investigating our edge is part of the embodiment process, and we are fooling ourselves if we believe there will be no more edge if we have awakened. Part of the continuing deepening of embodiment is the willingness to know our edge. One way to determine an edge is to ask yourself what you are avoiding. An edge can also be a current question, issue, or inquiry that is not yet clear or aligned with our deepest understanding. We might find an edge in dealing with difficult neighbors or with an elderly parent who is in need of care but whom we feel might not have cared for us with much compassion. An edge might be a question involving a particular conditioned response or deeply held pattern in the body-mind or in our relationships with others. Our edge might be a question about what it means to love or to move undividedly in a political landscape that feels dangerous or unjust. As Adyashanti often remarks, it is in living our realization that "the rubber meets the road." Understanding and awakening hold the possibilities of living more fully what we may have realized, but they do not guarantee how deeply that may happen. Once again, it is useful to ask, *What is our deepest desire?*

BEING TRUTHFUL

Truth itself and our beliefs about it are not the same thing. The deepest Truth is unspeakable and ungraspable. It cannot be gained or lost; yet each moment Truth is giving and receiving itself freely. Giving and receiving are actually a single movement. Whether we are giving love or attempting to control, speaking from truth or untruth, we receive what we give. If our interest lies in awakening and living from the truth of our deepest Being, we are called to realize the Truth of who we are. When we deeply receive this Truth, we cannot help but give it away. Giving it is *being* it.

To live in Truth means being truthful—full of truth. This means seeing from Truth, functioning from that openness, receiving the moment fully, giving what we actually *are* rather than our defenses against it. How different this feels from continually giving our conditioned opinions, trying to control life, insisting on being right, "winning" by imagining someone else must lose, demanding to be loved before we are willing to love. A life lived from Truth is a life of authenticity, not pretense. Sometimes, in living authentically, we will feel vulnerable. Whatever moment, whatever feeling, whatever thought—it is all happening in the Heart of Awareness, the Unborn Buddha mind.

LIVING AUTHENTICALLY

What does it mean to live an authentic life, to live with integrity, awareness, and devotion to what is most true within? Living authentically is quite different from living in imitation, living from a rulebook, or living in a trance state of identification with a "me" frightened of "doing it wrong" or "having to be right."

What might it be like to live without strategies to escape feeling the fears that direct egoic life? Until we begin to live from our true nature, we may not even be aware of the fears that silently run our life—fears of not being enough, not being loved, not fitting in, not being in control. Or we may be totally identified with our fears, unaware that there is also fearlessness inside. Many of our habitual patterns of coping are so deeply ingrained that we are not even aware of their operation. Are we open to looking? Can we investigate without judgment the beliefs we have taken to be true about our identities?

To live in truth is not about fixing an illusory "self" that is broken. It is about being awake to who/what we really are and living from the vast openness that includes even the parts of ourselves we may wish were different. As a friend once remarked, "In the Infinite you are, where would you send something you wanted to be rid of?" Our essential freedom is not a refusal of life; it is living awake, moving spontaneously from the deep silence of our true nature rather than from ideas about it.

It is difficult for the mind to see its own self-deception, but the Truth within continually sees untruth, shining its light and compassion into the darkness. Our greatest ally is our own integrity. No one can give us our integrity or take it away. It is ours to care for. Our essence is shared with all of life, and yet each moment's authentic expression is unique. In the spiritual life, we are not seeking simply to transcend our humanness, but to fully express the truth of our Being through it. When we want authenticity more than we want to maintain an image, freedom will lead the way.

LIVING AWAKE
IS LIVING NOW

Step out of your thoughts.
Your timeless presence,
freedom, and being
exist only Now.

WE CAN ONLY BE AWAKE NOW

Contrary to the mind's projection, we can only be awake Now. We cannot hold on to yesterday's awakening, as powerful as it might have been, or think that tomorrow we might finally "wake up." What is aware in us this very moment is timeless, and it unfolds its beingness only now. The mind is always looking for another moment. It lives in time, in duality. Duality is not a mistake, for the Infinite needs duality to experience itself. The constructs of time and space allow the Infinite to experience itself as duration and form. However, what is awake sees from beyond time and is awake only in the timeless Now. When we imagine that we can be awake in some other time than now, in some other place than here, we delude ourselves. Even our memories and projections occur in the Now.

The seeker imagines he is traveling in time toward a goal called "enlightenment" and wants to find the best path. There's a wonderful story that illustrates the seeker's dilemma. It includes an exchange in which a student asks his teacher whether the path to enlightenment is difficult or easy. He is told it is neither. When the student questions why, the teacher responds that there is no path to enlightenment; one does not travel to a goal. It is a journey that has no distance. When we stop traveling, we arrive.[1]

TIME AND THE TIMELESS COLLAPSE IN THE NOW

Time is actually the timeless manifesting as Being. When the timelessness of Being is seen through the mind, it is called "time." We perceive time when we perceive change. For the mind, time can seem to move fast or slow, but in fact, our life is simply now. When we are totally present *now*, beyond ideas, we are living awake, no longer identified with past memories or future expectations. The eternal *Now* is timeless, yet it appears as this moment—fresh, mysterious, alive, and free. *Now* is our timelessly awake Self *being*.

This very moment, this very breath, this very experience, this very sensation, all are objects in the Heart of Awareness that is here now. What is awake in us lives in the Now and cannot be separated from what is occurring. Whatever our fantasy may be about a spiritual journey that will take us from "here" to "there," we eventually see that it has only been a journey back to here and now. To be *here* consciously, and fully present *now*, is to experience our awake Presence. For a moment, consider being here without a past or projected future. Whom or what would you be?

WHERE AM I?

Along with the question *Who am I?* we might also ask *Where am I?* No matter where the body travels or what experiences arise, aren't you always *here*? Here, in the car moving the body to the grocery store. Here, in the phone conversation. Here, in the cooking of dinner. Here, in the argument with your partner. Here, in the perusing of the internet. Here, as your body sleeps. YOU are always here. Awareness is that which is here/now—not a body, not a mind, not an object that comes and goes, but that which is ever present.

A great liberation comes from living now as our Self, but it costs us our desire to live "then" or "when." This moment is a doorway into the timeless, awake dimension of our Being. Just this! What happens when we allow everything to be as it is now? The mind cannot understand how there could be peace if the moment is not peaceful, but peace is what is underlying all moments, all experiences—timelessly here now.

TIME DOES NOT TAKE US TO THE TIMELESS

Awakened living is all about returning again and again to Now, which is the timeless dimension right in front of us, not a thought in the back of the mind's memory. We can only breathe now, live now, and love now.

Can you love tomorrow? Tomorrow is imagination, fantasy. The love you will give or receive tomorrow, "when . . . ," is a fantasy that disappears with the illusion of time. It does not take *more* time to experience the timelessness of Being—the radiance in a flower, the life energy in a bird winging its way across the sky, the mystery of who you are. Why wait? Tomorrow never comes, for when it does, it's always today! Being awake is now; it does not operate in past or future tenses, and it actually steps out of the present tense as well in its timeless Presence. Even if we have had powerful and authentic awakenings or openings in the past, we must return to now if we are to live awake.

RETURNING TO ZERO

Minds want to know: Does a sage think, feel, walk, talk, have a spouse, a job, ever become ill? Does he ever feel frustration, sadness, anger, fear? To live awake, will it be necessary to drop out of my normal life and live in a cave? Does everyone who has had an awakening experience become a spiritual teacher?

The mind is always comparing itself with what it considers to be the ideal of a person living the awakened life. "The ideal looks like this; no, it looks like that." But however it looks, the mind is quite convinced it does not look like the one he or she is. Ramana would frequently be asked questions along this vein. He usually responded by asking, "Why do you want to know about someone else when you do not yet know who you yourself are? Find out who you are first, then see if the question remains."[2]

Life moves, mind moves, feelings move, but not a single moment is taken to be personal or separate from the wholeness of Being. And the wholeness of Being cannot be separated from the Source of Being, which is infinite, indescribable, nonconceptual, and incapable of being objectified in any way. The Source is where all concepts, forms, and differentiation dissolve. This is what I call "zero." It does not have a name. But whatever appears in/as *Being* arises from such a Mystery and returns to it, including the mind that creates an experience of self, world, and other. When this movement of mind "returning" to its home ground happens spontaneously in consciousness, we might call it "returning to zero." But the infinite zero does not move and thus has no need of returning anywhere; it is attention that returns to the silence and stillness of the Heart of Awareness.

THE WILLINGNESS TO BE TRANSFORMED

Egoic thought cannot know itself as "pure awareness"; rather, it is awareness that sees egoic thought. The infinite Ocean of Awareness awakens *itself* within its own expression of Being. And it is that same awake *beingness* that will transform our way of being in the world. If we are looking for a "permanent" state of embodiment or a knowing of pure awareness that is "remembered" every single moment, we are still operating from the mind of separation.

When there has been a true awakening, it is the Mystery and not the "me" that then begins to transform our thoughts, our heart, and our actions. At this point many seekers move away from what they have realized and return to the mind to try to figure out how to live from this truth. However, as soon as we go back to the mind's thoughts about "how," we have departed from the mystery of *Being*, which is the agent of living more deeply, directly, and simply from what we *are*. So this often becomes a source of confusion, and many either return to egoic transformation techniques, which are now directed by a spiritualized ego, or they become passive rather than grounded in *Being*, which is simultaneously alive, present, intimate with the moment, and functioning with wisdom and compassion. In either case, realization may not truly flower because of one's attempts to either control or avoid acting from that deeper dimension.

OUR LOCUS OF OPERATION SHIFTS

What happens is that our locus of operation shifts from conditioned thought to the openness of not-knowing mind. Conditioned thought may remain when it is useful, but we are now available for what Consciousness wants to say or do, knowing that it is always relating to itself from within itself. Responses simply happen spontaneously without the kind of deliberation our ego might once have engaged in. We experience "being lived." We trust the discriminating wisdom of the Heart of Awareness to move us.

When the inner knowing is informing our speech and actions without the filter of ego trying to stay safe or trying to be seen in a certain way, we may not, initially, always feel comfortable following "instructions." Yet here is where Emptiness begins dancing effortlessly, at times in surprising ways.

Of course, there are no guarantees that we will always be perfect in our responses. When we begin to realize the truth of what we are, we may feel that we are free, but our minds, emotions, and bodies may be acting and reacting from old identifications. It is our deep and sincere devotion to Truth and to *living* from Truth that opens the heart and mind and creates willingness for all false views to be deconstructed. Realization does not create a new identity; it keeps shedding old ones.

LIVING WITHOUT A MAP

To the egoic mind, living awake is imagined to be living in an ultimate state of knowing—always knowing what to say, where to go, what to do, how to respond, what the next thing should be. Actually, living awake is living without a map. We are not given a ten-year plan, not even a ten-minute plan or even a ten-second plan, which does not mean that we never make plans. It's just that we understand today's plan may not be tomorrow's reality. Our mind learns to live in not knowing, which, of course, was always the state of affairs, if we are being honest; but we imagined we were in control and had a mental map for living. We may have spent years trying to find the "right" map to tell us how to move in life and in relationships.

Now, there is nothing wrong with having a moral compass, or values based on kind and compassionate ways of behaving in life, or helpful ways of thinking about oneself or interacting with others. But living awake is not about knowing ahead of time what may be called for in any given moment or what compassion will look like. We actually are living without a map or a goal.

To the Western mind, living without a goal, without a map, having nowhere to go and nothing to do sounds like sheer madness—boring at best, lazy, irresponsible, and an invitation to chaos at worst. But nothing could be further from the truth. It might mean, in living awake, that we are finally available for Truth to move spontaneously within us in the Now, allowing action to come from the dimension of our being that is clear and at peace. Doing is coming from Being. It does not mean living stupidly or passively or being unable to make plans. It means not being attached to those plans. It means being open to what is here now rather than judging it, being curious rather than fearful about this moment's expression. It means being authentic, real, engaged, and intimate with experience.

By all means, if you want to drive to an unknown destination in your car, use a map. But if you want Truth, be guided from the deep, silent Source within that gives the mind no security but, rather, continually invites it to the unknown and to the lifelong adventure of living openly now.

WHAT MIGHT BE CALLED
FOR IN ANY GIVEN MOMENT

In any given moment or situation what might be called for could simply be a warm smile, a hug, compassionate listening, giving bread to someone who is hungry, or offering love to someone starving from its lack. What might be needed is changing our baby's diapers, washing dishes, watering plants, visiting a shut-in, giving our partner a kiss. Or what could be called for is a confrontation to an ego. In times of emergency, when there is no time to reflect, action may happen to save lives or avert accidents. When we experience being in the flow, we are not thinking about it; life is simply flowing effortlessly. We might be playing an instrument, singing in the shower, making a piece of art, running without thinking about running, enjoying cooking a new dish.

We will also be faced with challenges, difficult decisions, people who seem to thrive on creating conflict, drama, or argument. Are we willing/ able to stay connected to what is most deeply true, even as we have to be clear, set boundaries on our time, or refrain from engaging in dramas that are no longer interesting to us? Each time we relate, we may be tempted to return to old conditioned ways of being, but here is where it may take courage to live from what we have realized—and love from an open heart. We do not become doormats. When we take a seat in our true Self, we have great respect for our own expression of Being and what is true for us, at the same time honoring that others are deserving of the same respect and freedom to be who they are.

When life is simply happening spontaneously, with seemingly unexpected and sometimes miraculous outcomes, the ego wants to know how to stay in the flow. But the ego is not in charge of the flow. It is life without the continual story of "me"; it is simply the flow of life itself. We ARE life, not the separate "one" experiencing ourselves as its victim or its victor. The river of life keeps flowing.

THE MINDSTREAM

Each of us has a stream running through our life that has been called a "mindstream." It is the flow of *Being* itself, carrying with it the moment-to-moment continuation of both mental and sense impressions that pass through consciousness. It includes the impersonal stream of karmic conditions and imprints, both positive and negative. From these impermanent moments that appear in the river of

Being, we construct a seemingly permanent "self." But like a flowing river, it never stays the same for a single moment. It is awareness itself that provides our sense of *continuing*. Impermanent moments or trace memories appearing in consciousness do not produce a separate entity.

While the mindstream carries impressions from prior lifetimes to this one, giving rise to the concept of reincarnation (past lives or karma for a separate "me" or separate "soul"), these ideas are dependent on identification with both time and our time-bound mind. Our deepest nature is timeless, whole, undivided, and compassionately awake in the Now. It is not personal, has no separate "self," and yet here it is, awake and aware in each of us, each a unique, moment-to-moment expression of Totality. Some of us carry memories of what I would now call "past-life dreams," for even *this* life is a dream, from one perspective. What we carry in the karmic stream are memories of past actions, experience, or feelings, both negative and positive, that arise in present experience to be liberated back into the wholeness of Being or to continue an evolutionary journey.

Imprints or impulses appear in our experience in the Now; a certain flavor seems particular to us, and yet it is simply the conditioned movement of life itself. These impressions, flowing in consciousness, appear in order to be seen and liberated from the illusion of separation. The melting of separation comes through the power of Presence and love in the Now. The past has no hold when we are intensely focused on experience now. If there is something "past" that needs to be seen or healed back into wholeness, it will arise in present experience. We do not have to dig up pebbles from the streambed.

Whether we call this continuation a mindstream of Consciousness, a river of Being, or what is passed along in the lineage of our forefathers and foremothers through our genetic heritage and life experience, the mindstream does not define us but plays a part in our functioning and in where we may feel resonance. The stream is always flowing, yet it is simply a current and not an identity.

While our time-bound mind imagines the stream will eventually merge with the Ocean in the future, it is actually occurring within the Ocean of Awareness right now. The timeless does not require time.

Our awakening and freedom are present now. Through our devotion to Truth, we begin to see more and more deeply the ways the egoic mind holds on to a time-bound identity of separation.

Experientially, our lives are a continually changing happening in Consciousness itself. While we are conditioned to believe our body or mind contains a separate "self," in fact, upon deeper examination, we find no such entity—only the flow of thoughts, feelings, experience, memory, sense impressions, all happening in the river of Being. Or we could envision our life and experience as being a bit like popcorn popping—now a thought, now a feeling, now a rosebud, now a sip of water, now being at work, now a moment of fatigue, now a moment of joy, now a moment of sorrow, on and on, each popping up in the dimensionless space of awareness, seemingly real and yet totally ephemeral. To live more and more consciously as this transparent awareness is living more and more in the peace of our true nature.

SURPRISE AND JOY

Sometimes, in the midst of a suffering world, we forget that joy exists. Many of us are too busy worrying about life to enjoy the precious moments of living it. Our minds attempt to wrap meaning around each and every occurrence, and in doing so, we cannot experience the fullness of the moment as it is, much less find any joy in it. Without awareness, there could be no thinking, but thinking is not the same as simply being aware. Each moment is fresh and new. No moment repeats itself—ever! Only ideas repeat themselves; interpretations repeat themselves; stories repeat themselves.

Surprise, astonishment, wonder, amazement are frequent experiences when we are open to the moment as it is instead of as we think it should be. That is why the whole world is fascinating to a small child who still lives moment to moment without many ideas. A dead bird, a cloud in the sky, a tiny flower, a green bean, all equally fascinate the unconditioned mind of a child. He finds joy in unimaginable places; so does the sage.

To live awake means to be truly aware, to be open to surprises, to taste the joy of simply Being, whether we are listening to music, looking at the stars, or tasting a strawberry. It means being present to one another, walking on this earth, experiencing our breathing, being wholeheartedly involved with life. Joy and suffering frequently trade places and are sometimes different interpretations about life rather than different actual experiences. The death of one moment brings a new one. Both mourning and welcoming are possibilities.

There is a sense of wonder, a sense of joy and spontaneity that often feels lost as we live so much of our lives in the virtual reality of our mind instead of the actual reality of the moment we are experiencing. Wake up! The grass underneath your feet is astonishing; the pattern of light on the carpet is fascinating; the fact that your body knows how to heal itself is amazing; the billions of galaxies are unfathomable. But none is as wondrous as the truth of YOU and the gift you give the world of loving your Self as all of it!

AWAKENING
AND SURRENDER

Surrender comes when you no longer ask,
"Why is this happening to me?"[1]

ECKHART TOLLE

Awakening and surrender are always holding hands, dancing as a single movement, whether we speak of sleeping and waking in our daily life, the birth and death of the body, or awakening to the deepest Truth of who we are and dying to the illusion of what we are not. Spiritual egos love the idea of awakening, but not the idea of surrender. Neither awakening nor surrender can be accomplished by an illusory ego, even a spiritual ego. Living awake is living open to the moment and surrendering into its reality, the truth of now. This is not a passive way of living, but one that sees life from its perspective of wholeness—both the emptiness of its Source and the fullness of its infinite expressions. Surrender is simply yielding to rather than opposing the unfolding flow of life, opening fully to what is here now. It is in the absence of resistance that we experience the Presence that flows from the Heart of Awareness.

AWAKENING FROM AND
SURRENDERING TO THE ABSOLUTE

Every morning, when we awaken from nighttime dreaming and from dreamless sleep, the feeling "I am" appears, and with it we begin to put on our identity clothing. Yet in deep, dreamless sleep, there is no perception of a self, a world, an "other," or a god. We do not know if we are a man or a woman, Asian or Hispanic, married or single, parent or child. We do not know what we believe or even that we "exist." In other words, our mind has temporarily disappeared in the Absolute dimension, and in the morning we awaken from our rest in the Absolute. If we dream, something in us may remember a dream we had while sleeping. What remembers? Were you there? What was there? Every night, we surrender our daytime wakefulness into sleep. We usually are happy if we can fall asleep quickly; it is generally something we look forward to. Consciousness appears to go to sleep, but what is Awake does not. Mind has been surrendered into essence.

When we are born, we awaken from a dark, wet world in utero, where we lived with the steady beat of our mother's heart and the sloshing sounds of amniotic fluid as we moved about. We enter into a bright world of air rather than water, of the unmuffled sounds of voices, traffic, planes, music boxes, the wind blowing, people speaking to us—not through the medium of fluid, but through air. Our life in form takes another leap into consciousness.

When the body dies, we must surrender everything we have held on to—the life we called our own, the friends or family that may surround us, all of our possessions, our hopes for what we thought we wanted to accomplish or enjoy, everything we thought we were. At this point, there is no choice. Death will happen; we will be surrendered to the experience whether we want to surrender to it or not. We begin life surrendering the familiar warmth and wetness for a bold new world. We die surrendering whatever we cannot take with us, and we awaken to whatever continues. If, before the transformation called "death" of the body, we have discovered that our essential being is unborn and thus is undying, we know that is what continues. The Mystery that manifested as form is the same Mystery that continues with or without form.

WE SURRENDER OUR ILLUSORY
SELF, NOT OUR AUTHENTICITY

When we speak of surrender, we are not talking about surrendering what is authentic in ourselves, nor are we talking about becoming submissive in our human relationships; we are talking about surrender of the illusory self. *Surrender* is a word fraught with associations with weakness, passivity, defeat, and vulnerability—all things that egos want to avoid. But when we realize that we have never had a moment's breath, feeling, thought, or experience apart from the Spirit that animates our body-mind or the Awareness in which all is experienced or known, we realize we have never actually had a separate "self" to surrender! This recognition is very humbling to the ego, which has imagined it has been in control. As the egoic "self," we have certainly had the perception of choice and have perceived the exercise of "will," yet life's causes and conditions have moved us moment to moment. As the Self, the Heart of Awareness, we are infinite potential. When we take a seat in our true Self, there is a power, presence, and authority within our Self. We feel it, sense it, and this allows us to be authentic, to live with integrity, to be real. To live in Truth is not about fixing an illusory "self."

CHOICE POINTS

In egoic life, there are very few *real* choices, because our conditioned mind is operating unconsciously. As we are learning to live from a deeper, truer dimension of ourselves, however, there are choice points, points at which something in us sees the arising of the illusion of separation, blame, judgment, or self-induced suffering. These choice points require consciousness. Do we follow thoughts or emotions, believing these experiences are "truth," or do we return to zero, willing to be still in the midst of the moment? The stillness within us is not refusing our thoughts or feelings, but neither does it give our anxieties any real ground to stand on. In fact, when we are in touch with our open heart, we may feel love for our worrying mind. We have the opportunity time and again to remain steadfast, still, silent,

217

open, and awake to what is arising—not strategizing about how to get rid of something, not simply discharging it, but willing to see it all the way through. We appear to have choice points many times each day. If we get caught up in a philosophical stance regarding "Who chooses?" we will miss the opportunity to inquire more deeply, to experience more thoroughly and more lovingly the moment we are in.

There comes a time when we experience choiceless awareness and choiceless action, but this comes about only when we are more devoted to the Heart of Awareness than to life looking a certain way. Life looks the way it looks in any given moment; our response can come from any dimension of our Being—conditioned mind, conditioned emotions, a defended heart, the energetic body, or the deepest dimension of openheartedness and nonseparation. To awaken to What Is is to surrender to its truth and to see and respond to the moment from the light within us. When life presents a choice point and we do not get bogged down in philosophical debate, we can choose to invite conscious light to shine in the darkness, in the moments of contraction, negativity, fear, and unconscious resistance. If we want our frozen concepts or conditioned reactions and judgments warmed, thawed, and melted by the sun—the Heart of Awareness—we turn to face the sun. We are no longer defending against the reality of what is here now.

LIFE WITHOUT A WHY

> The wind blows where it will,
> and you hear the sound of it,
> but you do not know whence it comes
> or whither it goes; so it is
> with everyone who is born of the Spirit.[2]
> JOHN 3:8

Our mind is always searching for an answer to "Why?" This is fine for science, technology, an automobile engine that has stopped running, a cake that has failed to rise, or countless other things in one's daily functioning. But the mind trying to discover why life is moving this way and not that way will eventually become frustrated. Life simply moves; Truth moves within us, and it does not tell us why it is moving as it does. It just moves. This way of living does not give the mind any particular place to reside except in the experience of Now.

Whenever I see a leaf floating on water or being blown by the wind, my heart is deeply touched. For me, these images have come to represent the life of surrender—to Truth, to the Divine, to life. The leaf does not ask why the wind is blowing in one direction and not the other. It does not worry about its destination. A life lived in harmony with reality does not refuse the moment-to-moment unfolding of life. One legend holds that the aimless flight of a dry leaf was supposed to have been the immediate, apparent cause of Lao-Tzu's sudden illumination. He saw that his very *effort* to see into his true nature was what had obscured his seeing.[3]

> A leaf floating on the wind,
> without time,
> without worry,
> without a destination.
> True surrender.[4]

In awakened living, we open to the "what" and become less and less engaged in the "why." The floating leaf is content to be moved by the wind. It is a different way of living once you know you are "being lived," yet *You* are what is living you, dreaming you, intimate with you, and loving you. You realize you are both the Ocean of Awareness and the movement of its waves, the emptiness of Spirit and the fullness of expression—including your human expression.

SURRENDER IS NOT RESIGNATION

To the ego, surrender to what *is* is often misinterpreted as resignation. Relinquishing inner resistance, saying yes to the present moment, is not the same as resignation, which carries judgment and emotional negativity. Nor is surrender a passive stance toward life. To yield to the moment as it actually is allows us to be moved by the deeper dimension of our *Being* that is freed to move with compassion, intelligence, and wisdom. We can say no, when necessary, from love rather than resistance or conditioned reactivity; we can take action; we can respond sensitively and wisely. We surrender our allegiance to the false god of ego and are opened to responding rather than reacting. As identification with conditioned mind is seen more clearly and dismantled by truth, we realize that there is no psychological self to uphold, no separate "self" to promote or protect, no separate "doer." In this realization, there is great freedom.

DOING WITHOUT A "DOER"

Living without identifying as a separate "doer" does not mean being passive. Ego is the leaf, but *You* are the wind, moving your unique expression of reality. The experience or action of the moment is free to be as it is without egoic thought needing to control, defend, or will anything. Although it might appear to an observer that there is a "someone" doing all of these things, the inner experience is that Life—your life—is simply happening, an appearance in the Heart of Awareness, which is what you truly are.

Indeed, as "doing" happens without a "doer," the mind can remain open to the moment that appears and to whatever is to happen next. With regard to future decisions, the attitude is, "It will be interesting to see what happens." There is no sense that ego needs to control the creation of a moment or the outcome of one's life, yet this way of living does not feel passive or uninvolved. In not imagining you are separate from the moment of your living, you are more completely and intimately involved than when the mind is continually thinking, judging, interpreting, or worrying. But the involvement is not a personal one that imagines there is a "right" way or a "wrong" way for the moment to turn out. It is simply what it is, and you are not separate from its actions, including the ones that appear in yourself.

Likewise, a surrendered life does not feel passive because in the absence of a feared outcome, the mind is more relaxed in the midst of whatever expressions appear in the moment. Life is not "mine," nor is it "other" than mine. Absolute and relative cannot be separated. There might be a boldness of expression or gentle tenderness; there might be laughter, tears, or silence; there is freedom to experience the moment exactly as it is. When ego's illusion of control is surrendered to our deeper knowing, we trust the flow that is here today, aware that it might change tomorrow. We realize that what is awake is equally awake in both the "hellish" moments of our lives and the "heavenly" ones.

RIGHT VIEW, RIGHT ACTION

When the sense of doer-ship falls away, there is simply the experiencing of things being just what they are, accepted in the openness in which they are appearing or disappearing. Action arises spontaneously when we are responding to life from wholeness. An innate wisdom is present beyond our conditioned mind's view of right/wrong or good/bad. For example, say you encounter a beggar on the street. The beggar is your Self, but your limited mind does not know what is the most compassionate action to take in this particular situation. Whether you give or do not give, the action arises from the spontaneous action of wisdom and compassion in the moment. You are moved from a deeper, truer understanding of things than what appears from conditioning, than what you think you should or should not do in that situation. Regardless of the action of giving or not giving, you may find yourself experiencing love for this expression of your Self.

The mind would like to have rules of conduct for every situation. And there are religions that try to oblige. Having an ethical, compassionate perspective is part of the practice of any tradition (or any healthy upbringing), and rightly so. However, the fact of the matter is that one can never know what is right for every situation every time. So how can you decide ahead of time what the right action is for a moment that has not yet happened? "Right action," from a Buddhist perspective, comes from "right view," but right view is not an idea, ideology, or egoic point of view. It is, rather, the true viewing from what is timelessly awake, aware, and whole. It arises from the insight we have into reality. Love and wise action can have many faces. Love can nourish and protect; it can push out of the nest; it can give what is needed; it can take away what is not needed.

Doing happens without a separate "doer." Thoughts appear, but there is no separate "thinker." Ego's identification with separateness is so embedded that it does not seem possible that that which drives the wildflowers to bloom in springtime, the ant to search for food, birds to know migration patterns, the cow to have a calf, or the newborn baby to cry when it is hungry could possibly be the consciousness, energy, and motivating force behind the actions of an adult human being.

A woman in a group I facilitate once told us about a profound shift that happened while walking her dog up a steep hill. She was noticing the aches and pains of her aging body, wondering if she was too old for this, when out of the blue a question arose in her: "Am I the walker, or is walking simply happening?" Immediately, when the idea of being the "walker" slipped away, walking continued up the hill, but with total ease. She was astounded at the difference in experience. As we sat together, we continued to explore: "Am I the sitter, or is sitting simply happening?" You might ask yourself right now, "Am I the reader, or is reading simply happening?"

EGO'S ARGUMENT THAT NOTHING WOULD GET DONE

Egoic thought imagines that nothing would get done in a life in which one did not consider herself the "doer." "But I have a family to feed!" "I must make money to pay my rent!" "I can't take just any old job; I need to care about what I am doing and where!" "Who would be responsible for my work [or kids, health, et cetera] if I weren't doing it?" The mind of separation can become quite adamant in its view that nothing would get done if "it" weren't planning it and worrying about it, doing it and evaluating it. It becomes quite adept at arguing for its continued separate identity.

When the sense of separation ends, however, it is seen that no "one" has ever been a *separate* "doer," "thinker," "parent," "worker," "scientist," "teacher," "starving child," "saint," or "sinner." That which lives as itself is living as yourself this very moment, only you cannot imagine such a thing, because if it were true, you think you or your life would look some other way. Does it ever occur to you that the action of your life—that which motivates you, energizes you, and makes your life's choices—might be the very Being Consciousness that the ego imagines it is separate from? Could you imagine that it might be our sense of separation that creates most of our suffering and not life's unfolding as it does? Can you imagine that the so-called ego is itself a mere shadow of that which you seek? We do not even question our autonomy, except when life presents a situation over which we have no control and in the face of which we feel helpless. Then we use that situation to provide ammunition for our judgments that we, life, or God are not what we all are "supposed" to be.

The ego mind imagines life would fall apart if it weren't in charge. Yet everything that needs to happen continues to happen. In the midst of life, however it appears, you are free—free to let it be what it is, free to respond in ways that seem appropriate in the moment, free from the whole long list of "if onlys" you have carried around for so long. You are free to be yourself without self-consciousness for maybe the first time since you were a small child. There is an acceptance of whatever conditioning the body-mind may continue to have, as well as the willingness to investigate what is actually true. This is the freedom that comes from trusting the movement of the whole. It is a freedom that is free even from freedom.

22

FREEDOM FROM FREEDOM

Dissolve the seeker of freedom,
and all will be found timelessly free.

To desire liberation is to believe in separation. That which was never bound has no need of being liberated. When we discover our true nature, we have acquired nothing, and yet the felt sense is one of freedom. Openness has no agenda, no goal, and does not proclaim any identity. It does not elevate formlessness over form. It is not seeking to maintain a position, does not call itself a subject or an object. It is free of concepts and free from the "me." Because it is not separating itself from life in any form, it is free to have the experiences called "birth" and "death" within its unborn nature. It is free to play at "two-ness." The Heart that is boundlessly awake is free even from freedom; it is not attempting to escape from anything.

Truth liberates. It is dependent on nothing, has no cause, and has nothing to defend. To glimpse truth is relative easy; to see into our mind's untruth is more difficult. We all want to know Truth, but how many want to pay the price of illusion—the illusion that our mind can figure out the Mystery, that life should move for a "me" according to "my" desires, that we are "right" and others are "wrong," that freedom means maintaining a "state," that we can be free and still be "in control"?

HOW MUCH FREEDOM DO WE WANT?

How much freedom do we want? This is an important question, because once there is awakening, we realize we can only *be* truth. *Being* what we are is not the same as thinking about it or talking about it. To *be* truth is to see through our mind's illusions, the ones that we continually find fascinating or entertaining, the ones we continually exchange for the peace of our *being*. To *be* truth is to move from what is undivided. There will be many moments when this is not the experience, however, as we begin to see more and more clearly our habit patterns. Awakened seeing has the clarity of discernment but is infused with the compassionate understanding of the Heart.

WORKING WITH HABIT PATTERNS

All of us have habit patterns that come from both our experiences in this lifetime and whatever karmic threads we are carrying. These habit patterns may be held deeply in the neurobiology of the brain, in our thoughts, in our emotional or subtle body, and in our physical sensations. When we notice ourselves accepting as a "truth" about ourself one or more of these habit patterns, we can first accept that the feelings we are having are here; they feel real. But we may begin to see that the trigger for these feelings in the current circumstance is not the real reason for the reaction.

It is in compassionately allowing and then looking deeply into our actions or reactions that we may find certain knots of resistance and separation. When we do not judge them, but rather hold them in the Heart of Awareness with compassion, we may deepen our understanding of our habitual patterns of beliefs or emotions. When we become more interested in what is true than in judging ourselves for our conditioned views, these knots begin to loosen—from the deep and compassionate seeing alone. We may need reminding that habit patterns do not create, affirm, or define a separate "self."

Even if you experience hard, tight contractions, know that they are much like a baseball—seemingly hard on the outside, but only made up of layers of yarn wound over a central core. In the case of our contractions, threads of memory, feelings, beliefs, and interpretations are seemingly wound over a core of emptiness, each ultimately discovered to be quite insubstantial when seen from Presence. If we are deeply interested in awakening to Truth, we will not spend a lifetime trying to unwind every thread but rather will seek to find out what is the core, the truth of who we are. We will seek to discover what lies at the root of our idea of a separate self.

You are not a problem to be "solved." You are not your time-bound wounds. You are not your thoughts about a "self." You may want to find more skillful ways of living or relating, but trying to rid yourself of each unwanted aspect simply fuels your idea that you are a separate person who must strive to be different in order to be what you have always been—divine, whole, pure in essence, beautiful inside and out, free to simply *be*, deeply loved by the love you are, and free to express that love in your living.

FREEDOM FROM THE KNOWN

> When we are free from the known,
> we are free to live from the Unknown.

Are we willing to consider that we do not live in freedom because we are afraid to step out of what is known into the unknown? The mind lives in what it knows. It lives in thought, in duality, in its remembered, then projected, pains and pleasures. What is it like to live in the unconditioned? To live from the unborn? Life in its totality blooms, blows, moves, grows, gives birth, and dies in its own continual and undivided flow. Are we free enough to open to the flow, whatever it may contain?

To live in the unknown is our freedom. Yet this freedom is not at all what the mind imagines it will be. The mind believes that its security depends upon knowing something and that spiritual realization will be the ultimate state of knowing—knowing who we are, what we should do, how we should act. The irony is that our deepest freedom is really a state of continual insecurity for the mind that is searching for a place to arrive, a position to maintain, or something to "know." Peace is beyond the known and much simpler.

When we are telling the truth, we cannot say with any certainty that we know what the next moment will bring. We do not know how life will move, what events, thoughts, feelings, pleasures, or pains will appear or disappear. When we begin to sincerely investigate the question of who or what we truly are beyond our ideas, here, too, we eventually have to admit, "I don't really know." In the face of the mysteries of life and the vast silent Mystery of our Being, how do we respond? Do we want freedom more than we want life to look a certain way? Are we *being* life, or are we struggling to control life? A student once asked Adyashanti:

> "Isn't enlightenment the ultimate state of knowing?"
> No, it is the ultimate state of Being; knowing is the price.[1]

FREEDOM TO HAVE OUR HUMAN EXPERIENCES

When we encounter the vast openness and freedom of our true nature, understandably, our thinking mind then imagines it must become "only awareness," or it must "remember awareness," as if awareness were an object one could obtain and hold. Mind then begins to judge all human experience as somehow separate from the truth of formless awareness or Spirit. But this is more subtlety of ego, attempting to "become" what the Self already is. Can we simply notice that what is awake is already aware of this very moment, this movement of mind or emotion, this very experience?

Out of the infinite potential of our true nature, all phenomena arise, manifesting as *Being*. In awareness, the "ten thousand things" each have the freedom to *be* what they are, including the ten thousand moments of our experience that pop up in our Consciousness on any given day. Out of the dark womb of the unborn arises all that we know as Being, as form, as energy, and what is awake to all moments, all experiences, all phenomena. None of us is separate; none of us is where we do not belong; none of us is more or less advanced as essence. There is *only* God, *only* Buddha nature, *only* the Heart of Awareness. All forms, including our own, arise from the same ground and manifest the same universal awareness. In the openness of our true nature, we are free to be a human form, a feeling form, a thought form, a moment of anxiety or sadness—free to be real instead of needing to be perfect.

Without having to protect a self-image and without the fear that we are not "spiritual" or "love worthy," we are no longer pretending we do not feel what we feel or that life should only look a certain way. When we do not take ourselves to be separate from the action of Totality, we are neither blaming ourselves nor congratulating ourselves, neither feeling guilt nor needing to forgive—unless, of course, we do. Our actions are not always totally on the mark.

Compassion arises naturally, but it may not always be emotional compassion. Sometimes compassion moves to draw one to a deeper truth, a deeper authenticity. Those who are familiar with Manjushri, the bodhisattva of wisdom, know that the sword of wisdom and compassion cuts through illusion in ways that may not always feel comfortable to one's egoic identifications. Yet there is a great compassion of clear seeing in the midst of our very human experiences.

When we are truly living in the openness of not-knowing mind, we are not attached to the absolute dimension or the relative dimension. We are awake to whichever side of the coin is showing up in any given moment, knowing they are not separate. We have discovered that the essence of our ordinary mind cannot be separated from the essence of awakened mind. Thus we are free to have the experiences that appear in our human incarnation and to see that the truth and beauty of what we are is found in the most ordinary moments of our life.

THE EXTRAORDINARY WITHIN THE ORDINARY

> Greatness hides in smallness
> Simplicity in complexity.
> Nakedness has no preference
> for the clothing that
> wants to cover it.[2]

Concealed within the ordinary tasks, relationships, landscapes, and events of our everyday life lies the extraordinary. Habitual patterns of perception and response obscure our vision and dull our sensitivity to the miraculous nature of life unfolding in all its rich detail. We wait impatiently for a sense of the extraordinary to make itself known in our lives while failing to notice that the peace, love, presence, and beauty we yearn for are already present.

When we are truly open and deeply present to the moment of our experience—any experience—something amazing begins to happen. What once seemed hidden becomes visible. Simple acts of daily life can touch our heart and bring joy and clarity. The ground on which we stand appears holy, and so does the turnip we are peeling, or the person sitting before us, or the warm, fragrant tea we are sipping. Mindfulness of the ordinary brings experience of the extraordinary. As Mother Teresa put it, we may not be able to do great things, but "we can do small things with great love." It simply requires a shift from the mind to the true heart.

It is never life as it is that is boring or mundane but our thoughts that render it so. It is not our life that is constricted but our minds. It is not our daily activity that makes the extraordinary seem distant but our failure to be present to the ordinary moments as they appear in their exquisite variety and fullness.

FREEDOM FROM OUR OWN FREEDOM

When we have ceased striving for a different or better experience, ceased efforting to be someone else or somewhere else, ended the mind's incessant demand for some extraordinary state, we are no longer attached to an "experience" called freedom, no longer wanting to be "done" with our humanity. Rather, we realize that our freedom is to simply *be* what we are. Struggling for a goal or for an identity has ceased, not because the mind has figured out how to stop the struggle, but because we are intimate with that which has no need for struggling, no need for an identity built on striving. We are simply, naturally, and without fanfare *here* for what is here.

What is our response to the gift of freedom? Gratitude. Unending gratitude for the preciousness of this human life, for the unborn Spirit that is our essence through and through, for the mix of both light and darkness in experience, for the moment of this breath.

23

MYTHS OF THE
SPIRITUAL LIFE

Ocean and wave cannot be separated.

The only way to discover the myths of the spiritual life is to wake up to who/what you are and see for yourself. Prior to the search ending, we may have many beliefs about what it means to be "spiritual" or to be "awake." Take a moment to assess the myriad ideas you may have about spirituality, awakening, and living an awakened life. How many of the following thoughts do you believe?

- It is a person who wakes up.

- Experiencing my true nature is a goal requiring years (or lifetimes) of personal effort.

- The most I can hope for is a better "next life."

- Awakening to the absolute/transcendent Truth is the end of the journey.

- If I were awake, life would always feel beautiful and peaceful.

- Awakening is maintaining an unending experience in time.

- My intellectual understanding will deliver Truth.

- My (egoic) mind can tell who is awake and who is not.

- If I found the right teacher or guru, he or she could deliver enlightenment.

- One must always remain on the same path or continue the same practice in order to awaken.

- In order to experience my divine nature, I must kill my ego.

- Losing my separate identity would mean my life would fall apart, my children would go untended, work would go undone.

- To be truly spiritual is to live in a state of bliss all of the time.

- To be awake means there is total detachment from all things and all moments at all times.

- In an awakened state, one would have great powers, such as clairvoyance, omniscience, telepathy, and the power to heal.

- The experience of "no self" means an end to all conditioning, personality traits, and the like.

- Being awake means continually living in a different world than the one I live in.

- I must renounce my life as a householder, worker, et cetera in order to find spiritual freedom.

- Spiritual awakening means an end to all of my personal or relationship issues.

• Awakening is the ultimate state of knowing.

• The goal of awakening is to continually transcend
  the experience I am having.

• If I were awake, I would always feel
  _____ (fill in the blank).

• If I were a spiritual person, I would never feel
  _____ (fill in the blank).

I would invite you to wake up and find out if *any* of these ideas are true! But below are a few hints about the misconceptions minds have about the Ocean of Awareness, within which all things live and move and have their Being.

TEN MISCONCEPTIONS ABOUT THE SHORELESS OCEAN AND ITS WAVES

1. That a wave has a solid, permanent, separate "self," separate from the Ocean that gives it its life, its existence, its breath, its movement, its senses, its experience.

2. That the wave must eradicate all faults and delusions, control all of its movements, do many special practices, train for eons, accumulate special powers, and so become worthy in order that one day it may become water.

3. That the wave can know the Ocean as an object, can produce the Ocean, can possess the Ocean, can control the Ocean, can "attain" the Ocean, can judge what should or should not be the Ocean's movements. *(It is the Ocean that understands the wave, not the other way around.)*

4. That the Ocean prefers one wave over another, that only a very special, holy wave gets to be Ocean water, that the Ocean only pervades certain forms, waves, movements, and that only calm, "good" waves get to live in the Ocean.

5. That a storm at sea means the wave has misbehaved or is unworthy or that the clarity or muddiness of Ocean water is the accomplishment or failure of the wave.

6. That it is a wave that is enlightened rather than the Ocean that wakes itself up from its own forgetfulness. (*It is the movement of Consciousness itself to identify with its own creations, to imagine its life is only the surface waves.*)

7. That once its true nature is remembered, the wave will always behave according to a fixed set of rules, will never be moved by feelings of joy or sorrow, like or dislike, and that it must hold on to a still mind, hold on to the Ocean's still depths. (*As if a still mind is like a block of ice that movement could hold on to! A still mind is one that moves freely, responding wholeheartedly to whatever it encounters or reflects. It is empty and thus can move fluidly, according to circumstance.*)

8. That a "master" wave can give or bestow upon another wave its wetness.

9. That in order for a wave to become the Ocean, there is a shore where the wave needs to arrive in the shoreless Ocean!

10. That a wave's arising or disappearing means the beginning or ending of its life as the Ocean.

24

AN AFTERWORD
ABOUT WORDS

Before there was a word,
Where was separation?
Now that there are words,
Where is separation?[1]

I f you have finished reading this book, you will have read a great number of words describing a great number of concepts. Not a single *concept* is Truth. If there has been any understanding, please forget the words. If there has been no understanding, please throw the words away. Printed words on a page that try to describe the so-called spiritual journey are simply lines on paper, like a map, that attempt to give the mind a sense of the terrain and a framework for understanding experience. A menu does not deliver the taste of food, however; a verbal description of a rose cannot deliver its fragrance.

Neither a map nor words are the place you currently find yourself, nor can they ensure you arrive at a desired destination. Words and ideas are neither the present moment nor a destination, and nothing that can be spoken with words is ultimate Truth. *Nothing*. Truth lies beyond words, beyond ideas, beyond anything the finite mind can *think* about. Words are only for the purpose of going beyond words. There is a place for understanding of the mind, but true understanding transcends the mind and does not depend on it.

If there has been any understanding of what these words are trying to point to, you will understand that there is nowhere to go and no separate one who needs to get there. You will understand that *that* which drives the seeking mind and *that* which ends the seeking is who/what you already *are*, yet that Source cannot be "found" as an object.

Imagine if I were to put my finger someplace on a photo of planet earth near the area you take to be home and say, "There you are." You no doubt *were* photographed if you were alive when this picture of the earth was taken, but you will not find yourself in the photograph of the earth. Indeed, you could show me a recent photograph of yourself, a close-up of nothing else but the person you imagine is you, and still, if we pointed, you would not find yourself there. You will not find yourself in a photograph of the earth or in a photograph of your body. You will not find yourself in a mirror or in a still reflecting pond. You will not find yourself in the stories about the self you carry in your mind. You are neither a picture on a piece of paper nor a story in your memory. *So who are you?*

This book has emphasized Self-inquiry as a method to discover the truth about who you are. But methods are for those who take themselves to be separate, and you are not separate from anything or anyone—least of all, from the Heart of Awareness that is the living and the knowing of your experience—regardless of your thoughts, your mood, or who you imagine yourself to be. Methods are simply methods, a point of departure among teachers, but there is nothing from which to depart in the openness that is your true nature.

SUMMARY OF A JOURNEY

In my 2004 book *Only This!*, I summed up my own journey this way:

> I searched in scriptures, sutras, and endless books,
> imagining truth could be found in words or ideas. I
> meditated with mantras, breaths, incense, Catholic
> rosaries and Buddhist malas, sitting before statues and
> pictures of holy ones, on black cushions facing white

walls, with teachers whose Silence was their teaching. I searched for what I imagined was "there," until in stillness something turned around to notice what is here.

What is here when we stop trying to arrive there? What is here, so close that we do not notice? Words will never answer. What knows cannot be known except to Itself. It is what we are. . . . This is what silences every thought and every concept, even the concepts of truth, God, Buddha, world, and "me"; yet it is simultaneously their source. . . . Here is an ever-present Silence that knows no separation between background and foreground, divine and human, teacher and student, enlightened and unenlightened, God and flea. It is undivided Silence, empty of nothing, continually moving, continually still. It is what we are. Only This![2]

WHEN THE SEARCH ENDS

When the search ends, we realize that that which we were seeking is who/what we have always been! When the search ends, we realize that the Heart of Awareness, our true Self, has always been *here*, now. Here reading these words; here as the body is headed to work; here waiting for a doctor's appointment; here cooking dinner; here gazing at the ocean; here hugging our child; here holding the hand of a dying parent; here sitting in silence; here as the ten thousand things; here as the awake emptiness from which objects arise. When the search ends, we return to the ordinary, freely dwelling in the present moment, open to what is, content to live an ordinary life, and yet that life is infused with the understanding, compassion, and love that want to flow from its true heart.

Perfection lies in the whole, in Totality, and in its natural balance. Trying to perfect a limited "self" reflects one's identification with the body-mind. When your identification is no longer limited to the body, you will honor the body's ability to anchor you in the present moment, to respond to life, and to show you when you feel out of alignment with truth, but the body will not define who you are. Life may continue to empty you of your limited beliefs, but you are content to be where you are, doing what you are doing, for you know that you are not the "doer." You deny neither your humanness nor your divinity, knowing they are not separate. Your life in form may be touched by joys and sorrows, health and illness, contractions and expansion, moments of feeling stuck and moments of flowing. Life is whatever presents itself in your particular form of the formless; you know that resistance is futile. And yet that which is living its life in you may move in unexpected ways, wiser or funnier or more loving than your egoic mind could imagine.

NO NEED TO BE SEEN AS EXTRAORDINARY

While you sense the extraordinary in each moment and each form *as it is*, including your own, there is no need to be seen to be extraordinary. Dwelling in the ordinary, you can appreciate the natural unfolding of life, moments, thoughts, feelings, body sensations, spontaneous actions, whatever appears and disappears. Even though awareness may see places of separation still wanting to be liberated, you bow to that seeing, no longer judging that you need to be somewhere else, being someone else, doing something else. Dwelling in the ordinary means laughing when something is funny, crying when something is sad, enjoying the taste of food when you eat, feeling compassion in the face of pain or suffering, accepting what comes and accepting what goes, with love infusing it all.

DWELLING IN PEACE

Ultimately, dwelling in the Heart of Awareness is dwelling as the simple and transparent peace of our true nature and the love that flows from our open heart. Peace comes not from changing life, but from changing identification, changing perspective; yet egoic ambition will not change it. It is your thoughts that "you" are separate and that "you" must change yourself or your world that keep you from being open to the moment as it presents itself in its radiant reflection of the whole. You are God's reflection in your particular form, unfolding yourself each moment as what is. What Is sees its reflections everywhere. Consciousness, Being, the Tao, God, the Self, Buddha nature, and the Heart of Awareness are all names that have been named. But no name can contain or define what you are. No words, no concepts are it. Who you are is hidden in every moment, unseen, and yet appears in every moment, seen. What is beyond words gives rise to words. In the words of Chuang Tzu:

> How can I find someone who's forgotten words,
> so we can have a few words together?[3]

Like a leaf floating on the river or drifting on the breeze, life is moving itself. Peace is not divided from the moment at hand. Life continues on its course with or without our worry, with or without our words. The river can be trusted. The breeze knows where it blows. Our life knows its destination even though our mind does not. Our thoughts have never been driving the bus. Perhaps it is possible to relax and let yourself be taken, to celebrate your precious life, to enjoy your Self. What began your search will end it when you least expect it . . . or perhaps there was never anything to begin or to end.

> Finished, finished,
> When it is completely finished,
> There is nothing to finish.[4]
> SOEN NAKAGAWA

THE INVITATION

When God comes in your house
it is only by your invitation,
but even your invitation is God's,
for she has always been
landlady and tenant,
windows and walls,
the fire in your hearth
and the cold wind blowing at your door.

At first, her visits seem so welcome.
She brings tea and cookies and loves you
so sweetly inside your own heart.
You keep inviting her back
by your prayers and meditations,
imagining you've found the one you always wanted
who will hold you on her endless lap
and take away your pain forever.

But pretty soon, she starts arriving
unexpectedly, at odd hours of the day and night,
and every time she comes,
she takes something away—
a pretty picture here, a bookcase there,
maybe even some trash
you are happy to be rid of
in your basement.

But at some point, it occurs to you
she intends to move in completely.
And now the mind starts backing up:
"Perhaps you could come back another day,

after I've worked on my house,
after I've bought nicer furniture,
after I've finished my fight with evil,
after I've planted a peace garden."

But you must know
that if you invite God in,
sooner or later she will set up house,
and when she does, beware;
for she tosses out every single thing
she does not need, which,
in the case of the personality,
is every single thing you thought you were.

Every thought and cherished belief
she just throws out on the garbage heap;
and that might be fine if she replaced them,
but she never replaces those sacred thoughts;
she utterly destroys them. She strips the coverings
off the walls, and peels the paper from the window glass,
opens the door to invite in the wind,
and every creature you wanted kept out.

Sometimes she cleans your house gently,
dismantling it room by room.
But often, she just comes in with a torch,
and you feel in your gut the fire burn
in the center of your separate comfort,
and you watch the contents of your house
melt and turn to ash,
and the roof blow off.

And just when you think
there is nothing more that she could take,
she opens the ground beneath

the barely intact shell of your house,
and all the levels of your being
fall into the space that has no name;
and you are left alone in all the world,
without a map, without a path, without a point of view.

And you know you are creator of your dreams,
your dreams of mountains and rivers,
calm seas and storm clouds,
crashes of lightning and spacecraft,
beautiful babies asleep at the breast,
joyful dancing and puppies at play,
Spring's new blossoms,
and the threat of Winter's war.

And at this point,
what you are inside your house
is simply What is looking out.
Nothing's left but what is looking,
yet everything you see is you.
Now your life turns inside out.
Your body is the world of being
looking out of Just What Is.

And strange as it seems
to the mind of your memory,
you enjoy each dance of yourself,
even the pains you hoped to be rid of,
you experience fully without regret.
For everywhere your eye may look,
all it sees is infinite love
displaying itself in creation.
And just to be completely honest,
there are times you might be tempted
to rebuild your house of concepts,

for the mind just loves to think;
but the fire of Truth resides within you,
where it always lived before you knew,
and it keeps revealing moment to moment
what is false and what is true.

So what can be said about what happens
when God takes over her house?
She laughs and simply sips her tea,
washes her dishes and sleeps when it's time,
then goes to find another house
where there has been an invitation,
an invitation to come in
from the deep, deep love of Herself.

Dorothy Hunt

ACKNOWLEDGMENTS

Like each moment, the words on these pages simply appeared from the Mystery that moves our minds, our hearts, and our lives. This book began many years ago with the title *Riding an Ant to the Moon: Spiritual Ambition and the Search for Enlightenment.* I never sent it anywhere, but when a delightful editor at Sounds True, Melissa Valentine, contacted me about possibly writing something, I gave her the original manuscript, which has now been updated and transformed to become the book you see today. While the basic premise has not changed over the years, understandings have deepened, and the heart continues to open to an ever-expanding love. I am deeply grateful to Melissa for her invitation, encouragement, warmth, editing skills, and reassurance when it was needed. I also wish to thank the Sounds True staff for their many kindnesses extended in our work together.

No words can express the great love and unending gratitude I feel for the spiritual teachers who appeared most powerfully in my life: Ramana Maharshi and Adyashanti. Yet our lives contain many profound and perfect teachers. I bow especially to those in my immediate family—my husband, Jim, whose generous, loving spirit, even after his passing, still lives intimately in my heart; our children, Julia and Daniel; and our children's families, including three grandsons, whose joy, uniqueness, and love are continuing gifts.

In addition, I would like to express my deep appreciation for the many friends, students, clients, volunteers, and staff at Moon Mountain Sangha who have shared their lives, talents, questions, insights, and love. You have taught me so much about the power and intimacy of listening and sharing from the heart.

Dear Reader, may you and all beings realize your true Self, the Heart of Awareness that is your essence and birthright. May you recognize the deep wisdom and love within and be showered with the blessings that both begin and end your search in what is timelessly awake right now in each one of us.

NOTES

Epigraphs and poems without attribution are by the author.

Epigraph

1. Thomas Byrom, excerpts from *The Heart of Awareness: A Translation of the Ashtavakra Gita* (Boston: Shambhala Publications, 1990), 75, 77.

PART I. BEGINNING THE SEARCH

1. Dorothy Hunt, excerpt from "The Invitation," in *Only This!* (San Francisco: San Francisco Center for Meditation and Psychotherapy, 2004), 87.

Chapter 1. What Ends the Search Begins the Search

1. Idries Shah, "The Tale of the Sands," in *Tales of the Dervishes: Teaching Stories of the Sufi Masters over the Past Thousand Years* (New York: Arkana, 1967), 23.
2. T. S. Eliot, "Little Gidding," in *Four Quartets* (New York: Harcourt, Brace, and Company, 1943), 59.

Chapter 2. Spiritual Impulse and Spiritual Ambition

1. Kabir, *Kabir: Ecstatic Poems*, versions by Robert Bly (Boston: Beacon Press, 2004), 50.

Chapter 3. Silence and Stillness: The Greatest Teachers

1. Ramana Maharshi, *The Spiritual Teaching of Ramana Maharshi* (Boston: Shambhala Publications, 1988), 64.
2. Fynn, *Mister God, This Is Anna* (New York: HarperCollins Distribution Services, 1974).

Chapter 4. Paths and Practices in the Search for Truth

1. Nisargadatta Maharaj, *I Am That: Talks with Sri Nisargadatta Maharaj*, trans. Maurice Frydman, rev. and ed. Sudhakar S. Dikshit (Durham, NC: Acorn Press, 1973), 140.
2. Psalm 46:10, *The Oxford Annotated Bible* (New York: Oxford University Press, 1962), 691.
3. Lex Hixon, *Great Swan: Meetings with Ramakrishna* (Boston: Shambhala Publications, 1992), 297.

Chapter 5. Peace, Ego, and Inquiry

1. Nisargadatta Maharaj, *I Am That*, 142. Here the word *mind* means the thinking mind, not what some call *Original Mind*, a term that could be used as a synonym for Self, true nature, or the limitless Heart of Awareness.
2. Ramana Maharshi, *The Spiritual Teaching*, 76.
3. Meister Eckhart, "True Hearing," sermon IV of *Meister Eckhart's Sermons*, Christian Classics Ethereal Library, ccel.org/ccel/eckhart/sermons.vii.html.

PART II. SEEN AND UNSEEN

1. Dorothy Hunt, "The Footprint of the Divine." Unpublished poem.

Chapter 6. Background and Foreground

1. Rumi, *Mystical Poems of Rumi 1: First Selection, Poems 1–200*, trans. A. J. Arberry (Chicago: University of Chicago Press, 1968).
2. Kazuaki Tanahashi, ed., *Moon in a Dewdrop: Writings of Zen Master Dogen* (San Francisco: North Point Press, 1985), 71.

Chapter 7. The Heart of Awareness

1. Ramana Maharshi described his own meditation in this way in *The Sage of Arunachala: A Documentary*, a film directed by Dennis J. Hartel, produced by Arunachala Ashrama, and

distributed by Sri Ramanasramam, Tiruvannamalai, Tamil
Nadu, India, 1992.
2. Ramana Maharshi, *Talks with Sri Ramana Maharshi*
(Tiruvannamalai, Tamil Nadu, India: T. N. Venkataraman,
Sri Ramanasramam, 1984), 130.
3. Nisargadatta Maharaj, *I Am That*, 211.
4. Ramana Maharshi, *The Spiritual Teaching*, 91.

Chapter 8. Presence and Personhood

1. H. W. L. Poonja, *The Truth Is* (San Anselmo, CA: VidyaSagar
Publications, 1995), 335. For those unfamiliar with the terms
used: *karma* is action based on past causes and conditions.
Maya is the play of Consciousness manifesting as illusion in
the dream of Separation.
2. David Godman, ed., *Be As You Are: The Teachings of Sri Ramana
Maharshi* (London and New York: Arkana, 1985), 68–69.

PART III. CAUGHT IN THE JAWS OF THE TIGER

1. Dorothy Hunt, excerpt from "The Invitation," in *Only This!*, 87.

Chapter 9. Caught in the Tiger's Mouth

1. Ramana Maharshi, *The Spiritual Teaching*, 9–10.
2. Mooji, *White Fire: Spiritual Insights and Teachings of Advaita
Zen Master Mooji* (Oakland, CA: Mooji Media, 2014), 287.

Chapter 10. Dying for Truth, Yet Afraid of Disappearing

1. Demi, *The Empty Pot* (New York: Henry Holt, 1990).
2. Kabir, *Kabir*, 50.
3. "Meditation without Memory" is adapted from one of Douglas
Harding's "Experiments," The Headless Way, headless.org.
4. Rumi, "Chickpea to Cook," in *The Essential Rumi*, trans.
Coleman Barks (San Francisco: Harper, 1995), 132–33.

Chapter 11. Enlightenment Cannot Be Bought or Sold

1. Matthew 5:3, *The Oxford Annotated Bible*, 1175.

2. Raymond B. Blakney, trans., *Meister Eckhart* (New York: Harper and Row, 1941), 227.

3. Seng-Ts'an, *Hsin-hsin Ming: Verses on the Faith-Mind*, trans. Richard B. Clarke (Buffalo, NY: White Pine Press, 2001).

Chapter 12. Burning in Love's Fire

1. Dorothy Hunt, excerpt from "The Invitation," in *Only This!*, 88.

PART IV. THE SEARCH ENDS IN WHAT NEVER ENDS

1. Dorothy Hunt, excerpt from "The Invitation," in *Only This!*, 89.

Chapter 13. The End of Seeking

1. The story of Liang-shan and his teacher, T'ung-An, is from *The Record of Transmitting Light: Zen Master Keizan's Denkoroku*, trans. Francis H. Cook (Los Angeles: Center Publications, 1991), 190.

2. Dorothy Hunt, "When Seeking Ends," in *Only This!*, 90.

Chapter 14. Awakening Is Only the First Step

1. Sekito Kisen (Shitou Xiqian), *The Sandokai: Identity of Relative and Absolute*.

Chapter 15. Resting the Mind in the Heart of Awareness

1. *The Dhammapada*, verses 153–54.

2. Mooji, *White Fire*, 327.

PART V. UNDIVIDED LOVE

1. Dorothy Hunt, a variation of "Until we have fully . . . ," in *Leaves from Moon Mountain* (San Francisco: Moon Mountain Sangha, 2015), 109.

Chapter 16. Love Flows from Emptiness

1. Dorothy Hunt, "What Can Be Said about Love?" in *Leaves from Moon Mountain*, 102.

Chapter 17. Love Contains Both Joy and Suffering

1. The Buddha's first Noble Truth, the Dhammacakkappavattana Sutta.
2. David Hinton, trans., *Chuang Tzu: The Inner Chapters* (Washington, DC: Counterpoint, 1998), 87.

Chapter 18. Fierce Grace

1. C. S. Lewis, *The Problem of Pain* (New York: HarperOne, 2001) 1.
2. C. S. Lewis, *A Grief Observed* (New York: HarperOne, 1994). Also portrayed in the play and film versions of *Shadowlands*.

PART VI. LIVING AWAKE, LIVING NOW

1. Dorothy Hunt, excerpt from "The Invitation," in *Only This!*, 89.

Chapter 20. Living Awake Is Living Now

1. Anthony de Mello, "Arrival," in *One Minute Wisdom* (Garden City, NY: Doubleday, 1986), 50.
2. The words of Ramana Maharshi are from the film *The Sage of Arunachala*.

Chapter 21. Awakening and Surrender

1. Eckhart Tolle, *Stillness Speaks* (Novato, CA: New World Library, 2003), 70.
2. John 3:8, *The Oxford Annotated Bible*, 1287.
3. Ramesh S. Balsekar, *A Duet of One: The Ashtavakra Gita Dialogue* (Los Angeles: Advaita Press, 1989), 158–59.
4. Dorothy Hunt, "A Floating Leaf," in *Leaves from Moon Mountain*, 4.

Chapter 22. Freedom from Freedom

1. Adyashanti, "The Only Price," from Adyashanti's website, 2014, adyashanti.org/index.php?file=writings_inner&writingid=1.
2. Dorothy Hunt, "Nakedness Has No Preference," in *Only This!*, 38.

Chapter 24. An Afterword about Words

1. Dorothy Hunt, *Leaves from Moon Mountain*, 34.
2. Dorothy Hunt, "Silence Empty of Nothing," in *Only This!*, 263.
3. David Hinton, trans., *Chuang Tzu: The Inner Chapters*, xviii.
4. Soen Nakagawa (1907–1984) was a Rinzai Zen master.

BIBLIOGRAPHY

Adyashanti. *Emptiness Dancing.* Los Gatos, CA: Open Gate
  Publishing, 2004.
Balsekar, Ramesh S. *A Duet of One: The Ashtavakra Gita Dialogue.*
  Los Angeles: Advaita Press, 1989.
Barks, Coleman, trans. *The Essential Rumi.* San Francisco: Harper,
  1995.
Blakney, Raymond B., trans. *Meister Eckhart.* New York: Harper and
  Row, 1941.
Byrom, Thomas. *The Heart of Awareness: A Translation of the
  Ashtavakra Gita.* Boston: Shambhala Publications, 1990.
Cook, Francis H., trans. *The Record of Transmitting Light: Zen Master
  Keizan's Denkoroku.* Los Angeles: Center Publications, 1991.
de Mello, Anthony. *One Minute Wisdom.* Garden City, NY:
  Doubleday, 1986.
Demi. *The Empty Pot.* New York: Henry Holt, 1990.
Eliot, T. S. *Four Quartets.* New York: Harcourt, Brace, and Company,
  1943.
Godman, David, ed. *Be As You Are: The Teachings of Sri Ramana
  Maharshi.* London and New York: Arkana, 1985.
Hinton, David, trans. *Chuang Tzu: The Inner Chapters.* Washington,
  DC: Counterpoint, 1997.
Hixon, Lex. *Great Swan: Meetings with Ramakrishna.* Boston:
  Shambhala Publications, 1992.
Hunt, Dorothy. *Leaves from Moon Mountain.* San Francisco: Moon
  Mountain Sangha, 2015.
———. *Only This!* San Francisco: San Francisco Center for
  Meditation and Psychotherapy, 2004.
Kabir. *Kabir: Ecstatic Poems.* Versions by Robert Bly. Boston: Beacon
  Press, 2004.
Kisen, Sekito (Shitou Xiqian). *The Sandokai: Identity of Relative and
  Absolute.*

Lewis, C. S. *A Grief Observed.* New York: HarperOne, 1994.

———. *The Problem of Pain.* New York: HarperOne, 2001.

Mooji. *White Fire: Spiritual Insights and Teachings of Advaita Zen Master Mooji.* Oakland, CA: Mooji Media, 2014.

Nisargadatta Maharaj. *I Am That: Talks with Sri Nisargadatta Maharaj.* Translated by Maurice Frydman. Revised and edited by Sudhakar S. Dikshit. Durham, NC: Acorn Press, 1973.

The Oxford Annotated Bible, Revised Standard Version. New York: Oxford University Press, 1962.

Poonja, H. W. L. *The Truth Is.* San Anselmo, CA: VidyaSagar Publications, 1995.

Ramana Maharshi. *The Spiritual Teaching of Ramana Maharshi.* Boston: Shambhala Publications, 1988.

Seng-Ts'an. *Hsin-hsin Ming: Verses on the Faith-Mind.* Translated by Richard B. Clarke. Buffalo, NY: White Pine Press, 2001.

Shah, Idries. *Tales of the Dervishes: Teaching Stories of the Sufi Masters over the Past Thousand Years.* New York: Arkana, 1967.

Tanahashi, Kazuaki, ed. *Moon in a Dewdrop: Writings of Zen Master Dogen.* San Francisco: North Point Press, 1985.

PERMISSIONS

Epigraph, page xii: Excerpts from *The Heart of Awareness: A Translation of the Ashtavakra Gita*, translated by Thomas Byrom (Boston: Shambhala Publications, 1990). Copyright © 1990 by Thomas Byrom. Reprinted by arrangement with The Permissions Company, Inc., on behalf of Shambhala Publications Inc., Boulder, Colorado, shambhala.com.

Epigraphs for parts 1, 3, 4, 6, and chapter 12: Excerpts from "The Invitation," in *Only This!* by Dorothy S. Hunt (San Francisco: San Francisco Center for Meditation and Psychotherapy, 2004). Copyright © 2004 by Dorothy S. Hunt. Reprinted by permission of the San Francisco Center for Meditation and Psychotherapy.

"Nakedness Has No Preference" and "Silence Empty of Nothing": From *Only This!* by Dorothy Hunt. See above.

Poem in chapter 2, pages 14–15: From *Kabir: Ecstatic Poems* by Robert Bly (Boston: Beacon Press, 2004). Copyright © 2004 by Robert Bly. Reprinted by permission of Beacon Press.

"Meditation Without Memory," on page 110, is adapted from one of Douglas Harding's experiments. Used here by permission of Richard Lang, coordinator of The Shollond Trust, the UK charity set up in 1996 to help share Douglas Harding's The Headless Way, headless.org.

Rumi poem on pages 116–117: "Chickpea to Cook," in *The Essential Rumi*, translated by Coleman Barks (San Francisco: Harper, 1995). Reprinted by permission of Coleman Barks.

ABOUT THE AUTHOR

Dorothy Hunt serves as spiritual director of Moon Mountain Sangha in San Francisco, California, teaching in the spiritual lineage of Adyashanti, who invited her to share the Dharma in 2004. She is the founder of the San Francisco Center for Meditation and Psychotherapy and has practiced psychotherapy since 1967, though she is now semiretired from that practice. Dorothy is the author of *Only This!* and *Leaves from Moon Mountain*, and she is a contributing author to *The Sacred Mirror* and *Listening from the Heart of Silence* (volumes 1 and 2 in the Nondual Wisdom and Psychotherapy series), as well as to the online journal *Undivided*. Her poetry has been published in several journals, and she is a featured spiritual teacher in the book *Ordinary Women, Extraordinary Wisdom*.

Dorothy has a long and deep connection with the teachings of Ramana Maharshi and the path of Self-inquiry, as well as with the nondual teachings of Zen, Advaita, and the Christian mystics. In meeting Adyashanti, she was invited beyond identification with either the absolute or relative dimensions of Being, finding freedom in what is timelessly awake here and now in each one of us, regardless of the changing faces of experience. She lives in San Francisco and is a mother and grandmother. Dorothy offers satsang, retreats, and private meetings in the San Francisco Bay Area; Sonoma, California; and elsewhere by invitation.

For more information, please visit dorothyhunt.org. You may contact Dorothy at moonmountainsangha@sbcglobal.net.

ABOUT SOUNDS TRUE

S ounds True is a multimedia publisher whose mission is to inspire and support personal transformation and spiritual awakening. Founded in 1985 and located in Boulder, Colorado, we work with many of the leading spiritual teachers, thinkers, healers, and visionary artists of our time. We strive with every title to preserve the essential "living wisdom" of the author or artist. It is our goal to create products that not only provide information to a reader or listener, but that also embody the quality of a wisdom transmission.

For those seeking genuine transformation, Sounds True is your trusted partner. At SoundsTrue.com you will find a wealth of free resources to support your journey, including exclusive weekly audio interviews, free downloads, interactive learning tools, and other special savings on all our titles.

To learn more, please visit SoundsTrue.com/freegifts or call us toll-free at 800.333.9185.

sounds True
many voices, one journey